T0301390

Intellectual Property and Sustainable Markets

ELGAR INTELLECTUAL PROPERTY AND GLOBAL DEVELOPMENT

Series Editor: Peter K. Yu, *Professor of Law and Co-Director of the Center for Law and Intellectual Property at Texas A&M University School of Law, USA*

Rapid global economic integration and the increasing importance of technology and information goods have created the need for a broader, deeper and more critical understanding of intellectual property laws and policies. This uniquely designed book series provides an interdisciplinary forum for advancing the debate on the global intellectual property system and related issues that intersect with transnational politics, international governance, and global economic, social, cultural and technological development. The series features the works of established experts and emerging voices in the academy as well as those practising on the frontlines. The series' high-quality, informed and accessible volumes include a wide range of materials such as historical narratives, theoretical explanations, substantive discussions, critical evaluations, empirical analyses, comparative studies, and formulations of practical solutions and best practices. The series will appeal to academics, policy makers, judges, practitioners, transnational lawyers and civil society groups as well as students of law, politics, culture, political economy, international relations and development studies.

Titles in the series include:

The Global Governance of HIV/AIDS
Intellectual Property and Access to Essential Medicines
Edited by Obijiofor Aginam, John Harrington and Peter K. Yu

Access to Information and Knowledge
21st Century Challenges in Intellectual Property and Knowledge Governance
Edited by Dana Beldiman

Trademark Protection and Territoriality Challenges in a Global Economy
Edited by Irene Calboli and Edward Lee

Governance of Intellectual Property Rights in China and Europe
Edited by Nari Lee, Niklas Bruun and Mingde Li

Protecting Traditional Knowledge
Lessons from the Global Case Studies
Evana Wright

Intellectual Property and Sustainable Markets
Edited by Ole-Andreas Rognstad and Inger B. Ørstavik

Intellectual Property and Sustainable Markets

Edited by

Ole-Andreas Rognstad

Professor of Law, Department of Private Law and Centre for European Law, University of Oslo, Norway

Inger B. Ørstavik

Professor of Law, Department of Private Law and Centre for European Law, University of Oslo, Norway

ELGAR INTELLECTUAL PROPERTY AND GLOBAL DEVELOPMENT

Edward Elgar
PUBLISHING

Cheltenham, UK • Northampton, MA, USA

Published by
Edward Elgar Publishing Limited
The Lypiatts
15 Lansdown Road
Cheltenham
Glos GL50 2JA
UK

Edward Elgar Publishing, Inc.
William Pratt House
9 Dewey Court
Northampton
Massachusetts 01060
USA

A catalogue record for this book
is available from the British Library

Library of Congress Control Number: 2021938656

This book is available electronically in the **Elgar**online
Law subject collection
http://dx.doi.org/10.4337/9781789901351

ISBN 978 1 78990 134 4 (cased)
ISBN 978 1 78990 135 1 (eBook)

Printed and bound by CPI Group (UK) Ltd, Croydon, CR0 4YY

Contents

Contributors

Catherine Banet is Associate Professor in the Scandinavian Institute of Maritime Law, Department of Energy and Resources Law at the University of Oslo, Norway. She specialises in energy law, environmental law, competition law, EU/EEA law and law of the sea. Banet has a background in private law practice (Norway, France), the European Commission (DG ENV), U.S. diplomatic mission and academia. She is a member of the Advisory Academic Group to the International Bar Association, Section for Energy, Environment and Natural Resources and Infrastructure Law (SEERIL), and Academic Fellow at the Center on Regulation in Europe (CERRE).

Janice Denoncourt (BA (McGill), LLB (West. Australia), LLM (Murdoch), LLM (Bournemouth), PhD (Nottingham)) is Associate Professor at Nottingham Law School, Nottingham Trent University, UK. Denoncourt is an interdisciplinary researcher and author of *Intellectual Property, Finance and Corporate Governance* (Routledge, 2018) and contributes to the LLM International Financial Transactions module on IP finance. She is a graduate of the Australian Institute of Company Directors (GAICD), a Senior Fellow of the Higher Education Academy (SFHEA) and formerly practised as a barrister and solicitor in Western Australia and a solicitor in England and Wales. Denoncourt has been affiliated with Nottingham Law School, Nottingham Trent University, UK since 2008. She is a Herbert Smith Freehills and Minter Ellison alumna and has advised start-ups, SMEs, large private and publicly listed companies.

Joel B. Eisen is Professor at the University of Richmond School of Law, USA and is an internationally recognized expert on energy law and policy. In addition to courses in energy law, he teaches federal administrative law and environmental law. He has authored the textbook, *Energy, Economics and the Environment: An Advanced Introduction to Renewable Energy*, and other books, chapters, treatises and articles on clean and renewable energy. His article on renewable energy was honoured as one of the top four environmental law articles of 2011. He was Richmond Law's inaugural Austin Owen Research Fellow, and Vermont Law School's 2019 Distinguished Energy Law Scholar.

Daniel J. Gervais is Professor and Milton R. Underwood Chair in Law at Vanderbilt University Law School, USA and Director of the Vanderbilt Intellectual Property Program. He also holds a Professor II appointment at the Faculty of Law of the University of Oslo. In 2017–2019, he served as President of the International Association for the Advancement of Teaching and Research in Intellectual Property (ATRIP). He has published a multitude of books and articles in the field of international intellectual property, including *The TRIPS Agreement: Drafting History and Analysis* (5th edn, Thomson/ Sweet & Maxwell, 2021) and *Restructuring Copyright: A Path Towards International Copyright Reform* (Edward Elgar, 2019). He is a member of the Academy of Europe and of the American Law Institute where he serves as Associate Reporter on the Restatement of Copyright (First) Project.

Hans Morten Haugen is Professor of International Diakonia at VID Specialized University, Oslo, Norway. He is Dr. Jur. from the University of Oslo (2006), with the dissertation *The Right to Food and the TRIPS Agreement*, published by Brill in 2007. His other IP-related book is *Technology and Human Rights: Friends or Foes?* (Republic of Letters, 2012). He has nine articles in *The Journal of World Intellectual Property*, two being reprinted: 'Human rights and TRIPS exclusion and exception provisions', reprinted in *Intellectual Property and Human Rights*, ed. Laurence R. Helfer (Edward Elgar, 2013), and 'Patent rights and human rights: exploring their relationships', reprinted in *The Political Economy of Intellectual Property Rights* (vol. III), ed. Christopher May (Edward Elgar, 2010).

Inger B. Ørstavik, PhD, is Professor in the Department of Private Law at the University of Oslo, Norway. Ørstavik obtained her PhD in 2010 with the thesis 'The innovation spiral: questions in patent law, contract law and competition law relating to improvements of patented inventions'. The thesis was awarded H.M. the King's gold medal. She has experience from the Attorney General for Civil Affairs and from private practice. Ørstavik has published articles in intellectual property law, competition law and contract law. She teaches intellectual property law and property law, and has taught international human rights at Fudan University in Shanghai, China.

Kristen Jakobsen Osenga is Austin E. Owen Research Scholar and Professor of Law at the University of Richmond School of Law, USA as well as a Senior Scholar at the Center for the Protection of Intellectual Property, Antonin Scalia Law School, George Mason University. Her areas of expertise include patent law and other intellectual property law, law and language and legislation and regulation. Her latest publications include, inter alia, the journal articles 'Patent-eligible subject matter … still wielding the wrong weapon – 12 years later', 60 *IDEA* 104 (2020), and 'Institutional design for innovation: a radical proposal for addressing Section 101 patent eligible subject matter', 68 *American University Law Review* 1191 (2019).

Taina Pihlajarinne, LLD, is Professor at Helsinki University Faculty of Law, Finland and is researching and teaching intellectual property rights. Her research interests are focused on the impacts of digitalization and technological advances on law and on the relationship between sustainability, innovation and law. She has written extensively on these issues and she is a leader of research projects relating to these themes. Additionally, she serves as a Vice Dean responsible for research at the Helsinki University Faculty of Law.

Ole-Andreas Rognstad is Professor in the Department of Private Law and Centre for European Law at the University of Oslo, Norway and since 2021 has been Visiting Professor at the University of Helsinki, Finland. His authorship includes his doctoral thesis on 'Distribution of copies of copyright works' (1999), a textbook on (Norwegian) copyright law, a recent monograph (in English) on *Property Aspects of Intellectual Property* (Cambridge University Press, 2018), contributions to a (co-authored) textbook on EEA law as well as a large number of articles, mainly in the field of intellectual property. He has chaired, and been a member of, a number of public dispute settlement resolution bodies in Norway, is chairing the Norwegian Copyright Association and is a member of the European Copyright Society, Academy of Europe and the Norwegian Scientific Academy.

Peter K. Yu is Regents Professor of Law and Communication and Director of the Center for Law and Intellectual Property at Texas A&M University, USA. Born and raised in Hong Kong, he previously held the Kern Family Chair in Intellectual Property Law at Drake University Law School and was Wenlan Scholar Chair Professor at Zhongnan University of Economics and Law in Wuhan, China. He served as a Visiting Professor of Law at Bocconi University, Hanken School of Economics, Hokkaido University, the University of Haifa, the University of Helsinki, the University of Hong Kong and the University of Strasbourg.

Acknowledgements

The editors thank all contributors for their valuable contributions. Special thanks to Janice Denoncourt for her willingness to assist in finalizing the manuscripts, including language checks, and to research assistant Audun Nagelhus for final proofreading.

Ole-Andreas Rognstad and Inger B. Ørstavik
Oslo, December 2020

1. Intellectual property and sustainable markets: introduction

Ole-Andreas Rognstad and Inger B. Ørstavik

1. FROM THE EDITORS

The idea to investigate intellectual property and sustainability in a broader, market-based context was fostered within the Department of Private Law at the University of Oslo. In discussions with colleagues working within the fields of natural resources law, company law and intellectual property (IP) law, we observed that we all deal with many of the same overreaching challenges relating to sustainability and development in a broader sense. The approaches to the role of the law in solving these challenges, however, varied greatly. Nevertheless, a common denominator was the recognition of the need for society to tackle the challenges of securing sustainable development, and that sustainable development would depend on legal mechanisms for preserving knowledge and developing new knowledge. Furthermore, that those mechanisms, to contribute to both innovation and development of knowledge as well as sustainability, would likely have to be market-based and concrete. This book is the result of the discussions about the need to combine different fields of law in order to provide more depth and understanding to the topic of sustainability and IP law.

2. SUSTAINABILITY AND IP

The modern concept of sustainable development (SD) is often ascribed to the Brundtland report to the UN from 1987 but was then a rather toothless concept. It was defined as 'development that meets the needs of the present without compromising the ability of future generations to meet their own needs'.[1] It has later been suggested that this definition 'should ... be redefined to "development that meets the needs of the present while safeguarding Earth's

---

[1]   See *Chapter 4, fn. 5, infra.*

life-support system, on which the welfare of current and future generations depends"'.[2] As such, sustainability refers to all policies and developments, as is also clear from the UN global goals for sustainable development (SDGs), the '2030 Agenda'.[3] The 17 goals include diverse issues such as the ending of poverty and hunger and ensuring of healthy lives (goals 1–3), the ensuring of clean water and sanitation (goal 6), affordable and clean energy (goal 7), industry, innovation and infrastructure (goal 9) and climate action (goal 13), but also more general goals such as gender equality (goal 5), peace, justice and strong institutions (goal 16).

The role of intellectual property rights (IPRs) in order to achieve the SDGs is hardly visible in the agenda[4] (although it has been underscored elsewhere),[5] at the same time as the importance of technology and technological development are highlighted throughout. This emphasizes not only the importance but also the complexity and the ambiguity inherent in and surrounding IPRs as tools for promoting SD as well as pointing to possible supplements and alternatives to IP protection in furthering innovation to the benefit of SD. In this respect, simplistic approaches – such as a polarized discussion as to whether IPRs hinder access to resources or foster innovation essential to SD – should be avoided at least on a general level since the role and the impact of IPRs may differ in a multitude of respects.

The purpose of this book is to demonstrate and discuss the multi-faceted aspects of IP in relation to SD. Thus, the contributions evolve around several different SDGs as well as highlighting a whole range of different angles as to how IP can play a role in SD policy. In this respect, a general and universal approach is hardly possible. On the contrary, it is important to take account of 'local needs, national interests, technological capabilities and institutional capacities, and public health conditions', because 'the differences in economic conditions, imitative or innovative capacities, research and development productivities, and availability of human capital, [may imply that] an innovative model that works well in one country may not suit the needs and interests of another'.[6] Thus, although SD is a global phenomenon and responsibility, there

---

[2]   David Griggs et al. 'Sustainable Development. Goals for People and Planet', 495 *Nature* (2013), 305–330, 306.

[3]   'Transforming our World: The 2030 Agenda for Sustainable Development', United Nations – Sustainable Development knowledge platform, https://sustainabledevelopment.un.org/post2015/transformingourworld (accessed 23 August 2015).

[4]   See *Chapter 2, infra.*

[5]   See *Chapter 3, infra.*

[6]   Peter K. Yu, 'Realigning TRIPS-plus Negotiations with UN Sustainable Goals', *Chapter 3 in this volume, section 3.2 infra.*

are indeed problems concerned with seeking global or universal solutions to the IP/SD interface.

Overly simplified, sustainability is about choice of priorities, choosing the sustainable over the non-sustainable solutions, and demanding of all policies, investments and developments that they do not compromise the needs of future generations by contributing to SD.

3. SUSTAINABLE MARKETS: A CONTEXTUAL APPROACH TO IP AND SUSTAINABILITY

3.1 IP in Context

Moving into the IP/sustainability interface from the perspective of IP law enables us to look more closely at the role of IPRs in SD. IPRs provide incentives for private investment in innovation and creation. The legal right creates an exclusive position not otherwise inherent in knowledge and provides incentives to invest in innovation at a time when the result of the innovative/creative effort is still uncertain. However, the legal regulation of IPRs is general with regard to the outcome of innovative and creative processes and provides little flexibility to direct investments towards sustainable technologies and knowledge over other technologies.

The objectives of IPRs are the promotion of innovation and development of new knowledge. The basic rationale for awarding individuals exclusive rights to inventions or works of art or literature etc. is that innovation and creation lead to new knowledge to the benefit of society. On a theoretical and abstract level, it could be argued that innovation and new knowledge contribute to SD, as it enables us to make better, more sustainable choices based on enhanced knowledge. That assumption, however, requires that the context in which IPRs function incentivizes sustainable choices. IPRs are designed to work as legal instruments within an environment comprising other legal, factual and social mechanisms. A legal discussion of IPRs is incomplete if it is not contextual.

IPRs have proven to be robust against time and societal development, something that may also be partly ascribed to their contextual nature. International treaties regulating IPRs have existed for more than 130 years, and although corresponding national legal systems vary in tradition and experience, IPRs have survived revolutionary technical and societal developments. Apart from the fact that the international regime itself may serve as a barrier for radical reforms, as changes require consensus, IPRs function within the current and local legal, factual and social context, contributing to knowledge development within those trends.

The contextual nature of IPRs as well as the overarching nature of sustainability makes the discussion of IP and sustainability multi-faceted and diverse, as is reflected in this book. The contributions discuss different SDGs, either from a broader perspective,[7] or individually. Several of the following chapters discuss environmental concerns and climate change related issues (pertaining to SDGs 7, 12 and 13 in particular). Other chapters deal with public health concerns, in particular in developing countries (pertaining to SDGs 1–3)[8] and cultural sustainability.[9] Furthermore, several of the contributions touch upon the promotion of inclusive and sustainable industrialization and the fostering of innovation (SDG 9).

As IP interrelates with the goal of SD, a number of different legal issues arise. While not writing off radical changes to IP law as a means to promote SD, this book primarily discusses the interrelation between IP and other legal fields or issues, thereby contributing to a discussion of the role of IP in promoting and ensuring that development is sustainable. The first two chapters take an overarching approach to IP and sustainability, discussing the appropriateness of the international legal IP framework to deal with SD. Chapter 4 discusses the concept of cultural sustainability, its impact and importance. Chapters 5 and 6 take an IP integrated approach, discussing the openness of IP law to include sustainability considerations in the concrete application of the law. Chapters 7, 8 and 9 ask how IPRs and IP policy can contribute to SD, in particular, in the current technological environment and how other areas of law and policy are interrelated with IP law. Finally, Chapter 10 discusses alternative models for fostering innovation to the benefit of SD. There are past lessons learned, including what seem to be success stories, and future perspectives on how to improve on the IP/sustainability interface.

The diverse angles taken and problems discussed show the importance of examining IPRs in a legal, factual and societal context, especially when discussing the overarching goal of sustainability. This is not one, but many discussions. There are also important background trends in the context of IP that are merely touched upon in this book but are nevertheless significant.

First, there is the traditional silo approach of law and policymakers to IPRs as innovation policy and sustainability as environmental and development policy. On an international level, IPRs are remarkably non-addressed in the UN sustainability goals or in important international legal instruments dealing with environmental issues, such as the Paris Agreement. While not surprising, as there are only so many compromises between diverging interests that can be aligned within one set of international treaties or instruments,[10] the trend is to

---

[7]   *Chapter 2, infra.*
[8]   *Chapter 3, infra.*
[9]   *Chapter 4, infra.*
[10] See, for example, Abdel Ahmed Latif, 'Intellectual Property Rights and the Transfer of Climate Change Technologies: Issues, Challenges and Way Forward', 15 *Climate Policy* (2015), 103–126.

under-communicate the interrelation between the various areas of law relevant to achieve the SDGs.

At the level of national law, the same divide can be found. This book makes an important contribution to the international debate on the IP and sustainability interface by pointing to the interrelation between IP law and other areas of law, when considering how IPRs may play a role in achieving the SDGs. As the concept of sustainability is holistic, this work should also impact the debate within the different legal fields.

Despite this divide in the regulatory framework, there are numerous initiatives for cooperation between policymakers on international,[11] regional and national levels, as well as an emerging willingness of lawmakers to include sustainability in market-based regulation.[12] This book provides useful insights for these discussions.

Second, market dynamics form a factual context for the role that IPRs play in innovation processes and in the market. In some markets, IPRs do not appear necessary to provide incentives to develop new technology and bring it to the market. The solar PV industry is an example. Licence fees are only a small part of the costs in the industry value chain, indicating that IPRs are not a significant source of income for developers and producers in the solar PV industry. In wind technology, on the other hand, patent rights are highly concentrated, in that access to IPRs is likely to form a significant barrier to entry. The role that IPRs play for the development of technology and for market dynamics differs fundamentally in diverse markets.

In some markets, technology risks are high, as in markets with extreme network effects (such as telecommunications) and, as discussed here, in energy supply, i.e. the development of the grid. In these markets, there can be only one or a select few technology winners. When the risk of developing technology that is immediately obsolete is high, IPRs can be necessary. The discussion then turns to how other legal instruments work together with IPRs to facilitate efficient technology development and deployment. The development of technical standards is one aspect of this.

Finally, society is in constant development, and the role of IPRs is affected by trends and social innovation. An important current social development is the transformation of the passive consumer into a 'prosumer' who is actively

---

[11] Cf. the interesting cooperation between the European Patent Office (EPO) and the International Energy Agency (IEA), see https://www.iea.org/news/epo-and-iea-team-up-to-shed-light-on-trends-in-sustainable-energy-technologies (accessed 29 October 2020).

[12] See on a European level, the European Green Deal launched by the EU Commission, see https://ec.europa.eu/info/strategy/priorities-2019-2024/european-green-deal_en (accessed 29 October 2020).

participating in the market, either by 3D printing their own medical equipment or by delivering excess energy from their solar panel into the electric grid. Two-, or multi-sided business models are rapidly becoming the new standard in many economic areas. Multi-sided business models are important from a sustainability perspective, as they reduce transportation, facilitate reuse and recycling, and enable faster roll-out of renewable energy. The interface between IPRs and sustainability includes questions relating to the effects and limitations of IPRs: Do they facilitate or hinder the development of new business models? Are IPRs necessary as an incentive to innovate in these types of markets?

To conclude, the role of IPRs in developing sustainable markets is multi-faceted and partly ambiguous and dependent on how the potential to reconcile the traditional justifications of and approaches to IPRs with sustainability goals is exploited, or for that sake, the potential to reform IP law if necessary. In this book, various aspects of these questions are addressed and discussed.

3.2   Sustainable Markets: The Contextual Approach in this Book

The book begins with an overarching discussion of the relationship between IP law and the UN SDGs by Hans Morten Haugen. In his contribution, he addresses the divide between IP law and the international policies under the UN SDGs and provides a discussion of possible reasons for this divide. The chapter observes that IP has not been central in the formulation of the UN SDGs. Only one reference to IP is made in the 2015 Transforming Our World resolution, introducing the 17 SDGs (UN 2015, objective 3b), namely on the flexibilities to protect public health as allowed for in the TRIPS Agreement. Numerous reports under the Millennium Project analysed the role of science and technology in fulfilling the SDGs, criticizing the functioning of the present IP system in different ways. Based on the strong links between a well-functioning IP system and successful application of science and technology for sustainable development, the chapter presents five hypotheses in order to explain why IP is not highlighted in the context of the SDGs. These hypotheses are tested by analysing UN-wide processes relating to technology, processes within the World Intellectual Property Organization (WIPO), and TRIPS flexibilities.

Chapter 3, authored by Peter K. Yu, discusses more closely the interrelation between the SDGs and the TRIPS regime, with particular emphasis on the challenges faced by developing countries in promoting and fulfilling the SDGs. He observes that the UN SDGs were adopted at a time when countries were busy negotiating TRIPS-plus bilateral, regional and plurilateral agreements. The chapter explores how developing countries could attain more success by realigning TRIPS-plus intellectual property negotiations with the SDGs. It begins by discussing the intersection between the SDGs and the development of the intellectual property system – at both the domestic and international levels. The chapter then outlines the direct and indirect impediments to the promotion and fulfilment of the SDGs that have been generated by the recent and ongoing negotiations for TRIPS-plus trade agreements. These agreements include the Anti-Counterfeiting Trade Agreement, the Trans-Pacific Partnership Agreement (now the Comprehensive and Progressive Agreement for Trans-Pacific Partnership) and the proposed Regional Comprehensive Economic Partnership Agreement. In view of the potential dangers and complications caused by TRIPS-plus IP negotiations, this chapter concludes by identifying six distinct strategies that developing countries may deploy to ensure greater promotion and fulfilment of the SDGs.

In Chapter 4, Daniel J. Gervais discusses cultural sustainability as reflected in several of the SDGs. He notes the interrelationship between cultural and environmental sustainability and emphasizes that cultural sustainability is about the empowerment to develop and propagate values in a given society, including via art, literature and information. The chapter discusses in particular two vehicles that can contribute to human progress, the creation, dissemination and availability of Socially Responsible News (SRN) and literary and artistic creations. The allegation is that the continued role of those two vehicles is in serious peril, in that their very existence depends on factors wrongly taken for granted: the existence of professional creators, including journalists, on the one hand, and of organizations that support them such as publishers and news organizations, on the other. The author examines the situation of current markets for SRN and literary and artistic productions, and in particular the disruption caused by the shift to a few major digital platforms. Reform suggestions are made in relation to one important IP policy level: copyright, including a possible overhaul of the norms contained in the most important copyright treaty, the Berne Convention.

In Chapters 5 and 6, the authors take a concrete and national or regional view on how sustainability can be integrated into IP law. The preface for the discussion is the societal demand for more sustainability in the trade in goods, and the call that the law should contribute to repair and reuse of goods rather than mere consumption under SDG 12. Trade mark and patent rights do provide an exclusive right to ensure that the right holder recaps the full worth of the first sale of the product, but the actual scope of the right has not been discussed in the context of sustainability. Both contributions ask whether there is elasticity in patent and trade mark law to include a sustainability perspective in the application of national and regional law.

In Chapter 5, Taina Pihlajarinne examines repair activities and use of recycled materials from European patent and trade mark law perspectives.

The chapter focuses on two examples that demonstrate a strong property right impact on recycling efforts. The first is the consideration of normal lifespan in the repair or reconstruction dichotomy in the patent context, and the second involves the possibility to use trade marks in so-called upcycling activities. The chapter assesses the structures and interpretations of exclusive rights as impediments to the circular economy achieving its full potential in terms of repairing products or re-using materials. The author suggests that a concept of a 'sustainable lifespan' could be adapted into the IPR framework. The dichotomy between infringement and repair and reuse should be realigned around a 'normal, sustainable lifespan for that particular product' or an 'environmentally friendly lifespan' to cohere with a sustainable trade in goods.

Following the direction of Pihlajarinne's contribution, in Chapter 6 Ole-Andreas Rognstad discusses a judgment from the Norwegian Supreme Court where the Court rejected the relevance of sustainability arguments where iPhone screens were imported from Hong Kong to Norway for repair purposes. The screens were originally provided with Apple logos affixed without the consent of Apple Inc. but were de-branded with a removable ink marker prior to import into Norway. The Supreme Court found that the import infringed Apple's trade mark right, and held that competition and sustainability arguments were not relevant since the outcome only concerned trade mark use and not the use of screens. The Court nevertheless discussed whether the import negatively affected trade mark functions, a question answered in the affirmative. In the author's opinion, the Court's reasoning is based on postulates rather than any real assessment of harm to the trade mark, making the rejection of the relevance of sustainability arguments off target. The chapter points out that there is potential inherent in the doctrine of trade mark functions to take sustainability concerns into consideration, provided that more solid evidence is required for finding that these functions are harmed.

Chapters 7 to 10 discuss the process of innovation from various angles. Recognizing that innovation is paramount to promote and fulfil the UN SDGs, IP law alone does not support innovation, as the efficiency of IP law is largely dependent on other law and policy.

The primary objective of IPRs such as patents, designs and copyright is to provide incentives to invest in innovation and creation. However, the exclusive rights in themselves are hardly adequate to guarantee access to capital for innovators and creators. In Chapter 7, Janice Denoncourt discusses the role of IPRs in financial regulation, suggesting that financial regulation should facilitate a financial market better adapted to providing financing for innovation. Green finance (climate change mitigation and adaptation and related risks) and blue finance (to support ocean resilience) depend on innovation, so there is arguably a more prominent role for IPRs in sustainable finance initiatives. The chapter critically examines the activity of the Basel Committee on Banking

Supervision (BCBS) and the Basel Accords[13] bank asset classification system as applied to intangible assets as loan security (collateral).[14] Through an interdisciplinary traditional law and qualitative analysis, the author builds an exploratory case to support a new approach to the prudential regulation capital adequacy ratios (CARs) when transactions involve registered granted IPRs, such as patents, as loan security. The author evaluates why and how registered IPRs could be an important component of the evolving sustainable finance market with a role to play in unlocking critical innovation financing.

In Chapter 8, the discussion of IP moves from the context of financial markets to energy markets. Inger B. Ørstavik discusses how the transition from fossil to renewable energy, i.e. the fulfilment of SDG 7, is dependent on innovation in renewable energy technologies. The chapter uses the solar PV industry as an example, arguing that a coherent approach to energy policy and innovation policy is necessary due to the externalities of the technology neutrality of patent law. Patent law inadequately incentivizes innovation in renewable energy technologies over fossil technologies. Furthermore, patent law does not stimulate sustainability in the renewable energy industry as such, evidenced by the reliance on coal-fired utilities in the production of solar PV systems. The author argues that energy or environmental policies that support sustainability in the dynamics of the market will indirectly include sustainability in patent law, as market dynamics are integrated into the normative rationale of patent law. The chapter discusses how such policies can support the functions of patent law, driving innovation in renewable energy technologies and contributing to ensure that energy and industry markets are sustainable. The discussion concretizes an example of the argument made above, that a discussion of sustainability must take a holistic view.

Chapter 9 deals further with the energy market and ties into the societal trend that the supply of electricity is no longer a traditional one-sided supply, but a multi-sided business. An important development is the transition to a 'Smart Grid'. Joel B. Eisen and Kristen Jakobsen Osenga discuss how the United States is transforming its electric grid with Smart Grid initiatives that aim to overhaul the grid with modern, digital technologies, incorporate new resources, reduce carbon emissions, and provide consumers with new options for generating, using, conserving and transferring electricity. Interoperability standards have been recognized as central to the Smart Grid in the US. A fast-track process was established to develop and approve these standards,

---

[13] The BCBS was established in 1974 and issued the first Basel Accord in 1988 followed by the second, third and fourth of the Basel Accords over the next two decades.

[14] Although they have no legal force, the Basel Accords are voluntarily adopted by member nations, see https://www.bis.org/bcbs/about/overview.htm?m=3%7C14%7C573 (accessed 29 October 2020).

working in conjunction with standards developing organizations (SDOs). The authors find that patenting and standard setting are complementary and foster competition for speedier innovation. To protect companies other than patent holders, SDOs require that a patentee disclose any patents that are necessary to practise the standard and provide a licence under [fair], reasonable, and nondiscriminatory ([F]RAND) terms. This has struck an appropriate balance between the need for rapid standards development and the goal of IP protection, instrumental in the development of a centralized Smart Grid in the US.

In the final chapter, Catherine Banet explores innovation policy beyond IP law and discusses the concept of 'open innovation' in the context of the energy transition and the development of low carbon technologies. The chapter explores the interaction between energy law and IP law in the ecosystem of the energy sector, especially in relation to the development of low carbon technologies. The chapter includes a discussion of open innovation as a concept and the involvement of IPRs, providing a concrete analysis of how the development of low carbon technologies is increasingly reliant on open innovation models. The author also considers the implications of open innovation models on IP law and energy market regulation. The discussion provides the basis for reflections on the inter-regulation between IP law and energy law. This final chapter returns the discussion to the agenda for this book: the contextual and market-based analysis of IP and sustainability.

4. SUSTAINABLE MARKETS: A REALISTIC AND HOLISTIC APPROACH

Earlier in this introductory chapter, we pointed out that the discussion of IPRs and sustainability must take into account local needs, interests and overall differences, especially along the highly contentious axis of developing vs developed countries. The discussions in this book show that by taking a contextual and market-based approach to IP and sustainability, the discussion of how IPRs may include or promote sustainability becomes more nuanced. We believe that a holistic approach, where IPRs are discussed in a market context and the requirement for sustainability is applied to the market outcome, will provide a more realistic approach. However, one should not be afraid to introduce radical reform proposals in the IP field in order to achieve sustainability goals. To use *Drahos'* words: 'The world should not enter its longest night of crisis with globally extractive intellectual property institutions.'[15] And bearing in mind the challenges that the Covid-19 pandemic have posed to the global

---

[15] Peter Drahos, 'Six Minutes to Midnight – Can Intellectual Property Save the World?', in Kathy Bowrey, Michael Handler and Dianne Nicol (eds), *Emerging*

society, there might – as one commentator has put it – be 'a need to translate the collective solidarity we experience today into legally enforceable measures that balance patent protection and global access'.[16] This statement resonates with other IPRs and sustainability concerns as well.

Challenges in Intellectual Property, Oxford University Press: Australia (2011), Chapter 2.

[16]   Geertrui van Overwalle, 'Will Covid Patents Save the World?', 69 *GRUR Int.* (2020), 883–884, 884.

2. Why are intellectual property rights hardly visible in the United Nations Sustainable Development Goals?

Hans Morten Haugen

1. INTRODUCTION

The term sustainable is a flexible concept, but two crucial elements must be included in any appropriate use of the term: the holistic and the inter-generational. The holistic implies that there shall be simultaneous improvements – or at least no retrogression – within the three pillars of economic, ecological and social. The term inter-generational implies that the current fulfilment of needs shall not be to the detriment of future generations' possibilities to have their needs fulfilled. Sustainable market actors must acknowledge these crucial elements and have a business strategy that encompasses them.

Only one express reference to IP is made in the 2015 UN General Assembly Transforming Our World resolution, introducing the 17 SDGs.[1] The wording is on using flexibilities to protect public health as allowed for in the TRIPS Agreement, and is similar to the wording of the last summit resolution under the previous Millennium Development Goals (MDGs).[2] In the 2005 summit resolution, and in the Millennium Declaration itself, there are no references to IP at all.

Technology was, however, highlighted in two of the MDG targets, formulated subsequent to the adoption of the Millennium Declaration: Target 8E (access to affordable essential drugs); and Target 8F (new technologies, especially information and communications). Both Targets emphasized cooperation with the private sector, and this sector is dependent upon a well-functioning IP system. Technology is also emphasized in SDG targets 9.5, 9b and 17.6–17.8.

---

[1] UN, A/RES/70/1, Transforming Our World: The 2030 Agenda for Sustainable Development (2015a), target 3b.

[2] UN, A/RES/65/1, Keeping the Promise: United to Achieve the Millennium Development Goals (2010), para 78(t).

This chapter seeks to analyse the lack of emphasis on the role of IP in the SDGs. It develops five hypotheses, formulated under five C's as follows:

(i)   the *complexity* of IP in the context of both climate change and development;
(ii) lack of *communication* between relevant governmental offices as regards IP;
(iii) *compartmentalization* of IP issues in the UN, particularly between secretariats and delegations in Geneva and New York;
(iv) strengths of different *campaigns* in various countries and on the global level; and
(v)   an overall *cautious* approach on IP as evidenced by legislative changes and court rulings in both industrialized countries and developing countries.

I will return to whether these five hypotheses are strengthened or weakened in the discussion towards the end of the chapter. The chapter is structured as follows: Section 2 sets out overall perspectives on IP and development, embedded in quantitative studies. Section 3 provides a brief review of the IP and innovation studies submitted in the context of the MDGs, while Section 4 investigates how IP was addressed in the process leading up to the adoption of the SDGs and in the initial phase of the SDG era. Section 5 investigates how the SDGs are influencing the World Intellectual Property Organization's (WIPO) Development Agenda. Section 6 analyses how the WHO (World Health Organization), WIPO and WTO (World Trade Organization) Trilateral Cooperation on Public Health, IP and Trade has sought to promote development, through the lens of IP and pharmaceuticals. Section 7 identifies some of the recent controversies concerning IP on a national level, particularly with regard to the least-developed countries (LDCs), asking to what extent IP rights are shrinking their 'development space'. Section 8 provides an overall discussion, embedded in the five C's, while Section 9 concludes.

2.   THE RELATIONSHIP BETWEEN IP AND SOCIO-ECONOMIC DEVELOPMENT

While sustainable development must be seen holistically, as specified above, the shifts that have taken place within the understanding of what brings about socio-economic development warrants an in-depth assessment. Rather than merely emphasizing economic growth, development must be understood within a framework of opportunities, capabilities and liberties.[3] Development can be understood as societal transformation towards:

> a situation where people can control their own resources and claim their rights, where they enjoy a minimum of economic and human security and are thus able to make choices that will improve their future.[4]

This shift towards a human-centred concept of development – emphasizing opportunities, control and choices – began around 1990, with the first Human Development Report by the United Nations Development Program (UNDP). A new paradigm emerged in 2000, emphasizing a human rights-based approach to development. In 2003, this approach was defined in the so-called 'Statement of Common Understanding' adopted by all of the UN's specialized agencies, funds and programmes:

> Human rights standards contained in, and principles derived from, the Universal Declaration of Human Rights and other international human rights instruments guide all development cooperation and programming in all sectors and in all phases of the programming process.[5]

While this definition specifies development programming, this term is wide enough to encompass any efforts for development. The term 'all sectors' implies a high ambition for the concrete application of human rights. Human rights *principles* are essentially about minimum requirements for an inclusive decision-making process. The seven principles most commonly referred to are human dignity, non-discrimination, rule of law, transparency, accountability, participation and empowerment.[6]

Keeping these three development concepts – sustainability, socio-economy and human-centred – in mind, there is a need to gain more insight into the IP logics. On the face of it, IP is the legal system that seems most contradictory to human rights logics. Human rights concerns *enhanced access* to necessities. The IP system seeks to achieve *controlled access* to new technologies and creative work, implying that the right holder is to determine conditions for

---

[3]   Norwegian Government, *Report No. 13 to the Storting (2008–2009). Climate, Conflict and Capital – Norwegian Development Policy Adapting to Change* (Norwegian Ministry of Foreign Affairs 2009) 13.

[4]   Ibid.

[5]   UN Development Group, *The Human Rights-based Approach. Statement of Common Understanding* (2003) https://www.unicef.org/sowc04/files/AnnexB.pdf (accessed 22 June 2020).

[6]   Tahmina Karimova, *Human Rights and Development in International Law* (Routledge 2016) 76, referring to UN Food and Agricultural Organization (FAO).

others' use. Moreover, the enjoyment of human rights is based on a holistic approach that views the various rights as mutually interdependent, indivisible and interrelated, while IP are instrumental rights, serving societal needs by rewarding particular innovative or creative contributions.

There are of course links between the two, expressed through the *droit d'auteur* concept. France and several Latin American countries took the lead in proposing what became Article 27.2 of the Universal Declaration of Human Rights and subsequently Article 15.1(c) of the International Covenant on Economic, Social and Cultural Rights (ICESCR) on recognition of the right to enjoy the moral and material interests of those contributing with literary, artistic or scientific productions. Moreover, the European Court of Human Rights (ECtHR) understands IP to fall under the property rights protection of Article 1 in Additional Protocol 1 to the European Convention for the Protection of Human Rights and Fundamental Freedoms.

The tensions between human rights and IP are also evident if we take the perspective of time into account. Human rights implementation involves measures for regular and predictable enjoyment of basic necessities. IP protection concerns creating predictability for producers of technology and creative works, and the societal benefit of such a policy shift will be seen only after a certain period. The logic of the patent system has been formulated as: 'by slowing down the diffusion of technical progress it ensures that there will be more progress to diffuse.'[7] In other words, the perceived predictability of the patent system induces technology developers to invest in R&D efforts.

This long-term positive contribution of IP must be generally acknowledged. The theory and practice of IP does not always match, however. First, technological improvements can be hindered by too many patents, the so-called 'patent thickets', which is also termed the 'tragedy of the anti-commons'.[8] Second, it is estimated that only when reaching a GDP/capita level of 7750 US dollars will a given country be expected to benefit from a stronger patent system.[9] Third, the same author notes that even if LDCs are not required to comply with the substantive parts of the TRIPS Agreement – the extension

---

[7]   Joan Robinson, *The Accumulation of Capital* (3rd edn, Macmillan 1971) 87.

[8]   Michael A. Heller, 'The Tragedy of the Anti-commons: A Concise Introduction and Lexicon' (2013) 76 *Modern Law Review* 6; Michael A. Heller and Rebecca S. Eisenberg, 'Can Patents Deter Innovation? The Anti-Commons in Biomedical Research' (1998) 280 *Science* 698.

[9]   Keith Maskus, *Intellectual Property Rights in the Global Economy* (Institute for International Economics 1998) 108.

period is currently until 2021,[10] and 2033 for pharmaceutical products[11] – the mere existence of the TRIPS Agreement implies adoption of higher IP standards than a country's technological level would indicate.[12]

Summing up, we see that there are obvious tensions between IP and human rights, and the sequence for introducing high IP protection can affect a country's development prospects. However, technology promotion – which includes IP legislation – is an integral part of any development policy.

3.   IP: AN IMPORTANT CONCERN IN THE MILLENNIUM PROJECT REPORTS

Under the so-called UN Millennium Project commissioned by the UN Secretary-General, a total of 13 Task Force reports and an overall final report (*Investing in Development*) were published. High-ranking experts analysed the policy shifts needed to meet the MDGs.[13] Many of the Task Force reports addressed technological innovation, with the impacts of IP identified as a concern in several of the reports.

Investing in Development did not encompass an in-depth analysis of IP, but after a brief assessment of inadequate flexibility mechanisms in the TRIPS Agreement noted: 'There is a clear case for revisiting more of the rules to examine their impact on developing countries and any additional flexibility required.'[14] The term 'revisiting' reveals an inadequate understanding of the complexities in renegotiating provisions of the TRIPS Agreement. This has only happened once, in the context of compulsory licensing for states without production capacity for pharmaceutical products (Article 31*bis*), an amendment that entered into effect in 2017, 11 years after the decision to amend the

---

[10]   WTO, WTO Doc IP/C/64 Extension of the Transition Period Under Article 66.1 of the TRIPS Agreement for Least Developed Country Members (2013). Chad, on behalf of LDC members, has proposed an extension until 2033: see IP/C/W/668 (2020).

[11]   WTO, WTO Doc IP/C/73, Extension of the Transition Period Under Article 66.1 of the TRIPS Agreement for Least Developed Country Members for Certain Obligations with Respect to Pharmaceutical Products (2015a).

[12]   Maskus, fn. 9, *supra*, 108.

[13]   An overview of the various Task Force reports is found in UN Millennium Project, *UN Millennium Development Library: Investing in Development: A Practical Plan to Achieve the Millennium Development Goals. Report to the UN Secretary-General* (Earthscan 2005a) xi.

[14]   UN Millennium Project, *Investing in Development: A Practical Plan to Achieve the Millennium Development Goals* (Earthscan 2005a) 219; note that there is nothing on TRIPS in the shorter version; see UN Millennium Project, *Investing in Development: A Practical Plan to Achieve the Millennium Development Goals. Overview* (Earthscan 2005b).

TRIPS Agreement, and 16 years after the Doha Ministerial Conference that started the renegotiating process.

To foster production of medicines for tropical diseases, *Investing in Development* highlighted three ways to mobilize private research efforts in the absence of a sufficiently strong market: (i) *Ex post* prizes; (ii) direct funding; and (iii) pre-commitment purchase agreements.[15] We see that these three strategies are promoted in the absence of IP protection, or where prospects for profit from commercializing IP-protected products are too meagre. When IP is addressed in the specific reports, this quote is illustrative:

> Commitment is also required from the international community to alleviate the restrictive features of [TRIPS] ...[16]

Another report acknowledges the efforts of a specific alliance, the TB Alliance, enabling it to 'balance health equity with incentives ...'.[17] Moreover, country-level guidance on how access to medicines is affected by IP is recommended.[18]

In line with the findings by Maskus,[19] the Task Force on trade poses the rhetorical question:

> Should intellectual property rights have been included in the WTO? From an economic point of view, probably not, because they require a very delicate balance of market forces and public action – a balance unlikely to be the same for all countries.[20]

The former President of Mexico (1994–2000), Ernesto Zedillo, was the coordinator for this Task Force. His reign was in the initial years of WTO and the North American Free Trade Agreement (NAFTA), both of which included comprehensive protection for IP. We see that a person who played a role in,

---

[15]   Earthscan 2005a, 229; see also UN Millennium Project, *Prescription for Healthy Development: Increasing Access to Medicines. Report of the Task Force on HIV/AIDS, Malaria, TB, and Access to Essential Medicines, Working Group on Access to Essential Medicines* (Earthscan 2005c).

[16]   UN Millennium Project, *Coming to Grips with Malaria in the New Millennium. Task Force on HIV/AIDS, Malaria, TB, and Access to Essential Medicines, Working Group on Malaria* (Earthscan 2005d) 7; see also 53.

[17]   UN Millennium Project, *Investing in strategies to reverse the global incidence of TB. Task Force on HIV/AIDS, Malaria, TB, and Access to Essential Medicines* (Earthscan 2005e) 130.

[18]   UN Millennium Project 2005c, fn. 15, *supra*, 110.

[19]   Maskus, fn. 9, *supra*.

[20]   UN Millennium Project, *Trade for Development. Task Force on Trade* (Earthscan 2005f) 7.

at least the implementation of, these new IP standards subsequently chaired a Task Force that argued against the inclusion of IP in the WTO negotiations.

Proposals for a diverse approach to IP protection was promoted in the report from the Task Force on Science, Technology and Innovation, proposing a 'three-tier system', based on states' GDP/capita. Less onerous obligations should be placed on states with less than 5000 US dollars, and even less onerous obligations should be placed on states with less than 1000 US dollars.[21]

In light of Maskus' findings, quoted above, in the author's opinion this is a reasonable proposal. As the extension period for TRIPS demonstrates, this is partly practised, but only for LDCs, in accordance with Article 66 of the TRIPS Agreement. For other developing countries Article 65 of the TRIPS Agreement applies, but the last year that a state was permitted to 'delay the application' of the TRIPS Agreement was 2005, and only for product patents. Hence, any developing country – exempting LDCs – that becomes a member of the WTO after 2005 must comply with all substantive provisions of TRIPS. One exception exists, however: the so-called 'non-violations approach', as outlined in Article 64.2 and Article 64.3 of the TRIPS Agreement, is still not being applied, despite pressure from the USA and Switzerland.[22]

We see that none of the Task Forces nor the overall report from the Millennium Project had an active endorsement of the global IP system as it currently operates.

4.   IP IN THE NEGOTIATION PROCESS AND INITIAL ERA OF THE SDGS

How did the IP concerns in the Millennium Project reports – written by highly regarded international experts in their respective disciplines – influence the process towards the 2015 adoption of the SDG agenda? There can be no doubt that a well-functioning IP system and successful application of science and technology is important for sustainable development. In order to identify how the UN views IP in the context of science, technology and innovation (STI), we will first focus on the General Assembly, and return to the IP work of the various UN bodies in the next two sections.

A report on the progress in formulating the SDGs emphasized that a 'balanced IP rights framework' is part of a well-functioning national STI ecosystem, in addition to institutions, an educated workforce, a research and

---

[21]   UN Millennium Project, *Innovation: Applying Knowledge in Development. Task Force on Science, Technology, and Innovation* (Earthscan 2005g) 112–113.

[22]   WTO secretariat, 'Non-violation' complaints (Article 64.2) (2019) https://www.wto.org/english/tratop_e/trips_e/nonviolation_e.htm (accessed 22 June 2020).

education infrastructure, private–public innovation linkages, and enterprises committed to R&D.[23]

Over the last decade, the UN General Assembly has adopted three kinds of resolutions highlighting technology in the context of the SDGs: the annual resolutions on ICT for sustainable development[24] and the biannual resolutions on science and technology and on agricultural technology, respectively.[25] All are based on comprehensive reports from the UN Secretary-General.[26] Moreover, a resolution to give directions for the multi-stakeholder forum (STI Forum) under the Technology Facilitation Mechanism (TFM) established by the Third International Conference on Financing for Development[27] mentioned under SDG target 17.6 is relevant. The STI Forum will be analysed below, and not the overall TFM. As the resolution primarily addresses procedural issues, it will not be included in the analysis below, which will be limited to the most recent resolutions and reports.

In the ICT resolution, IP right is not referred to at all explicitly, only implicitly, by encouraging 'legal and regulatory frameworks conducive to increased investment and innovation' and 'universal access strategies'.[28] There is no *explicit* reference to IP in the UN Secretary-General's report, but an implicit reference to IP by highlighting Research4Life, a public–private partnership fostering affordable access to new scholarly, peer-reviewed research in the realms of health, agriculture, environment, development and global justice. Research4Life involves the WHO, FAO, WIPO, the UN Environmental Programme (UNEP) and the International Labour Organization (ILO).

---

[23] UN, E/CN.16/2014/2, Science, Technology and Innovation for the Post-2015 Development Agenda. Report of the Secretary-General (2014) para 11.

[24] UN, A/RES/74/199, Information and Communications Technologies for Sustainable Development (2020a).

[25] UN, A/RES/74/229, Science, Technology and Innovation for Sustainable Development (2020b) (earlier the title only referred to development; see A/RES/72/228); UN, A/RES/72/215, Agricultural Technology for Sustainable Development (2020c).

[26] UN, A/74/62-E/2019/6, Report of the Secretary-General on Progress Made in the Implementation of and Follow-up to the Outcomes of the World Summit on the Information Society at the Regional and International Levels (2019a); UN, A/74/230, Science, Technology and Innovation for Sustainable Development. Report of the Secretary-General (2019b); UN, A/74/238. Agricultural Technology for Sustainable Development. Report of the Secretary-General (2019c).

[27] UN, A/RES/69/313, Addis Ababa Action Agenda of the Third International Conference on Financing for Development (2015b) para 123. The most recent element of the TFM is the online platform 2030 Connect; see Hans Morten Haugen, 'Does TRIPS (Agreement on Trade-related Aspects of Intellectual Property Rights) Prevent COVID-19 Vaccines as a Global Public Good?' (2021) *Journal of World Intellectual Property* (online first), particularly note 5; DOI: 10.1111/jwip.12187.

[28] UN 2020a, fn. 24, *supra*, para 41.

The overall science and technology resolution asserts that IP and innovation strategies must be aligned with states' development strategies, asking WIPO to help to 'design, develop and implement' such strategies.[29] Another paragraph highlights 'an efficient, adequate, balanced and effective intellectual property framework, while encouraging access to science, technology and innovation by developing countries'.[30] The term 'balanced' must be read so as to provide for technology producers and technology consumers simultaneously.

Nothing is said about IP in the resolution on agriculture, even if the resolution encourages states to promote 'innovative and sustainable food systems'.[31] In the UN Secretary-General's report on agriculture, IP is mentioned once, identified as a challenge in the context of genetic editing.[32] By reviewing the last three sessions of the UN Commission on Science and Technology for Development (CSTD), concerns are expressed over IP for smallholder farmers in the UN Secretary-General's report to the 2017 CSTD session,[33] and with a different emphasis in his report to the 2019 CSTD session.[34] No reference to IP is found in the reports from these three sessions. In this context of agriculture, it is relevant that one of two main themes at the 2017 session was the role of STI in ensuring food security by 2030.

Hence, we see that there is relatively limited emphasis on IP in both the reports and the resolutions, yet WIPO is identified as the core UN body. This is probably not surprising, but FAO and WHO do have important roles to advise states on IP in their respective fields, without being acknowledged by the UN General Assembly.

IP issues are, however, addressed in the context of the TFM that consists of a UN Interagency Task Team (IATT), the STI Forum and the online platform 2030 Connect, all with the purpose of harnessing STI for the SDGs. The summary from the 2017 STI Forum highlights 'effective IP rights protec-

---

[29]   UN 2020b, fn. 25, *supra*, para 29; see also para 10, and preambular para 26.

[30]   UN 2020b, fn. 25, *supra*, para 7 (the wording was previously in the preambular paragraphs; see A/RES/72/228).

[31]   UN 2020c, fn. 25, *supra*, para 7; see also para 23.

[32]   UN 2019c, fn. 26, *supra*, para 21.

[33]   UN, E/CN.16/2017/3, The Role of Science, Technology and Innovation in Ensuring Food Security by 2030. Report of the Secretary-General (2017a) para 14 ('costly and externally input-dependent …'); see also para 66. Note that the report from the session merely lists the speakers at the session that discussed this report; see UN, E/2017/31-E/CN.16/2017/4, Commission on Science and Technology for Development. Report on the Twentieth Session (2017b) Annex II, paras 8–9.

[34]   UN, E/CN.16/2019/2, The Impact of Rapid Technological Change on Sustainable Development (2019d) para 37 (noting IP's 'unclear implications for smallholder farmers').

tions'.[35] The 2016 Forum refers to IP as one of many elements of 'robust legal environments that promote innovation'.[36] While these are merely summaries of the issues discussed at the STI Forums, terms like 'effective' and 'robust' indicate a somewhat other direction than the terms 'balanced' and 'access'.[37]

A positive and rather uncritical approach towards IP in an African context was expressed at the 2018 UN Integration Segment of the Economic and Social Council (ECOSOC).[38] These annual sessions discuss how to achieve sustainable development and poverty eradication. Despite the fact that technology and innovation were the two main topics in 2018, there was only one reference to IP in the 33-page-long 'Conference Room Paper', included in the context of 'disruptive innovations' like cloud computing and open source.[39]

A milestone so far in the UN's elaboration of positive STI–IP–SDG relationships is the 2020 Guidebook for the Preparation of STI for SDGs Roadmaps. The Guidebook presents the creation of the TFM as being 'of historic significance, as it brought back substantive STI discussions to … New York, after decades of political gridlock over IP rights and technology transfer issues'.[40] It remains to be seen if this identification of the STI–IP–SDG relationships will make IP issues appear in the reports from the annual UN High-level Political Forum on Sustainable Development, to whom the STI Forum reports.

In summary, despite the limited references to IP in UN documents, technology is essential in most of the SDGs, as will be seen below. Despite these many linkages between IP and SDGs, there was limited attention to IP in the lead up to the adoption of the SDGs. It is too early to assert whether the relatively strong pro-IP wording applied, particularly, in the 2017 STI Forum[41] will represent a new approach of acknowledging the importance of a stronger IP approach in the context of SDGs. As similar wording is not applied in the

---

[35]   UN, E/HLPF/2017/4, Multi-stakeholder Forum on Science, Technology and Innovation for the Sustainable Development Goals (2017c) paras 21 and 68.
[36]   UN, E/HLPF/2016/6, Multi-stakeholder Forum on Science, Technology and Innovation for the Sustainable Development Goals: Summary by the Co-Chairs (2016) para 21.
[37]   UN 2014, fn. 23, *supra*, para 11; UN 2020b, fn. 25, *supra*, para 7.
[38]   UN, ECOSOC/6912, Economic and Social Council Discusses Leveraging Technology, Innovation to Build More Resilient Africa, on Final Day of Integration Segment, (3 May 2018) session V.
[39]   UN, ECOSOC Integration Segment. Innovative Communities: Leveraging Technology and Innovation to Build Sustainable and Resilient Societies. Conference Room Paper (30 April 2018) 26.
[40]   IATT's Sub-Working Group on STI Roadmaps co-led by World Bank, DESA, UNCTAD and UNESCO, Guidebook for the Preparation of Science, Technology and Innovation (STI) for SDGs Roadmaps (2020) 68.
[41]   UN 2017c, fn. 35, *supra.*

summary from the 2018 and 2019 STI Forums, it seems justified to conclude that the launching of the STI Forum has not implied a radical shift in the approach on IP and the SDGs within the UN.

5.   WIPO'S COMMITTEE ON DEVELOPMENT AND INTELLECTUAL PROPERTY

While acknowledging that the TRIPS Council has sought to identify measures to promote technology transfer in the context of IP rights – with particular emphasis on climate change in 2013 and 2014 – this section will analyse efforts within the UN, more specifically WIPO's Committee on Development and Intellectual Property (CDIP).

WIPO's Development Agenda (DA) was launched in 2007,[42] and studies and conferences have been commissioned, embedded in the 45 adopted recommendations. The 45th recommendation specifies 'To approach IP enforcement in the context of broader societal interests and especially development oriented concerns ...' in accordance with Article 7 of the TRIPS Agreement, which is quoted in full.

Article 7 is found in Part I of the TRIPS Agreement and is resorted to when interpreting the provisions of Part II of the TRIPS Agreement. In this context it is relevant to note that Bangladesh asserted that the 'TRIPS Agreement was a consensus of the lowest common denominator of all countries'.[43] Based on the many examples of 'TRIPS plus' provisions in treaties negotiated between developing countries and the LDCs themselves,[44] this assertion can be problematized.

The 2016 International Conference on IP and Development concluded that an approach based on '*one-size-fits-all* was not a correct approach in making IP work for development'.[45] When commenting on the official report from

---

[42]   WIPO, A/43/16, General Assembly Report adopted by the Assembly (2007) 152; see also 153–157. Note also that the UN Conference on Trade and Development (UNCTAD) has a mandate relating to IP and development; see UNCTAD, TD/519/ Add.2, Declaration from the XIV UNCTAD Conference (2016) para 55(s).

[43]   WIPO, CDIP/18/11, Report of the 18th meeting of the Committee on Development and Intellectual Property (CDIP) (2017a) para 22.

[44]   Hans Morten Haugen, 'Inappropriate Processes and Unbalanced Outcomes: Plant Variety Protection in Africa Goes Beyond UPOV 1991 Requirements' (2015) 18 *Journal of World Intellectual Property* 196.

[45]   WIPO, CDIP/18/3, Report on the International Conference on Intellectual Property and Development. Prepared by the Secretariat (2016a) 15 (italics in original).

this Conference, Bangladesh, on behalf of the LDCs, made an interesting observation:

> It noted that all the speakers had agreed on the fact that the direct linkage between IP and innovation had yet to be proven beyond doubt. History and experience had proved that IP and development rights and responsibilities went hand-in-hand.[46]

Notwithstanding the lack of a clear understanding of the phrase 'development rights and responsibilities', it seems as if these two statements go in somewhat opposite directions. The first can be read as an implicit criticism of the IP system, while the latter is an implicit endorsement of the IP system. Bangladesh also noted the need to make IP beneficial for LDCs, without specifying how this was to be achieved. Another Conference on IP and Development was held in 2019, and similar conferences will be held in 2021 and 2023.[47]

Specifically addressing the SDGs, the debates over WIPO's contributions have taken place in the CDIP and have evolved considerably. The first submission on the SDGs by the WIPO Secretariat stated that SDGs 9 (innovation) and 17 (technology, as part of a global partnership) 'could be linked to the mandate and strategic objectives of WIPO'.[48] To use the term 'could', when explaining how WIPO's mandate and field of competence is relevant, is too passive, particularly when keeping in mind that innovation and technology are crucial elements for meeting almost all the SDGs. This is acknowledged when the document continues by listing SDGs 'with relevance to WIPO ...': SDGs 2 (food), 3 (health), 4 (education), 7 (energy), 8 (economic growth), 12 (waste) and 13 (climate).[49]

The group of developed countries, termed Group B, asserted that, 'as a first step, there was a need to clarify those SDGs which were relevant to WIPO's work',[50] and the United Kingdom underlined that 'the way forward was to build on the two SDGs identified ...'.[51] Nigeria, on behalf of the African Group, specified that WIPO's role must encompass other SDGs, emphasizing particularly how proprietary technologies 'were accessible and how access could be ensured using IP tools ...'.[52] As an illustration of the disagreement

---

[46] WIPO 2017a, fn. 43, *supra*, 7.
[47] WIPO, CDIP/24/5, Report on the International Conference on Intellectual Property (IP) and Development – How to Benefit from the IP System (2019a).
[48] WIPO, CDIP/16/8, WIPO and the Post-2015 Development Agenda. Prepared by the Secretariat (2015) Annex 5.
[49] Ibid, Annex, 6.
[50] WIPO, CDIP/16/10, Report of the 16th meeting of the Committee on Development and Intellectual Property (2016b) 5.
[51] Ibid, 62.
[52] Ibid, 57.

between developed and developing countries, Brazil held that 'arguments should be provided on why some SDGs should not be included in WIPO's work …'.[53]

There can be no doubt that technology is essential for most of the SDGs, and Uganda highlights nine: SDG 1 (poverty), 2 (food), 3 (health), 6 (water & sanitation), 7 (energy), 9 (innovation), 10 (inequality), 15 (on-ground resources) and 17 (technology, as part of a global partnership).[54] We saw that the WIPO Secretariat highlighted a different list, with four not included by Uganda: SDGs 4 (education), 8 (economic growth), 12 (waste) and 13 (climate).[55] Combining these two lists, only four SDGs (5 (gender), 11 (cities), 14 (life in water) and 16 (thriving communities)) are ignored, but the emphasis on gender at the 21st session of CDIP[56] indicates that gender equality and technology will receive more attention within WIPO.

China proposed that implementation of the SDGs become a standing agenda item of CDIP.[57] Despite support from several important states,[58] this proposal was not adopted. Rather, there is to be an annual report on WIPO's 'contribution to the implementation of the SDGs'.[59] The subsequent report built on discussions at three earlier sessions,[60] and specifies WIPO's roles, including in the IATT and the STI Forum under the TFM, and the subsequent reports were more substantive.[61]

---

[53]   Ibid, 59.
[54]   WIPO, CDIP/18/4, Compilation of Member State Inputs on SDGs Relevant to WIPO's work. Prepared by the Secretariat (2016c) Annex III.
[55]   WIPO 2015, fn. 48, *supra*, Annex, 6.
[56]   WIPO, CDIP/21/15, Report of the 21st meeting of the Committee on Development and Intellectual Property (2018a); WIPO, CDIP/21/12 REV, Project Proposal from the Delegations of Canada, Mexico and the United States of America on Increasing the Role of Women in Innovation and Entrepreneurship, Encouraging Women in Developing Countries to Use the Intellectual Property System (2018b).
[57]   WIPO 2016c, fn. 54, *supra*, Annex IV.
[58]   WIPO, CDIP/17/11, Report of the 17th meeting of the Committee on Development and Intellectual Property (2016d) paras 247 & 367 (China), paras 534 & 596 (Brazil); see also WIPO 2017a, fn. 43, *supra*, paras 27 & 191 (Indonesia), paras 36 & 188 (Nigeria, on behalf of the African Group), para 189 (China), para 190 (Chile, on behalf of GRULAC), para 197 (South Africa) and para 198 (India).
[59]   WIPO 2017a, fn. 43, *supra*, 77; see also 78–80; WIPO, CDIP/19/12, Report of the 19th meeting of the Committee on Development and Intellectual Property (2017b) 3–4; and WIPO, CDIP/20/13, Report of the 20th meeting of the Committee on Development and Intellectual Property (2018c) 87 [xiii–xiv in 'list of work'].
[60]   WIPO 2017a, fn. 43, *supra*, 51–61, WIPO 2016d, fn. 58, *supra*, 71–76, and WIPO 2016b, fn. 50, *supra*, 55–64.
[61]   WIPO, CDIP/21/10, Report on WIPO's Contribution to the Implementation of the Sustainable Development Goals and Its Associated Targets. Prepared by the Secretariat (2018d); WIPO, CDIP/23/10, Report on WIPO's Contribution to the Implementation

On the controversial issue of whether WIPO should adopt a broad or narrow approach towards the SDGs, WIPO's Director General highlighted four 'levels' for different SDGs: (i) Innovation *contributes directly* to the SDGs; (ii) innovation as a *policy setting* can assist in meeting the SDG; (iii) certain SDGs are *relevant* to the settings of an innovation policy framework; and (iv) SDG 17 is a *modality*.[62] The term modality is understood as the mode by which something is done. Several SDGs are listed under each of the first three categories. Hence, only SDG 16 (just, peaceful and inclusive societies) has never been identified by the WIPO Secretariat as relevant.[63]

The mandate of the CDIP goes, however, beyond the 45 recommendations adopted in 2007, as the CDIP is mandated to 'discuss intellectual property and development related issues as agreed by the Committee, as well as those decided by the General Assembly'.[64] The core of WIPO's work in the realm of development should be to identify how IP can foster technology transfer,[65] and how WIPO can provide technical assistance and capacity building for the purpose of technology promotion.[66] When the 2019 Conference on IP and Development was summed up by WIPO, however, a balanced IP system was

---

of the Sustainable Development Goals and Its Associated Targets. Prepared by the Secretariat (2019b); WIPO, CDIP/25/6, Report on WIPO's Contribution to the Implementation of the Sustainable Development Goals and Its Associated Targets. Prepared by the Secretariat (2020).

[62]   WIPO, Report on WIPO's Contribution to the Implementation of SDGs and its Associated Targets. Prepared by the Secretariat (2017c) Annex, 6–7 (italics added).

[63]   Ibid, Annex; WIPO 2015, fn. 48, *supra*, Annex.

[64]   WIPO 2007, fn. 42, *supra*, 152, decision 3c; see also WIPO 2018c, fn. 59, *supra*, 87 [xvi in 'list of work']; and WIPO, CDIP/21/8 REV, Compilation of Member State Inputs on Issues to be Addressed under the Agenda Item 'Intellectual Property and Development'. Prepared by the Secretariat (2018e).

[65]   WIPO 2018c, fn. 59, *supra*, 87 [x–xii in 'list of work']; see also WIPO, CDIP/19/11 REV, Project on Intellectual Property Management and Transfer of Technology (2017d).

[66]   WIPO 2018c, fn. 59, *supra*, 87 [vi–ix in 'list of work']; see also Carolyn Deere-Birkbeck and Ron Marchant, *The Technical Assistance Principles of the WIPO Development Agenda and their Practical Implementation. Issue Paper No. 28* (International Centre for Trade and Sustainable Development 2010). This chapter cannot analyse the many projects to implement the 45 recommendations of the DA, but as one example, Recommendation 8 on facilitating access to specialized databases for the purposes of patent searches has been promoted by the establishment of Technology and Innovation Support Centers (TISCs) (WIPO, CDIP/3/INF/2 (2009) Annex III). By 2019, there were 835 TISCs, each being categorized according to the range of services they provided; see WIPO, *WIPO and the Sustainable Development Goals. Innovation Driving Human Progress* (WIPO 2019c); see also WIPO, *Technology and Innovation Support Centers (TISCs) Report 2018. Celebrating 10 years of TISCs* (WIPO 2019d).

operationalized as 'to balance the issue of protection and enforcement'.[67] This is not the most common definition of a balanced IP system, as discussed above, as access for technology consumers is not acknowledged.

Notwithstanding the disagreements on whether the SDGs should be a standing agenda item of the CDIP and whether WIPO should relate to (almost) all the SDGs, the policy debates in WIPO demonstrate that WIPO takes its role as a UN agency seriously.

The governing challenges of WIPO must be noted, however, with the UN Joint Inspection Unit (JIU) calling for a review of the WIPO 'governance framework as well as current practices with a view to strengthen the capacity of the governing bodies to guide and monitor the work of the organization'.[68] In JIU's report, WIPO's DA was addressed specifically, noting 'an acute polarization between various groups of delegations …'.[69] The JIU recommends 'an effective system for reporting, monitoring and evaluating the implementation of the DA recommendations'.[70] This recommendation was not, however, among the ten main recommendations, and was not addressed explicitly by WIPO in its response.[71] Effective implementation of the recommendations of the CDIP will enhance WIPO's global legitimacy.

6.   THE WHO, WIPO, WTO TRILATERAL COOPERATION ON PUBLIC HEALTH, IP AND TRADE

The cooperation started earlier, but the first symposium of the Trilateral Cooperation held in 2010 marks an important strengthening of the common efforts by these three organizations and agencies. These have been renamed 'technical symposiums', and a total of eight have been held so far, in addition to 14 workshops on the TRIPS Agreement and public health.[72] Moreover, there

---

[67]   WIPO 2019a, fn. 47, *supra*, Annex 1, 14.

[68]   UN Joint Inspection Unit [JIU], JIU/REP/2014/2, Review of Management and Administration in the World Intellectual Property Organization (WIPO) (2014) recommendation 1 (extract); see also WIPO, WO/PBC/22/WIPO Response and Observations to JIU/REP/2014/2 (2014).

[69]   JIU/REP/2014/2, 10.

[70]   Ibid, 11.

[71]   WIPO 2014, fn. 68, *supra*.

[72]   WTO Secretariat, Trilateral Cooperation on Intellectual Property and Public Health (2020) https://www.wto.org/english/tratop_e/trips_e/who_wipo_wto_e.htm (accessed 22 June 2020). One of the 2020 webinars convened by WIPO was hosted by the Trilateral cooperation; see: https://www.wipo.int/meetings/en/topic.jsp?group_id=311 (accessed 22 June 2020).

have been three studies, one before and two after the launch of the Trilateral Cooperation.[73]

These studies are broad, and even though a 20-page section in the most recent study identifies IP-related determinants of access,[74] it can be argued that the study does not explore in depth the flexibilities provided by TRIPS. One example suffices, regarding the possibility to revoke or forfeit patents.[75] This provision of TRIPS is relatively seldom analysed as an example of TRIPS flexibility,[76] and here it will be used as an illustration.

Article 32 of TRIPS reads: 'An opportunity for judicial review of any decision to revoke or forfeit a patent shall be available.' Moreover, revocation or forfeiture is regulated by Article 5A(3) of the 1883 Paris Convention for the Protection of Industrial Property.[77]

As explained by the present author,[78] TRIPS does not prescribe what are the justified reasons for revocations – for correcting abuse or errors done before the patent grant – or forfeiture – for correcting abuse or errors done after the patent grant. Most commonly, revocation can be done in cases of non-compliance

---

[73]   WHO, WIPO and WTO, Promoting Access to Medical Technologies and Innovation. Second edition. Intersections between Public Health, Intellectual Property and Trade (2020) https://www.wto.org/english/res_e/booksp_e/who-wipo-wto_2020_e .pdf (accessed 10 November 2020); WHO, WIPO and WTO, Promoting Access to Medical Technologies and Innovation: Intersections between Public Health, Intellectual Property and Trade (2013) https://www.wto.org/english/res_e/booksp_e/pamtiwhowip owtoweb13e.pdf (accessed 22 June 2020); WHO and WTO, WTO Agreements and Public Health. A Joint Study by the WHO and the WTO Secretariat (2002) https://www .wto.org/english/res_e/booksp_e/who_wto_e.pdf (accessed 22 June 2020).

[74]   WHO, WIPO and WTO 2020, fn. 73, *supra*, 171.

[75]   WHO, WIPO and WTO 2020, fn. 73, *supra*, 59–60, notes 66 and 70 and accompanying text; note 70 refers to WIPO, SCP/18/4, Opposition Systems and other Administrative Revocation and Invalidation Mechanisms. Document Prepared by the Secretariat (2012).

[76]   Jayashree Watal, 'Implementing the TRIPS Agreement on Patents: Optimal Legislative Strategies for Developing Countries' in Owen Lippert (ed.) *Competitive Strategies for the Protection of Intellectual Property* (Fraser Institute 1999) 111.

[77]   Ibid; see also Hans Morten Haugen, 'The Right to Food, Farmers' Rights and Intellectual Property Rights: Can Competing Law Be Reconciled?' in Nadia Lambek, Priscilla Claeys, Adrienne Wong and Lea Brilmayer (eds) *Rethinking Food Systems: Structural Challenges, New Strategies and the Law* (Springer 2014) 206, contrasting Watal, fn. 76, *supra* and Andrea Gülland and Wanda Werner, 'Article 32' in Peter-Tobias Stoll, Jan Busche and Katrin Arend (eds) *WTO – Trade-Related Aspects of Intellectual Property Rights, Max Planck Commentaries on World Trade Law, Vol 7* (Brill 2009).

[78]   Hans Morten Haugen, *The Right to Food and the TRIPS Agreement – With a Particular Emphasis on Developing Countries' Measures for Food Production and Distribution* (Brill 2007) 245–248.

with any of the substantive patentability requirements, or inadequate disclosure of the patent. Forfeiture is most commonly done if annual patent fees are not paid or in cases of non-working of the patented invention, as for instance provided in Section 89 of the India Patent Act.

In the WIPO document, there is reference only to one piece of legislation that allows a state to 'cancel' a patent, if the patent 'is contrary to public order or morality'.[79] There are, however, other states, such as India, that allow for 'revocation of patent in public interest', as further specified in Section 66 of the India Patent Act. There is nothing in the TRIPS Agreement that prohibits the revocation of patents in the public interest.[80]

While cancellation procedures are by their nature controversial, the Trilateral Cooperation (WHO, WIPO and WTO) should at least identify all possible flexibilities that actually exist within TRIPS. In the latter study, there is, however, a review of so-called 'TRIPS plus' provisions in bilateral and plurilateral trade and investment agreements, for instance so-called 'border measures' beyond those required by TRIPS applying to copyright and trade marks (TRIPS Section 4; Articles 51–60).[81] Picking up on the World Health Assembly's call to all countries to take the impact on public health into account when adopting IP legislation,[82] the Trilateral Cooperation warned that TRIPS-plus provisions might affect both the creation of and access to medical technologies.[83]

References to TRIPS flexibilities are at the core of the disagreements regarding IP. TRIPS flexibilities were not included in the 2018 UN draft political declaration on tuberculosis that was first sent to the President of the UN General Assembly,[84] but the text was later revised, specifying that IP 'should be interpreted and implemented in a manner supportive of the right of Member States to protect public health …'.[85] This new resolution was approved at the

---

[79]   WIPO 2012, fn. 75, *supra*, 54, para 249 [The Philippines' Patent Act, Section 61.1(c)].

[80]   Watal, fn. 76, *supra*.

[81]   WHO, WIPO and WTO 2020, fn. 73, *supra*, 187.

[82]   WHO, Resolution WHA61.21, Global Strategy and Plan of Action on Public Health, Innovation and Intellectual Property (2008).

[83]   WHO, WIPO and WTO 2020, fn. 73, *supra*, 190.

[84]   UN intergovernmental consultations and negotiations on the modalities and outcomes of the High-Level Meeting on the Fight against Tuberculosis, United to End Tuberculosis: An Urgent Global Response to a Global Epidemic (20 July 2018) https://www.un.org/pga/72/wp-content/uploads/sites/51/2018/07/TB.pdf (accessed 22 June 2020).

[85]   UN General Assembly, A/RES/73/3, Political Declaration of the High-Level Meeting of the General Assembly on the Fight against Tuberculosis (2018a) para 19. See also UN General Assembly, A/RES/73/2, Political Declaration of the Third High-Level Meeting of the General Assembly on the Prevention and Control of Non-Communicable Diseases (2018b) para 36. The call for a rewording of this para-

high-level meeting of the UN General Assembly, which set aside one full day to discuss the fight against tuberculosis. In 2018, WIPO's Standing Committee on the Law of Patents agreed that 'Exceptions and Limitations to Patent Rights' should be a priority in its agenda item on future work,[86] and there was also an agenda item on patents and health.[87]

Innovation is the main emphasis in a report by WHO's Commission on Intellectual Property Rights, Innovation and Public Health (CIPRIPH). Hence, TRIPS Article 32 was not elaborated upon in this report, but the Commission analysed compulsory licences (TRIPS Article 31), parallel imports (TRIPS Article 6) and test data protection and data exclusivity (TRIPS Article 39.3). It specifies that Article 39.3

> does not create property rights, nor a right to prevent others from relying on the data for the marketing approval of the same product by a third party, or from using the data except where unfair (dishonest) commercial practices are involved.[88]

TRIPS Article 39.3, which applies to pharmaceutical or agricultural chemical products, only applies if states require such test data 'as a condition of approving the marketing' of such products.[89] If this is the case, such test data is to be protected against 'unfair commercial use' and 'disclosure, except where necessary to protect the public...'. As will be shown below, protection of test data in India has been repeatedly emphasized by Switzerland, without specifying whether the conditions specified in Article 39.3 actually apply to India, and the reality is that India does not require test data for approving medicines.[90] Moreover, India has the same approach for agricultural chemical products.

---

graph came from South Africa; see The Wire, 'UN Political Declaration on TB Likely to Be Re-Opened, With Pushback Against the US' (26 July 2018).

[86]   WIPO Standing Committee on the Law of Patents, SCP/28/11, Twenty-Eighth Session, Summary by the Chair (2018) 3–4; only compulsory licences have been discussed at the subsequent sessions; see WIPO Standing Committee on the Law of Patents, SCP/30/10, Thirtieth Session, Summary by the Chair (2019a) paras 5–7 [agenda item 5]; WIPO Standing Committee on the Law of Patents, SCP/31/9, Thirty-First Session, Summary by the Chair (2019b) paras 7–8 [agenda item 5].

[87]   Ibid (2019b) paras 15–19 [agenda item 7].

[88]   WHO's Commission on Intellectual Property Rights, Innovation and Public Health, Report of the Commission on Intellectual Property Rights, Innovation and Public Health (2006) 124, www.who.int/intellectualproperty/documents/thereport/ENPublicHealthReport.pdf (accessed 22 June 2020).

[89]   WHO, WIPO and WTO 2013, fn. 73, *supra*, 187.

[90]   LiveLaw, 'Patent Battle Over Breast Cancer Drug: Roche Withdraws Its SLP Against Delhi High Court's Approval to Biosimilars' (13 August 2017) http://www.livelaw.in/patent-battle-breast-cancer-drug-roche-withdraws-slp-delhi-high-courts-approval-biosimilars (accessed 22 June 2020).

Attempts to introduce a Pesticides (Amendment) Bill failed in 2008,[91] and it was again proposed to the Lok Sabha (Parliament) in 2015 but has still not been adopted.[92]

Moreover, the CIPRIPH underlined how 'improvements in "access" (availability, acceptability, accessibility and quality) are possible even in the face of weak infrastructure and poverty ...'.[93] Other issues analysed by the Commission include the facilitating of generic competition, by the means of an 'early working' exception in domestic patent law,[94] and how to avoid 'evergreening' of patents, more specifically that new patents are applied for based on the same inventions as existing patents, in order to extend the protection period.

The emphasis on access to medicines has been paramount in WHO's work, with a decision at the 2018 World Health Assembly (WHA) on a Roadmap for Access to Medicines and Vaccines, with a subsequent resolution on transparency in pricing at the 2019 WHA.[95] At the 2018 WHA, USA expressed opposition, particularly as concerns the use of compulsory licences to ensure access to affordable medicines.[96] The USA itself allows for compulsory licensing in its own legislation, with a high threshold in 28 US Code § 1498 for challenging the use of a patented invention without a licence from the owner. At the 2019 WHA, the opposition did not come from the USA, but from Germany, the United Kingdom and Hungary.[97]

Hence, despite more than 15 years of attempts to reconcile the rights of producers and users, and industrialized and developing countries, we still experience strong divides.

---

[91]　SpicyIP, 'Data Exclusivity Back on the Table for India' (27 March 2015).

[92]　Scroll, 'Draft Bill on Regulating Pesticides Could Punish Farmers who use Spurious Products, Experts Fear' (23 February 2018).

[93]　WHO's Commission on Intellectual Property Rights, Innovation and Public Health, fn. 88, *supra*, 107.

[94]　WHO's Commission on Intellectual Property Rights, Innovation and Public Health, fn. 88, *supra*, 130.

[95]　WHO, Resolution WHA71.12, Addressing the Global Shortage of, and Access to, Medicines and Vaccines (2018); see also WHO, A72/17, Access to Medicines and Vaccines, Report by the Director-General (2019a) and WHO, Resolution WHA72.8, Improving the Transparency of Markets for Medicines, Vaccines, and other Health Products (2019b).

[96]　Intellectual Property Watch, 'WHA Agrees On Drafting Of Roadmap For Access To Medicines And Vaccines; US Blasts Compulsory Licences' (24 May 2018).

[97]　Intellectual Property Watch, 'World Health Assembly Approves Milestone Resolution on Price Transparency' (28 May 2019).

7.   RECENT CONTROVERSIES CONCERNING IP

The main causes of tension tend to focus on pharmaceutical products, even if there are many examples of developing countries and LDCs taking upon themselves 'TRIPS plus' obligations within other fields of technology.[98] Moreover, India is the country that has received most attention recently, due to its large generic pharmaceutical industry and several rulings in the Supreme Court. As India is an important provider of affordable medicines also beyond its border, patent protection for pharmaceutical products in India will be highlighted.

Probably the most debated ruling is Novartis v. Union of India & Others (Supreme Court of India 2013). At the core of the ruling was Article 3(d) of India's 2005 Patent (Amendment) Act, adopted to comply with India's obligations under TRIPS. Article 3(d) – an example of an anti-evergreening law – states that 'inventions not patentable' includes (extract):

> the mere discovery of a new form of a known substance which does not result in the enhancement of the known efficacy of that substance or the mere discovery of any new property or new use for a known substance or of the mere use of a known process, ... unless such known process results in a new product ...

In brief, the Supreme Court found that Novartis' Gleevec did not meet the 'efficacy' test, but it also emphasized 'easy access to the denizens of this country for life saving drugs' and India's 'constitutional obligation of providing health care to its citizens'.

Over recent years, there have been several disputes between generic producers and Roche, also involving the Drugs Controller General of India (DCGI).[99]

---

[98]   Haugen 2015, fn. 44, *supra*.

[99]   High Court of Dehli, Roche v. Cipla [Erlocip], CS(OS) No.89/2008 & CC No.52/2008 (2012) [ruling in favour of Cipla, against Roche]; High Court of Dehli, Roche v. Cipla [Tarceva], RFA(OS) 92/2012 and RFA(OS) 103/2012 (2015a) [ruling in favour of Roche, against Cipla]; High Court of Dehli, Roche v. Glenmark Pharmaceuticals, CS(OS) No.402/2010 & CC No.50/2010 (2015b) [noting settlement between Roche and Glenmark Pharmaceuticals]; High Court of Dehli, Roche v. Drugs Controller General of India [Herceptin], CCP(O) No.69/2015, CS(OS) No.355/2014 (2016) [permitting Mylan and Biocon to manufacture and market generic products], High Court of Dehli, Roche v. Natco Pharma and Dr. Reddy's Laboratories, CS(COMM) Nos.29/2016 & 946/2016 (2017) [ruling in favour of Natco Pharma and Dr. Reddy's Laboratories, against Roche]. These judgments are available at http://delhihighcourt.nic.in/case.asp (accessed 22 June 2020), but the 3 March 2017 Order of the High Court of Dehli, in Biocon and Mylan v. Roche [ruling in favour of Biocon and Mylan] is available at http://delhihighcourt.nic.in/dhcqrydisp_o.asp?pn=50677&yr=2017 (accessed 22 June 2020). For an investigation against Roche, initiated by the Competition Commission of India, after a complaint brought by Biocon and Mylan, see

In addition, the DCGI has been obligated to comply with interim orders concerning labels and packaging.[100] The most recent disputes have been over Roche's cancer drug originally named Herceptin, which has appeared under new names.

Acknowledging that India has several flexibilities in its patent legislation, both generally and as regards pharmaceutical products and biotechnology inventions in the realm of agriculture,[101] it is interesting to review how India's Patent Act is viewed by other states. I have reviewed the examination of India's policies by the WTO's Trade Policy Review Body since 2005.

In 2007, Switzerland made a positive assessment of the 2005 Patent (Amendment) Act, and commented positively on the Act's pre- and post-grant opposition possibility, mailbox procedures (TRIPS Art 70.8(c)), new forms of a known substance and test data (TRIPS Art 39.3).[102] In 2011, however, Switzerland was more negative, noting that:

> legal uncertainty persists in the area of intellectual property rights protection and their effective enforcement. I can mention for example the uncertainty regarding the legal protection of undisclosed test data submitted to the authorities in order to get marketing approval for pharmaceuticals or plant protection products.[103]

We see that inadequate protection for test data is criticized, but the reality is that TRIPS only requires such test data to be protected if the domestic legislation requires such test data for approving marketing of products. The criticism by Switzerland was repeated in 2015,[104] but now with the addition that this

---

PatentsRewind, 'CCI Orders Investigation against Roche' (26 April 2017); for a subsequent (confidential) settlement and withdrawal of a case before the Supreme Court of India; see Centre for Biosimilars, 'Roche Withdraws SLP Against Biocon and Mylan's Trastuzumab Biosimilar' (14 August 2017). The 2016 judgment was appealed and has been heard at the High Court of Dehli; see FirstWorldPharma, 'Roche Plea in High Court on Cancer Drug not Maintainable: Mylan, Biocon' (10 January 2018). I have searched in vain for a subsequent judgment.

[100] High Court of Dehli, Roche v. Drugs Controller General of India, I.A. No.11225/2015 in CS(OS) No.355/2014 (2015c); High Court of Dehli, Roche v. Drugs Controller General of India I.A. Nos.2371/2014, 2988/2014, 2990/2014, 4649/2014, 4677/2014, 5956/2014, 9155/2014, 9157/2014, 14533/2014, 14534/2014, 791/2015, 11224/2015, 11225/2015, 12830/2015, 12831/2015, 12862/2015 & CCP(O) No.69/2015 in CS(OS) No.355/2014 (2015d).

[101] Haugen, fn. 77, *supra*, 215.

[102] WTO, WT/TPR/M/182, Trade Policy Review India. Minutes of Meeting (2007) para 157.

[103] WTO, WT/TPR/M/249, Trade Policy Review India. Minutes of Meeting (2011) para 115.

[104] WTO, WT/TPR/M/313, Trade Policy Review India. Minutes of Meeting (2015b) para 4.42.

criticism was echoed by the Chairperson when summing up the session, high-lighting protection of trade secrets and test data.[105] Further, the Chairperson noted that this and previous reviews had requested India to strengthen the enforcement of IP rights,[106] but the reality is that in 2015 several countries, including the USA, commended India for its measures to strengthen the enforcement of IP.[107]

Finally, to illustrate the tensions within global IP policies, the EU Counterfeiting and Piracy Watch-List is relevant. While the USA has for years applied the so-called 'Special 301' procedure as a basis for retaliating against any state that is believed to provide inadequate protection of IP, a new development is that the EU has adopted such a list, contained in a March 2018 report.[108] The EU Watch-List – categorizing 14 states under three different priorities, with China at level 1, India at level 2 and the USA at level 3 – has been criticized by several NGOs.[109] The basis of the criticism is that the criteria in the Watch-List build on standards that go far beyond the TRIPS Agreement for identifying inadequate IP protection. These include stricter patentability criteria, restrictions on compulsory licensing and requirements of test data pro-tection. Those criticizing the EU Watch-List assert that it blurs the distinction between generic medicines and counterfeit products. Hence, human rights, the objectives of the TRIPS Agreement and SDG target 3b are all undermined by the criteria applied in the Watch-List.

8.   DISCUSSION: WHAT EXPLAINS THE LACK OF ATTENTION TO IP IN THE SDGS?

In the introduction of the chapter, five C's were introduced as five hypotheses or possible explanations for the lack of emphasis in the 17 SDGs and the 169 SDG targets: (i) *complexity* of IP; (ii) lack of *communication* domestically; (iii) *compartmentalization* of IP issues in the UN; (iv) strengths of different *campaigns*; and (v) an overall *cautious* approach on IP. Which of these five hypotheses seems to be strengthened by the arguments put forth in this chapter?

---

[105]   Ibid, para 6.5.
[106]   Ibid, para 1.9.
[107]   Ibid, paras 4.77 (Colombia); 4.92 (USA); 4.217 (Brazil); 4.232 (Dominican Republic); 4.276 (Ecuador); and 4.350 (El Salvador).
[108]   EU Commission, *Commission Staff Working Document. Report on the Protection and Enforcement of Intellectual Property Rights in Third Countries*, SWD(2018) 47 final (EU 2018).
[109]   Access to Medicines Ireland and 32 others, 'Dear Commissioner Malmström' (2018) https://medicinesalliance.eu/wp-content/uploads/2018/04/Open-Letter-to-Com missioner-Malmstr%C3%B6m_-EU-Watch-List.pdf (accessed 22 June 2020).

The complexity of IP is never explicitly acknowledged by states, but the fact is that IPRs are not emphasized in the reports that feed into the UN system in New York nor feature in the resolutions emanating from these bodies. Even if there is no agreement between states on whether SDGs should become a standing agenda item in the CDIP, at least the WIPO Secretariat has taken the integral approach of the SDGs seriously. There is still a need to build mutual understanding between groups of states within WIPO faced with the 'acute polarization' between developed and developing countries that was noted by the UN Joint Inspection Unit.[110]

In addition to WIPO's CDIP, the UN has two additional bodies whose mandate relates to science and technology in the context of sustainable development: the CSTD (meeting in Geneva) and the STI Forum (meeting in New York). CSTD is formally a Commission under ECOSOC, presenting itself as 'the main platform in the UN system that addresses science and technology questions in the context of development',[111] giving 'high-level advice' to the central UN bodies.[112] The CSTD is not, however, adequately communicating specific recommendations from its sessions where experts are invited to speak.[113] As both WIPO and WHO are located in Geneva, it is fair to state that the most relevant UN bodies that are mandated to deal with issues related to technology and IP are located in Geneva – notwithstanding the fact that FAO is located in Rome, the UN Educational, Scientific and Cultural Organization (UNESCO) is located in Paris, and the UN Industrial Development Organization (UNIDO) is located in Vienna.

The location of WHO in Geneva has facilitated the cooperation between WHO, WIPO and WTO. Its most recent study identifies how provisions in certain bilateral trade and investment agreements go beyond the provisions in the TRIPS Agreement, particularly as regards 'patentability criteria, patent term extensions, test data protection, linkage of regulatory approval with

---

[110] UN Joint Inspection Unit, fn. 68, *supra*, 10.

[111] UNCTAD, 'United Nations to Address Rapid Technological Change and its Implications for Developing Countries' (10 May 2018) http://unctad.org/en/Pages/ PressRelease.aspx?OriginalVersionID=454 (accessed 22 June 2020).

[112] UNCTAD, United Nations Commission on Science and Technology for Development (CSTD) (2017) http://unctad.org/en/Pages/CSTD.aspx/en/Pages/.aspx ?Ne=11,5,,&An=,,ows_Country,ascending&In=,,ows_UNCTADLocation,descending &WG=,,ows_Title,ascending&Do=19,5 (accessed 22 June 2020).

[113] UN 2017a, fn. 33, *supra*, Annex II, paras 8–9, merely listing the speakers at the session held on 10 May 2017, during the CSTD session. The report from the intersessional panel, held in Geneva from 23 to 25 January 2017 (E/CN.16/2017/CRP.1) is not available from the CSTD home page, but there are five Q&A resources; see UNCTAD 2017, fn. 112, *supra*.

patents and enforcement of IP, including border measures ...'.[114] As seen above, there are other flexibilities in TRIPS that are not addressed adequately, for instance forfeiture of patents in the public interest, to enhance access to affordable medicines or vaccines. As developing countries are encouraged by SDG target 3b to use the TRIPS flexibilities 'to the full', all possible TRIPS flexibilities should have been identified, and this is not done in the report by the WHO's CIPRIPH.

There is therefore a basis for affirming that, even if there is an acknowledgement of the flexibilities, insufficiently detailed knowledge is included in various written reports in the UN system. The same argument applies to disagreements within the WTO, such as when India was criticized for its lack of test data protection,[115] when in reality TRIPS only requires such test data to be protected if the domestic legislation requires such test data for approving marketing of products.

Hence, hypotheses (i) and (iii) on complexity and compartmentalization are strengthened. Hypothesis (ii) on lack of communication on IP issues in the domestic realm, between different ministries and public bodies, has not been adequately analysed in this chapter, but I have identified a clear lack of communication in another article.[116]

Regarding hypothesis (iv) on the strength of various NGO campaigns, several successes through the efforts of NGOs during the last two decades have been reported.[117] Abbott notes that the TRIPS-plus provisions represent an *exception* to this overall trend of prioritizing access to medicines in the context of public health. This can be explained by the fact that pharmaceutical companies have undertaken advocacy efforts towards the presidents' offices, based on an observation that many developing countries' governments 'work with a lot of authority flowing down from the presidential office that affects the outcome of trade negotiations and legislative efforts'.[118] Lobbying and advocacy efforts by NGOs might not be as effective as those efforts undertaken by the pharmaceutical companies or their associations.

The fact that it is in the realm of medicines that we see the only explicit reference to IP among all the SDG targets is therefore no coincidence. The clear tension between (high) price and (less) affordability is relatively easy

---

[114] WHO, WIPO and WTO 2020, fn. 73, *supra*, 171; less emphasis on flexibilities are found in WHO and WTO 2002, fn. 73, *supra*.
[115] WTO 2015b, fn. 104, *supra*, para 4.42; WTO 2011, fn. 104, *supra*, para 115.
[116] Haugen 2015, fn. 44, *supra*.
[117] Intellectual Property Watch, 'Civil Society Key in TRIPS Flexibility Implementation' (4 May 2018).
[118] Ibid, sect. 'Role of Civil Society Key in Access to Medicines', quoting Professor Abbott.

to communicate. Some might argue that the same would apply to seeds and schoolbooks, but price effects of patented seeds and copyrighted material are not necessarily as obvious as in the realm of pharmaceuticals and health, as it is easier to get access to alternative products in the realm of education and food. Hence, a company selling seeds for ten times the price of its competitors' seeds would soon be outcompeted.

While patenting in the realm of medicines has received the most attention, there is no lack of awareness or critical voices in the realm of seeds patenting or use of copyrighted material for educational purposes. NGO pressure is not enough, however. Such pressure must correspond with a willingness among states to arrive at a formulation that could find enough common ground between the diverse groups of states to be specified as an SDG target. Hence, hypothesis (iv) relating to NGO campaigns may explain why there is an IP reference within the SDGs in the realm of access to medicines. While NGO campaigns have brought attention to the price effects of IP, other SDG targets are silent as regards IP.

Lastly, hypothesis (v) advocating a cautious approach seems difficult to uphold. There is no general opposition to IP among developing countries. Many consider strong IP standards and effective IP enforcement as critical for attracting foreign investment, not adequately acknowledging that there are a broad range of other policy measures that will foster predictability and facilitate any investment decisions.

9.   CONCLUSION

To find new and real solutions to the overwhelming challenges encompassed by the 17 SDGs requires inventiveness and innovative strategies. There can be no doubt that a well-functioning IP system is important for fostering such solutions. Developing countries – and particularly LDCs that are presently not required to comply with the substantive parts of the TRIPS Agreement – should not be pressured to adopt higher standards of IP protection than their development level indicates.

The SDG target 3b specifies that TRIPS flexibilities must be 'used to the full' by developing countries. The most recent UN resolution on STI for development underlines an IP framework that is aligned with their development strategies,[119] but that also is to be 'efficient, adequate, balanced and effective'.[120] As clarified above, 'balanced' implies providing for technology producers and technology consumers simultaneously, but a WIPO Director

---

[119]   UN 2020b, fn. 104, *supra*, para 29.
[120]   UN 2020b, fn. 104, *supra*, para 7.

operationalizes a balanced IP system so as 'to balance the issue of protection and enforcement'.[121] WIPO is not necessarily the best choice for advice on how to use TRIPS flexibilities.

While this chapter acknowledges that TRIPS flexibilities are applied, there is pressure on developing countries to apply strict IP standards, with the EU Commission Watch-List a prominent example of this approach. As access to medicines is so crucial for improving the social pillar within sustainable development, the chapter has devoted most attention to medicines in the context of identifying recent controversies such as India's legislation. Both the Watch-List and particularly Switzerland's approach towards India has been criticized.

Five hypotheses to explain the lack of emphasis on the role of IP in the SDGs were introduced and considered in this chapter. In conclusion, the first, third and fourth hypotheses on the complexity of IP, on the compartmentalization of IP issues in the UN and on NGO campaigns were strengthened. The fifth hypothesis on a cautious approach was not affirmed. The second hypothesis on lack of communication on IP domestically did not have adequate empirical material to be assessed in this chapter.

---

[121]　WIPO 2019a, fn. 47, *supra*, Annex 1, 14.

3. Realigning TRIPS-plus negotiations with UN Sustainable Development Goals[1]

Peter K. Yu

1. INTRODUCTION

The development of the intellectual property system goes hand in hand with efforts to promote sustainable development. Such development is explicitly mentioned in key documents involving both the World Trade Organization (WTO) and the World Intellectual Property Organization (WIPO), the two predominant multilateral intellectual property negotiation fora. The preamble of the Agreement Establishing the World Trade Organization '[r]ecogniz[ed] that ... relations in the field of trade and economic endeavour should be conducted with a view to ... allowing for the optimal use of the world's resources in accordance with the objective of sustainable development'. A few years ago, the United Nations also adopted a set of sustainable development goals (SDGs) to replace its earlier Millennium Development Goals (MDGs). As a UN specialized agency, WIPO is expected not only to play important roles in realizing the SDGs, but also to ensure the consistency between its multilateral negotiations and efforts to promote these goals.

This chapter begins by discussing the intersection between the SDGs and the development of the intellectual property system – at both the domestic and international levels. A deeper understanding of this interrelationship is urgently needed, considering the recurring debates at WIPO about whether its mandates, activities and strategic goals contribute to achieving these goals. This chapter then outlines the direct and indirect impediments that the recent and ongoing negotiations for TRIPS-plus bilateral, regional and plurilateral agreements have placed on the promotion and fulfilment of the

---

[1] This chapter draws on research that the author conducted for earlier articles in the *Florida Law Review* and the *WIPO Journal* as well as a book chapter published by Edward Elgar Publishing.

SDGs. These agreements include the Anti-Counterfeiting Trade Agreement (ACTA), the Trans-Pacific Partnership (TPP) Agreement, the Comprehensive and Progressive Agreement for Trans-Pacific Partnership (CPTPP) and the Regional Comprehensive Economic Partnership (RCEP) Agreement. In view of the potential dangers and complications caused by TRIPS-plus intellectual property negotiations, this chapter concludes by identifying six distinct strategies that developing countries may deploy to ensure greater promotion and fulfilment of the SDGs.

Greater alignment of international intellectual property negotiations with these goals is critically important to the development of sustainable markets at both the national and international levels. Whether in the area of public health, climate change, genetic resources or traditional knowledge, developing countries have important roles to play in the debate on intellectual property and sustainability.[2] Just as the Brundtland Commission called on us to 'ensure that [development] meets the needs of the present without compromising the ability of future generations to meet their own needs',[3] international intellectual property negotiations should be conducted in a way that will not compromise the developing countries' abilities to meet their present and future needs.

2.   SUSTAINABLE DEVELOPMENT GOALS

In December 2015, the United Nations completed its cycle for the MDGs, which were launched in September 2000 as part of the UN Millennium Declaration. Adopted in its place was the 2030 Agenda for Sustainable Development, which sought to achieve development for the next 15 years and featured 17 SDGs and 169 targets. The incorporation of these goals into WIPO's activities began to emerge as an important issue at the eighteenth session of the WIPO Committee on Development and Intellectual Property (CDIP) in fall 2016.[4] Given that the SDGs will continue until the end of 2030, this issue will likely remain important, relevant and perhaps even controversial at WIPO in the next decade.

---

[2]   Marie-Claire Cordonier Segger and Ashfaq Khalfan, *Sustainable Development Law: Principles, Practices and Prospects* 2 (Oxford: Oxford University Press 2004); World Commission on Environment and Development, *Our Common Future* 41 (Oxford: Oxford University Press 1987); Peter K. Yu, 'Five Decades of Intellectual Property and Global Development' (2016) 8 *WIPO Journal* 1, 9.

[3]   World Commission on Environment and Development, fn. 2 *supra*, 8.

[4]   Catherine Saez, 'WIPO Committee Debates SDGs, Review of Development Agenda Recommendations', *Intellectual Property Watch* 1 November 2016. See also Chapter 2 in this volume.

At that CDIP meeting, the committee members explored the relationship between the SDGs and WIPO's mandate, activities and strategic goals. Considered to be directly related to WIPO were SDG 9 ('Build resilient infrastructure, promote inclusive and sustainable industrialization and foster innovation') and SDG 17 ('Strengthen the means of implementation and revitalize the Global Partnership for Sustainable Development'). Also listed as relevant to WIPO's programmes and activities in a CDIP document were SDG 2 ('End hunger, achieve food security and improved nutrition and promote sustainable agriculture'), SDG 3 ('Ensure healthy lives and promote well-being for all at all ages'), SDG 4 ('Ensure inclusive and equitable quality education and promote lifelong learning opportunities for all'), SDG 7 ('Ensure access to affordable, reliable, sustainable and modern energy for all'), SDG 8 ('Promote sustained, inclusive and sustainable economic growth, full and productive employment and decent work for all') and SDG 13 ('Take urgent action to combat climate change and its impacts').[5]

Thus far, developing countries have actively pushed for a broadened focus on the relationship between the SDGs and WIPO's mandate, activities and strategic goals. In that direction, Brazil, China, Uganda and the Latin American and Caribbean Group (GRULAC) provided independent written submissions to the CDIP.[6] China took the position that 'in addition to the above-mentioned nine goals, many of the 17 SDGs and 169 targets are related to [intellectual property] and in particular to the work of WIPO'.[7] Likewise, Brazil declared:

> As one of the specialized agenc[ies] of the United Nations, WIPO presents the adequate technical capacity necessary to actively participate in the debates and actions related to the SDGs. Given its legal status, shaped by the Agreement between the United Nations and WIPO of 1974, WIPO must bring inputs that enable the implementation of the objectives, in collaboration with other relevant actors. Furthermore, the 2030 Agenda requests that international organizations mobilize, from all sources, 'financial and technical assistance to strengthen developing countries' scientific, technological and innovative capacities to move towards more sustainable patterns of consumption and production'. It is a role in which WIPO has the experience and human power demanded by those countries and the Organization [should] not evade its responsibility.[8]

By contrast, developed countries have been highly critical of the greater linkage between the SDGs and WIPO. Speaking on behalf of the Group B

---

[5]   Committee on Development and Intellectual Property, 'WIPO and the Post-2015 Development Agenda', 9 October 2015, CDIP/16/8.
[6]   Committee on Development and Intellectual Property, 'Compilation of Member State Inputs on SDGs Relevant to WIPO's Work', 8 August 2016, CDIP/18/4.
[7]   *Ibid*, annex I, 2.
[8]   *Ibid*, annex IV, 2.

developed countries, the delegate from Turkey declared, 'WIPO's work in relation to the SDGs must be in line with the organisation's mandate as per its Convention and focus on the areas of expertise of the organisation'.[9]

While it is not difficult to understand the developed countries' resistance to the consideration of a wide array of SDGs when reviewing WIPO's programmes and activities – which closely align with the traditional North–South divide – it is somewhat disingenuous to deny the direct relation between SDG 3 and WIPO's mandate and strategic goals.[10] Seeking to '[e]nsure healthy lives and promote well-being for all at all ages', that goal was the only SDG that explicitly mentioned the TRIPS Agreement and the Doha Declaration on the TRIPS Agreement and Public Health. Adopted on 14 November 2001, the Doha Declaration focused specifically on the interplay between intellectual property protection and the protection of public health. The first two paragraphs of the Declaration explicitly 'recognize[d] the gravity of the public health problems afflicting many developing and least-developed countries, especially those resulting from HIV/AIDS, tuberculosis, malaria and other epidemics ... [and] the need for the [TRIPS Agreement] to be part of the wider national and international action to address these problems'.

Moreover, in the past few decades, the intellectual property system has greatly expanded at both the domestic and international levels. Today, intellectual property issues have spilt over into many different areas. A case in point is the ongoing effort to create international instruments for the protection of genetic resources, traditional knowledge and traditional cultural expressions. Explicitly mentioned in SDG Target 2.5, such protection has impacted on a wide variety of policy areas, including agricultural productivity, biological diversity, cultural patrimony, food security, environmental sustainability, business ethics, global competition, human rights, international trade, public health, scientific research, sustainable development and wealth distribution.[11]

Finally, as WIPO and its CDIP continue to explore ways to better incorporate the SDGs into the organization's programmes and activities, there is no better support and guidance than the Declaration on the Right to Development,

---

[9]   Catherine Saez, 'WIPO Members Divided on IP Agency's Role in Implementation of UN Sustainable Development Goals', *Intellectual Property Watch* 2 November 2016.

[10]   One could note WIPO's sensitivity to the fact that the World Health Organization is the primary UN agency handling public health matters. However, this siloed approach, while understandable, is not conducive to addressing matters that have now impacted multiple issue areas, including both health and intellectual property.

[11]   Peter K. Yu, 'Traditional Knowledge, Intellectual Property, and Indigenous Culture: An Introduction' (2003) 11 *Cardozo Journal of International and Comparative Law* 239, 240.

which was adopted in December 1986 and affirmed by the Vienna Declaration and Programme of Action in June 1993. Article 1(1) of this Declaration expressly states:

> The right to development is an inalienable human right by virtue of which every human person and all peoples are entitled to participate in, contribute to, and enjoy economic, social, cultural and political development, in which all human rights and fundamental freedoms can be fully realized.

Although controversy continues to exist in the developed world concerning the necessity, validity, viability, usefulness and legal status of the right to development,[12] this Declaration has provided important insight into efforts seeking to tailor the intellectual property system to the needs of development. Article 2(1) of the Declaration explicitly states: 'The human person is the central subject of development and should be the active participant and beneficiary of the right to development.' The development of the intellectual property system should therefore be human-centred, rather than focus unduly on the interests of intellectual property industries. Such a human-centred approach will further require greater consistency between intellectual property laws and policies on the one hand and international human rights obligations on the other.[13] Examples of such obligations are those relating to the right to life, the

---

[12]   Isabella Bunn, *The Right to Development and International Economic Law: Legal and Moral Dimensions* (Oxford: Hart 2012) 1, 127. On this controversy, see Ahmed Abdel-Latif, 'The Right to Development: What Implications for the Multilateral Intellectual Property Framework?' in Christophe Geiger (ed.), *Research Handbook on Human Rights and Intellectual Property* (Cheltenham, UK and Northampton, MA, USA: Edward Elgar Publishing 2015); Philip Alston, 'The Shortcomings of a Garfield the Cat Approach to the Right to Development' (1985) 15 *California Western International Law Journal* 510; Jack Donnelly, 'In Search of the Unicorn: The Jurisprudence and Politics of the Right to Development' (1985) 15 *California Western International Law Journal* 473; Stephen Marks, 'The Human Right to Development: Between Rhetoric and Reality' (2004) 17 *Harvard Human Rights Journal* 137; Oscar Schachter, 'Implementing the Right to Development: Programme of Action' in Subrata Roy Chowdhury, Erik M.G. Denters and Paul J.I.M. de Waart (eds), *The Right to Development in International Law* (Dordrecht: Martinus Nijhoff Publishers 1992).

[13]   E.g. Sub-Commission on the Promotion and Protection of Human Rights, 'The Impact of the Agreement on Trade-Related Aspects of Intellectual Property Rights on Human Rights: Report of the High Commissioner', 27 June 2001, E/CN.4/Sub.2/2001/13; Committee on Economic, Social and Cultural Rights, 'General Comment No. 17: The Right of Everyone to Benefit from the Protection of the Moral and Material Interests Resulting from Any Scientific, Literary or Artistic Production of Which He or She Is the Author (Article 15, Paragraph 1(c), of the Covenant)', 12 January 2006, E/C.12/GC/17; Special Rapporteur in the Field of Cultural Rights (Farida Shaheed), 'Copyright Policy and the Right to Science and Culture: Report of the

right to health, the right to food, the right to freedom of expression, the right to education, the right to cultural participation and development, the right to enjoy the benefits of scientific progress and its applications, and the right to self-determination.[14] In addition, the Declaration on the Right to Development underscores the collective responsibility to promote and fulfil the SDGs. This responsibility should be borne by neither the Global North nor the Global South. Instead, it should be shared by the entire international community.[15] As article 2(2) of the Declaration stated, '[a]ll human beings have a responsibility for development, individually and collectively'. Although intellectual property laws, policies and treaties have been frequently criticized for favouring developed country interests, intellectual property rights per se are not biased towards either the Global North or the Global South. Thus far, developed countries have played a predominant role in creating and shaping international intellectual property norms. Nevertheless, with appropriate political support and technical guidance, these norms can be easily realigned to provide developing countries with greater benefits and stronger recognition of their intellectual property interests.

It is therefore no surprise that WIPO noted in a CDIP document that 'many of the SDGs are dependent upon the development and diffusion of innovative technologies'.[16] As the document explained:

Innovation and creativity are not goals in themselves; they are means and tools for creative solutions to development challenges and, being at the heart of the system,

Special Rapporteur in the Field of Cultural Rights', 24 December 2014, A/HRC/28/57; Special Rapporteur in the Field of Cultural Rights (Farida Shaheed), 'Cultural Rights', 4 August 2015, A/70/279.

[14] For the author's earlier articles on intellectual property and human rights, see Peter K. Yu, 'The Anatomy of the Human Rights Framework for Intellectual Property' (2016) 69 *SMU Law Review* 37 ('Anatomy of Human Rights'); Peter K. Yu, 'Digital Copyright Enforcement Measures and Their Human Rights Threats' in Geiger, fn. 12 *supra*; Peter K. Yu, 'Intellectual Property and Human Rights 2.0' (2019) 53 *University of Richmond Law Review* 1375; Peter K. Yu, 'Intellectual Property and Human Rights in the Nonmultilateral Era' (2012) 64 *Florida Law Review* 1045 ('Nonmultilateral Era'); Peter K. Yu, 'Reconceptualizing Intellectual Property Interests in a Human Rights Framework' (2007) 40 *U.C. Davis Law Review* 1039; Peter K. Yu, 'Ten Common Questions about Intellectual Property and Human Rights' (2007) 23 *Georgia State University Law Review* 709.

[15] Subrata Roy Chowdhury and Paul J.I.M. de Waart, 'Significance of the Right to Development: An Introductory View' in Chowdhury, Denters and de Waart, fn. 12 *supra*, 19; Khurshid Iqbal, *The Right to Development in International Law: The Case of Pakistan* (London: Routledge 2010) 86–7; Takhmina Karimova, *Human Rights and Development in International Law* (Abingdon: Routledge 2016) 110.

[16] Committee on Development and Intellectual Property, 'Report on WIPO's Contribution to the Implementation of the Sustainable Development Goals and Its Associated Targets', para. 8, 26 March 2018, CDIP/21/10.

have an impact on many of the SDGs. As such, innovation has a direct impact on SDG 2 (zero hunger), SDG 3 (good health and well being), SDG 6 (clean water and sanitation), SDG 7 (affordable and clean energy), SDG 8 (decent work and economic growth), SDG 11 (sustainable cities and communities) and SDG 13 (climate change). As a policy setting, innovation can assist in achieving SDG 1 (no poverty[)], SDG 8 (decent work and economic growth), SDG 14 (life below water), and SDG 15 (life on land). Moreover, certain SDGs are relevant to the settings of an innovation policy framework, notably SDG 5 (gender equality[)], SDG 8 (decent work and economic growth), SDG 10 (reduced inequalities), and SDG 12 (responsible consumption and production).

3.   TRIPS-PLUS AGREEMENTS

3.1   Recent and Ongoing Developments

Since the early 2000s, the European Union and the United States have been using bilateral and regional trade agreements to enhance their bargaining positions and to avoid deadlocks in international intellectual property negotiations. The need for such agreements was apparent following the collapse of the Millennium Round of Trade Negotiations in Seattle and the premature end of the Fifth WTO Ministerial Meeting in Cancún. As a result of these debacles, developed countries began searching for what Fred Bergsten described as 'competitive liberalization'.[17] Such liberalization calls for the development of preferential arrangements to liberalize trade by promoting competition among countries, especially those in small regional markets.[18]

Today, the United States has established standalone free trade agreements (FTAs) with Australia, Bahrain, Chile, Colombia, Israel, Jordan, Morocco, Oman, Panama, Peru, Singapore and South Korea. The United States is also a party to the Dominican Republic–Central America Free Trade Agreement, which it signed with Costa Rica, the Dominican Republic, El Salvador, Guatemala, Honduras and Nicaragua on 5 August 2004. More recently, the Trump administration completed its re-negotiation of the North American Free Trade Agreement (NAFTA), which was established close to three decades ago. Signed in November 2018, the United States–Mexico–Canada Agreement, which sought to replace its predecessor, entered into effect on 1 July 2020.

---

[17]   Fred C. Bergsten, 'Competitive Liberalization and Global Free Trade: A Vision for the Early 21st Century' (1996) *Institute for International Economics Working Paper No. 96-15.*

[18]   Renato Ruggiero, 'Comment' in Jeffrey J. Schott (ed.), *Free Trade Agreements: US Strategies and Priorities* (Washington, DC: Institute for International Economics 2004) 26.

Meanwhile, the European Union has established economic partnership agreements (EPAs) or FTAs with Canada, Colombia, Ecuador, Japan, Peru, Singapore, South Africa, South Korea, Ukraine, Vietnam and other countries. It is a party to the EPAs with the Caribbean Forum (CARIFORUM) and the South African Development Community (SADC). In addition, the European Union is awaiting signature of EPAs or FTAs with MERCOSUR, a common market comprising Argentina, Brazil, Paraguay and Uruguay, and a number of African countries. It is also negotiating EPAs or FTAs with Australia, Indonesia, New Zealand and the Philippines. Although EPAs generally provide broader coverage than FTAs, their goals are rather similar for the purposes of this chapter.[19]

In the intellectual property arena, EPAs and FTAs generally include intellectual property standards that go beyond what is required by the TRIPS Agreement or other WIPO-administered multilateral intellectual property agreements. To illustrate the high TRIPS-plus standards found in EPAs and FTAs, consider the Australia–United States Free Trade Agreement. Adopted on 18 May 2004, this pioneering US FTA includes in Chapter 17 distinct provisions on copyrights, trademarks, patents and other forms of intellectual property rights. Specifically, the agreement requires the contracting parties to ratify or accede to the WIPO Copyright Treaty, the WIPO Performances and Phonograms Treaty, the Patent Cooperation Treaty, the Protocol Relating to the Madrid Agreement Concerning the International Registration of Marks and the 1991 Act of the International Union for the Protection of New Varieties of Plants (UPOV), among others. The Australia–United States Free Trade Agreement also requires these parties to extend the term of copyright pro-tection beyond the international minimum standard and to provide detailed intellectual property enforcement provisions. Article 17.4.7(a) further requires each party to 'provide for criminal procedures and penalties to be applied where any person is found to have engaged wilfully and for the purposes of commercial advantage or financial gain in any of the above activities'. Finally, the agreement threatens the success and vitality of Australia's Pharmaceutical Benefits Scheme.[20] Article 17.9.4, in particular, bans the parallel importation of cheap generic drugs.

---

[19] For example, EPAs cover non-trade issues such as competition policy, invest-ment, improvement of business environment, cooperation in vocational education and training, labour and product standards, environmental protection, tourism, illegal migration and the resolution of other non-economic cross-border problems.

[20] Cynthia M. Ho, *Access to Medicine in the Global Economy: International Agreements on Patents and Related Rights* (Oxford: Oxford University Press 2011) 246–7.

In the mid-2000s, developed countries began to push for even higher TRIPS-plus intellectual property standards by negotiating plurilateral trade, investment and intellectual property agreements. Using a highly controversial 'country club' approach,[21] these agreements sought to bring together developed and like-minded countries to set new international intellectual property standards that exceeded those found in the multilateral trading system. The widely cited examples are ACTA, the TPP, the CPTPP and the RCEP.

Proposed by Japan,[22] ACTA aimed to set new and higher benchmarks for international intellectual property protection and enforcement. Among the countries participating in the negotiations were Australia, Canada, the European Union, Japan, Mexico, Morocco, New Zealand, Singapore, South Korea, Switzerland and the United States (along with Jordan and the United Arab Emirates, both of which participated in only the first round of the negotiations).[23] After three years and 11 rounds of formal negotiations, ACTA was finally adopted on 15 April 2011. Thus far, only Japan, the country of depositary, has ratified the agreement. Because this agreement will not take effect until six parties have deposited their instruments of ratification, it remains unclear if the agreement will ever enter into force.

While developed countries were busy negotiating ACTA, they also launched the negotiations on an equally controversial plurilateral agreement known as the TPP Agreement. This mega-regional agreement began as a quadrilateral agreement between Chile, New Zealand, Singapore and, later, Brunei Darussalam, which was known as the Trans-Pacific Strategic Economic Partnership Agreement or, more commonly, the 'P4' or 'Pacific 4'.[24] In March 2010, shortly before the eighth round of the ACTA negotiations in Wellington, New Zealand, negotiations began among Australia, Peru, Vietnam, the United States and the P4 members for an expanded agreement. Malaysia, Mexico, Canada and Japan joined the negotiations afterwards.

---

[21]   Daniel Gervais, 'Country Clubs, Empiricism, Blogs and Innovation: The Future of International Intellectual Property Norm Making in the Wake of ACTA' in Mira Burri and Thomas Cottier (eds), *Trade Governance in the Digital Age: World Trade Forum* (Cambridge: Cambridge University Press 2012); Peter K. Yu, 'The ACTA/TPP Country Clubs' in Dana Beldiman (ed.), *Access to Information and Knowledge: 21st Century Challenges in Intellectual Property and Knowledge Governance* (Cheltenham, UK and Northampton, MA, USA: Edward Elgar Publishing 2014).

[22]   Peter K. Yu, 'Six Secret (and Now Open) Fears of ACTA' (2011) 64 *SMU Law Review* 975, 980–83.

[23]   *Ibid* 1075.

[24]   Meredith Kolsky Lewis, 'Expanding the P-4 Trade Agreement into a Broader Trans-Pacific Partnership: Implications, Risks and Opportunities' (2009) 4 *Asian Journal of WTO and International Health Law and Policy* 401, 403–4.

From its inception, the TPP was negotiated as a highly ambitious and comprehensive trade agreement that sought to cover '40% of global [gross domestic product] and some 30% of worldwide trade in both goods and services'.[25] Targeted areas included market access, textiles and apparel, sanitary and phytosanitary measures, investment, financial services, telecommunications, electronic commerce, government procurement, competition, intellectual property, labour, the environment and regulatory standards. After nearly six years of formal negotiations, the TPP Agreement was finally signed in Auckland, New Zealand on 4 February 2016. The final text contained 30 chapters, with Chapter 18 devoted specifically to intellectual property matters. That chapter covered issues such as trademarks, country names, geographical indications, patents and undisclosed test data, industrial designs, copyright and related rights, enforcement and Internet service providers.

Although the US Obama administration considered the TPP 'a cardinal priority and a cornerstone of [its] Pivot to Asia',[26] the Trump administration reversed course by directing the US Trade Representative to withdraw from the TPP and related negotiations. With the United States' withdrawal, the TPP has now been placed on life support.[27] Nevertheless, the 11 remaining TPP partners successfully established the CPTPP, which was signed in March 2018 and has since entered into force. Even though the CPTPP kept intact a large part of the original TPP intellectual property chapter, it suspended the more controversial intellectual property provisions, such as those covering copyright and patent terms, undisclosed test or other data, biologics, technological protection measures, and legal remedies and safe harbours.[28]

Just as developed and like-minded countries were busy negotiating the TPP, ASEAN, Australia, China, India, Japan, New Zealand, South Korea began negotiating the RCEP. Launched in November 2012, these negotiations built on prior efforts to facilitate regional economic integration and cooperation under the frameworks of ASEAN+3 (ASEAN, China, Japan and South Korea), ASEAN+6 (ASEAN+3, Australia, India and New Zealand) and the Asia-Pacific Economic Cooperation Forum (APEC).[29] Together, the 16 RCEP negotiating parties would 'account for almost half of the world's population,

---

[25] David A. Gantz, 'The TPP and RCEP: Mega-Trade Agreements for the Pacific Rim' (2016) 33 *Arizona Journal of International and Comparative Law* 57, 59.

[26] Kurt M. Campbell, *The Pivot: The Future of American Statecraft in Asia* (New York: Twelve 2016) 268.

[27] Peter K. Yu, 'Thinking about the Trans-Pacific Partnership (and a Mega-Regional Agreement on Life Support)' (2017) 20 *SMU Science and Technology Law Review* 97.

[28] *Ibid* 105.

[29] Peter K. Yu, 'The RCEP and Trans-Pacific Intellectual Property Norms' (2017) 50 *Vanderbilt Journal of Transnational Law* 673, 678–85.

over 30 per cent of global [gross domestic product] and over a quarter of world exports'[30] – figures that compared favourably with those of the TPP. Upon establishment, the RCEP would cover not only China and India but also two high-income Asian economies (Japan and South Korea) and six other CPTPP partners (Australia, Brunei Darussalam, Malaysia, New Zealand, Singapore and Vietnam). After eight years and more than 30 rounds of negotiations, the RCEP Agreement was finally signed in a COVID-19-induced virtual cere-mony on 15 November 2020. The signatories included all negotiating parties except India, which withdrew a little more than a year before.

The final RCEP text contains 20 chapters, with Chapter 11 devoted specif-ically to intellectual property matters.[31] That chapter, which is as substantial as the TPP intellectual property chapter, includes 14 sections, 83 provisions and two annexes. It covers copyright and related rights, trademarks, geo-graphical indications, patents, industrial designs, genetic resources, traditional knowledge and folklore, unfair competition, country names, enforcement of intellectual property rights, and transitional arrangements. Although the high intellectual property standards revealed in a leaked negotiating draft initially surprised commentators,[32] the final text confirms that the RCEP Agreement is just another TRIPS-plus plurilateral agreement that aims to raise international intellectual property standards beyond the TRIPS requirements, similar to the TPP Agreement and the CPTPP.

3.2   Direct Impediments

The primary objective of TRIPS-plus bilateral, regional and plurilateral agree-ments is to set high standards of protection and enforcement that go beyond what the TRIPS Agreement requires. The need for such higher standards is understandable, considering that the agreement was adopted more than two decades ago. Because the agreement was negotiated before the Internet entered the mainstream, it does not provide adequate intellectual property protection and enforcement in the digital environment.[33]

---

[30] 'Regional Comprehensive Economic Partnership' (*Australian Department of Foreign Affairs and Trade*), http://dfat.gov.au/trade/agreements/rcep/pages/regional -comprehensive-economic-partnership.aspx, accessed 23 June 2019.
[31] On the intellectual property provisions disclosed in a leaked negotiating draft, see Yu, fn. 29 *supra*, 704–19.
[32] Jeremy Malcolm, 'Meet RCEP, a Trade Agreement in Asia That's Even Worse than TPP or ACTA' (*Electronic Frontier Foundation*, 4 June 2015), https://www.eff .org/deeplinks/2015/06/just-when-you-thought-no-trade-agreement-could-be-worse -tpp-meet-rcep, accessed 23 November 2020.
[33] Marci A. Hamilton, 'The TRIPS Agreement: Imperialistic, Outdated, and Overprotective' (1996) 29 *Vanderbilt Journal of Transnational Law* 613, 614–15; J.H.

To a large extent, the justification for intellectual property chapters in TRIPS-plus trade agreements is quite similar to what TRIPS proponents advanced in the late 1980s and early 1990s.[34] During the TRIPS negotiations, developing countries were repeatedly 'told to overlook the distasteful aspects of introducing or increasing intellectual property protection and enforcement in exchange for longer-term economic health'.[35] Although higher standards of intellectual property protection and enforcement can be beneficial, unsuitable standards can be highly problematic, especially for developing countries.

First, through the transplant of high developed-country standards, TRIPS-plus intellectual property chapters threaten to ignore developing countries' 'local needs, national interests, technological capabilities, institutional capacities, and public health conditions'.[36] Because of the differences in economic conditions, imitative or innovative capacities, research and development productivities and availability of human capital, an innovative model that works well in one country may not suit the needs and interests of another.[37] Thus, the unquestioned adoption of foreign intellectual property standards may not only fail to result in greater innovative efforts, industrial progress

---

Reichman, 'The Know-How Gap in the TRIPS Agreement: Why Software Fared Badly, and What Are the Solutions' (1995) 17 *Hastings Communications and Entertainment Law Journal* 763, 766; Peter K. Yu, 'TRIPS and Its Achilles' Heel' (2011) 18 *Journal of Intellectual Property Law* 479, 502–3 ('Achilles' Heel'). On the various digital intellectual property enforcement measures that have emerged after the conclusion of the TRIPS Agreement, see Peter K. Yu, 'Enforcement: A Neglected Child in the Intellectual Property Family' in Susy Frankel and Daniel Gervais (eds), *The Internet and the Emerging Importance of New Forms of Intellectual Property* (Alphen aan den Rijn: Wolters Kluwer 2016) 286–90.

[34]   On TRIPS negotiations, see Daniel Gervais, *The TRIPS Agreement: Drafting History and Analysis*, 3rd edn (London: Sweet and Maxwell 2008) 3–27; Duncan Matthews, *Globalising Intellectual Property Rights: The TRIPS Agreement* (London: Routledge 2002); Susan K. Sell, *Private Power, Public Law: The Globalization of Intellectual Property Rights* (Cambridge: Cambridge University Press 2003) 96–120; Jayashree Watal, *Intellectual Property Rights in the WTO and Developing Countries* (The Hague: Kluwer Law International 2001) 11–47; Peter K. Yu, 'TRIPS and Its Discontents' (2006) 10 *Marquette Intellectual Property Law Review* 369, 371–9.

[35]   Daniel J. Gervais, 'The TRIPS Agreement and the Doha Round: History and Impact on Economic Development' in Peter K. Yu (ed.), *Intellectual Property and Information Wealth: Issues and Practices in the Digital Age*, Vol. 4 (Westport: Praeger Publishers 2007) 43.

[36]   Peter K. Yu, 'The International Enclosure Movement' (2007) 82 *Indiana Law Journal* 827, 828.

[37]   Claudio R. Frischtak, 'Harmonization versus Differentiation in Intellectual Property Rights Regime' in Mitchel B. Wallerstein, Mary Ellen Mogee and Roberta A. Schoen (eds), *Global Dimensions of Intellectual Property Rights in Science and Technology* (Washington, DC: National Academy Press 1993) 93–7.

and technology transfers, but it may also drain away the resources needed for dealing with the socio-economic and public health problems generated by the new standards.[38]

Second, the introduction of reforms based on foreign laws may exacerbate the dire economic plight of many developing countries, as the newly transplanted laws would enable foreign rights holders in developed and emerging countries to crush local industries through litigation threats or actual lawsuits.[39] Even if the new laws were beneficial in the long run, many of these countries might not have the wealth, infrastructure and technological base to take advantage of the opportunities created by the system in the short run.[40] For countries with urgent and desperate public policy needs or a dying population that lacks access to essential medicines, the realization of the hope for a brighter long-term future seems far away, if not unrealistic. If protection were strengthened beyond the point of an appropriate balance, there is no doubt that the present population would greatly suffer.

Third, greater harmonization of legal standards, while potentially beneficial,[41] can take away valuable opportunities for experimentation with new regulatory and economic policies.[42] In addition, the creation of diversified rules can facilitate competition among jurisdictions. It could also enable the jurisdictions to decide for themselves what rules and systems they want to adopt.[43] Such decisions, in turn, would render the lawmaking process more accountable to the local populations.[44] In the digital age, when governments or legislatures hastily introduce laws, often without convincing empirical evidence, greater experimentation and competition are badly needed.[45]

Finally, whether intended or not, TRIPS-plus bilateral, regional and plurilateral agreements may call for higher levels of protection and enforcement than what is currently offered in developed countries.[46] Notably, the intellectual

[38] Yu, fn. 36 *supra*, 828.

[39] *See* Ellen 't Hoen, 'TRIPS, Pharmaceutical Patents, and Access to Essential Medicines: A Long Way from Seattle to Doha' (2002) 3 *Chicago Journal of International Law* 27, 30–31.

[40] Keith E. Maskus, *Intellectual Property Rights in the Global Economy* (Washington, DC: Institute for International Economics 2000) 237.

[41] *See* John F. Duffy, 'Harmony and Diversity in Global Patent Law' (2002) 17 *Berkeley Technology Law Journal* 685, 693–703.

[42] *Ibid* 707–8.

[43] *Ibid* 703–6.

[44] *Ibid* 706–7.

[45] Peter K. Yu, 'Anticircumvention and Anti-anticircumvention' (2006) 84 *Denver University Law Review* 13, 40–58.

[46] Carlos M. Correa, 'Bilateralism in Intellectual Property: Defeating the WTO System for Access to Medicines' (2004) 36 *Case Western Reserve Journal of International Law* 79, 93; Yu, fn. 45 *supra*, 41.

property chapters in these agreements have omitted the important limitations and exceptions that developed countries carefully introduced to ensure balance in their intellectual property systems. Among the oft-cited examples are the many exceptions found in the US anti-circumvention provision.[47] If a major intellectual property power like the United States did not even find it beneficial to have high anti-circumvention standards without pairing them with a multitude of qualifying exceptions, why would unqualified standards be appropriate for developing countries with limited resources, insufficient safeguards and inadequate correction mechanisms?[48]

3.3   Indirect Impediments

Although TRIPS-plus trade agreements have created alarming concerns in the intellectual property arena, the bilateral, regional and plurilateral approaches used to establish these agreements have sparked additional worries. By going outside the multilateral system, these agreements have undermined the existing multilateral approach to international norm-setting in both the intellectual property and trade arenas.[49]

As commentators have widely recognized, the development of ACTA and the TPP was not only an effort to strengthen the protection and enforcement of intellectual property rights, but also an indictment of the deficiencies in the TRIPS Agreement and the multilateral approach used in completing the WTO rounds of trade negotiations.[50] By inducing a change in national preferences for multilateral approaches, the establishment of TRIPS-plus trade agreements has therefore posed significant challenges to the stability of the international intellectual property and trading systems. These bilateral, regional and plurilateral negotiations may further alienate a country's trading partners, making it more difficult for the country to undertake multilateral discussions in the future.[51]

---

[47]   17 USC s 1201(d)–(j).

[48]   Commission on Intellectual Property Rights, *Integrating Intellectual Property Rights and Development Policy: Report of the Commission on Intellectual Property Rights* (London: Commission on Intellectual Property Rights 2002) 4; Maskus, fn. 40 *supra*, 237; Yu, fn. 36 *supra*, 890.

[49]   Peter K. Yu, 'Sinic Trade Agreements' (2011) 44 *U.C. Davis Law Review* 953, 976–7.

[50]   Jeffery Atik, 'ACTA and the Destabilization of TRIPS' in Hans Henrik Lidgard, Jeffery Atik and Tu Thanh Nguyen (eds), *Sustainable Technology Transfer: A Guide to Global Aid & Trade Development* (Alphen aan den Rijn: Wolters Kluwer 2012) 145; Catherine Saez, 'ACTA a Sign of Weakness in Multilateral System, WIPO Head Says' *Intellectual Property Watch* 30 June 2010; Yu, 'Achilles' Heel', fn. 33 *supra*, 511–14.

[51]   Cho Sungjoon, 'A Bridge Too Far: The Fall of the Fifth WTO Ministerial Conference in Cancun and the Future of Trade Constitution' (2004) 7 *Journal of*

Even worse, by fragmenting the international regulatory system and creating what Jagdish Bhagwati and other commentators have described as the 'spaghetti bowl'[52] or the 'noodle bowl',[53] the continued push for TRIPS-plus bilateral, regional and plurilateral agreements has forced countries to divert scarce time, resources, energy and attention from other international intergovernmental initiatives, including those designed to promote and fulfil the SDGs.[54] In developing countries with scarce resources and whose limited negotiating personnel is often stretched between negotiations inside and outside the multilateral fora, a greater focus on bilateral, regional and plurilateral negotiations will inevitably deplete resources that can otherwise be used to achieve the SDGs.

It is important to remember that not every country has the ability to undertake discussions in a multitude of negotiation fora. Even the European Union and the United States could not devote the same amount of time, energy and attention to the multilateral process had they been asked to negotiate a large number of bilateral, regional and plurilateral agreements alongside the ongoing multilateral negotiations.[55] With significantly more limited resources, developing countries most certainly will do much worse.

Moreover, as Eyal Benvenisti and George Downs insightfully observed, the growing proliferation of international regulatory institutions with overlapping jurisdictions and ambiguous boundaries could help powerful countries preserve their dominance in the international arena.[56] The growing complexities

---

International Economic Law 219, 239; Marshall A. Leaffer, 'Protecting United States Intellectual Property Abroad: Toward a New Multilateralism' (1991) 76 *Iowa Law Review* 273, 297; Yu, fn. 49 *supra*, 976.

[52]   Jagdish Bhagwati, 'US Trade Policy: The Infatuation with Free Trade Areas' in Jagdish Bhagwati and Anne O. Krueger (eds), *The Dangerous Drift to Preferential Trade Agreements* (Washington, DC: AEI Press 1995) 2–3.

[53]   Richard E. Baldwin, 'Managing the Noodle Bowl: The Fragility of East Asian Regionalism' (2007) *Asian Development Bank Working Paper on Regional Economic Integration* No. 7; Masahiro Kawai and Ganeshan Wignaraja, 'Asian FTAs: Trends and Challenges' (2009) *Asian Development Bank Working Paper* No. 144, 3; Wang Jiangyu, 'Association of Southeast Asian Nations–China Free Trade Agreement' in Simon Lester and Bryan Mercurio (eds), *Bilateral and Regional Trade Agreements: Case Studies*, 1st edn (Cambridge: Cambridge University Press 2009) 224; Yu, fn. 49 *supra*, 978.

[54]   Ruggiero, fn. 18 *supra*, 26–7; Yu, fn. 49 *supra*, 977.

[55]   Chad Damro, 'The Political Economy of Regional Trade Agreements' in Lorand Bartels and Federico Ortino (eds), *Regional Trade Agreements and the WTO Legal System* (Oxford: Oxford University Press 2007) 42; Jeffrey J. Schott, 'Free Trade Agreements: Boon or Bane of the World Trading System?' in Schott, fn. 18 *supra*, 16.

[56]   Eyal Benvenisti and George W. Downs, 'The Empire's New Clothes: Political Economy and the Fragmentation of International Law' (2007) 60 *Stanford Law Review* 595, 597–8.

could also result in what Kal Raustiala has described as 'strategic inconsistencies', which help alter, undermine or put pressure on unfavourable norms outside the international intellectual property regime.[57] Such complexities could further upset the existing coalition dynamics between international actors and institutions, thereby threatening to reduce the bargaining power and influence developing countries have obtained through past coalition-building initiatives.[58]

4. REALIGNMENT STRATEGIES

In view of the challenges posed by the negotiations surrounding TRIPS-plus bilateral, regional and plurilateral agreements, this section identifies six distinct strategies to help developing countries realign their international intellectual property negotiations with the SDGs. To provide a wide spectrum of illustrations, this section discusses strategies relating to public health, climate change, genetic resources and traditional knowledge. The examples also draw on various regional and international negotiations, including the TPP, CPTPP and RCEP negotiations as well as the ongoing WIPO negotiations for the development of multilateral instruments to protect genetic resources, traditional knowledge and traditional cultural expressions.

4.1 Enhance TRIPS and TRIPS-Plus Flexibilities

As the intellectual property system continues to expand at both the domestic and international levels, policymakers and commentators have widely noted the need to introduce flexibilities, safeguards, limitations and exceptions. This is what Daniel Gervais has referred to as the 'subtractive narrative'.[59] In the area of public health, for instance, Frederick Abbott reminded us that the TRIPS Agreement has preserved the following flexibilities:

> The TRIPS Agreement … does not … restrict the authority of governments to regulate prices. It … permits [compulsory or government use licences] to be granted. It permits governments to authorize parallel importation. The TRIPS Agreement does

---

[57] Kal Raustiala, 'Density and Conflict in International Intellectual Property Law' (2007) 40 *U.C. Davis Law Review* 1021, 1027–8; Yu, fn. 49 *supra*, 979.

[58] Ruth L. Okediji, 'The International Relations of Intellectual Property: Narratives of Developing Country Participation in the Global Intellectual Property System' (2003) 7 *Singapore Journal of International and Comparative Law* 315, 373; Peter K. Yu, 'International Enclosure, the Regime Complex, and Intellectual Property Schizophrenia' (2007) *Michigan State Law Review* 1, 17–18; Yu, fn. 49 *supra*, 981.

[59] Daniel Gervais, 'Of Clusters and Assumptions: Innovation as Part of a Full TRIPS Implementation' (2009) 77 *Fordham Law Review* 2353, 2357–60.

not specify that new-use patents must be granted. It allows patents to be used for regulatory approval purposes, and it does not require the extension of patent terms to offset regulatory approval periods. The TRIPS Agreement provides a limited form of protection for submissions of regulatory data; but this protection does not prevent a generic producer from making use of publicly available information to generate bioequivalence test data. The TRIPS Agreement provides substantial discretion for the application of competition laws.[60]

One development that has been rather controversial in the area of pharmaceutical patents concerns India's adoption of section 3(d) of the Patents (Amendment) Act 2005. Enacted to prevent 'the mere discovery of a new form of a known substance which does not result in increased efficacy of that substance or the mere discovery of any new property or new use for a known substance', that provision was challenged before the Madras High Court, which upheld the provision. Upon appeal, the Indian Supreme Court rejected Novartis' argument that the provision had violated both the Indian Constitution and the TRIPS Agreement.

Another development that is worth our attention and that has received longstanding interest in the public health arena relates to the expansion of the TRIPS-based compulsory licensing arrangement to cover countries that have limited or no capacity to manufacture pharmaceuticals that are needed to address public health crises, such as those relating to HIV/AIDS, malaria and tuberculosis. Adopted on 6 December 2005, article 31*bis* of the TRIPS Agreement allows countries with insufficient or no manufacturing capacity to import generic versions of patented pharmaceuticals. Although it took more than a decade for over two-thirds of the WTO membership to ratify this amendment, the amendment entered into force on 23 January 2017.

A third development that is of great relevance to the promotion and fulfilment of the SDGs pertains to proposals to introduce, retain or reintroduce the local working requirement in patent law. Thus far, the policy debates surrounding these proposals have been highly divisive. While developed countries take the position that such introduction would violate the TRIPS Agreement, developing countries insist that the agreement has preserved local working as a flexibility. The treaty language is as ambiguous as these policy positions. Although article 27.1 of the TRIPS Agreement states that 'patents shall be available and patent rights enjoyable without discrimination as to the place of invention, the field of technology and whether products are imported

---

[60] Frederick M. Abbott, 'The Cycle of Action and Reaction: Developments and Trends in Intellectual Property and Health' in Pedro Roffe, Geoff Tansey and David Vivas-Eugui (eds), *Negotiating Health: Intellectual Property and Access to Medicines* (London: Earthscan 2006) 30.

or locally produced', article 5(A)(2) of the Paris Convention for the Protection of Industrial Property states explicitly that '[e]ach country of the Union shall have the right to take legislative measures providing for the grant of compulsory licenses to prevent the abuses which might result from the exercise of the exclusive rights conferred by the patent, for example, failure to work'. The WTO Dispute Settlement Body has yet to have an opportunity to clarify the issue.[61]

Apart from these three developments, one could point to efforts to adjust the duration of intellectual property rights; set limits on patent protection for microorganisms and diagnostic, therapeutic and surgical methods; introduce exceptions for research, early working and the development of diagnostics; facilitate parallel importation; and advance more concrete language to promote transfer of technology. Greater effort to promote technology transfer is particularly urgent and important to the SDGs. Indeed, articles 66.2 and 67 of the TRIPS Agreement lay down explicit obligations relating to technology transfer and technical cooperation. Paragraph 11.2 of the Doha Ministerial Decision of 14 November 2001 further affirmed these obligations.

4.2   Advance Pro-Development Proposals

Owing to the power asymmetry between developed and developing countries, the latter rarely have opportunities to introduce new provisions based on their preferred intellectual property models. Nevertheless, a few exceptions exist. Virtually all of these exceptions build on the successful negotiation of international agreements at other multilateral fora, including those outside the intellectual property field.

A notable example is India's effort to introduce substantive provisions on genetic resources, traditional knowledge and traditional cultural expressions at the RCEP negotiations. Although the country withdrew in the late stages of the negotiations, it was one of the four negotiating parties that had advanced a negotiating text in October 2014.[62] Its submission specifically included a ten-paragraph proposal requiring patent applicants to disclose the traditional knowledge and genetic resources used in inventions. Drawing on laws contain-

---

[61]   On 30 May 2000, the United States did file a complaint against Brazil concerning the issue in *Brazil – Measures Affecting Patent Protection*. That case was quickly settled a year later after Brazil lodged a counter complaint in *United States – US Patents Code*.

[62]   '2014 Oct 10: ASEAN Proposals for RCEP IP Chapter, Also India' (*Knowledge Ecology International*, 8 June 2015), https://www.keionline.org/22781, accessed 27 November 2020.

ing a similar requirement in India and other parts of the world,[63] the proposal was consistent with the Nagoya Protocol on Access to Genetic Resources and the Fair and Equitable Sharing of Benefits Arising from Their Utilization. Adopted on 29 October 2010, that instrument aims to promote fair and equitable sharing of benefits arising from the utilization of genetic resources, thereby contributing to the conservation and the sustainable use of biological diversity. Thanks to India's proposal, the leaked draft of the RCEP intellectual property now includes a rather lengthy section on genetic resources, traditional knowledge and folklore. That section stands in sharp contrast to the more limited provisions in the TPP – and, by extension, the CPTPP.

Another example is the new requirement that countries accede to the Marrakesh Treaty to Facilitate Access to Published Works for Persons Who Are Blind, Visually Impaired or Otherwise Print Disabled. Adopted on 27 June 2013, this landmark treaty aims to provide easy or ready access to copyrighted publications to hundreds of millions of individuals with print disabilities. The Marrakesh Treaty is not only the first WIPO agreement devoted solely to limitations and exceptions, but is also the first WIPO agreement providing references to international human rights instruments.[64] Although the treaty entered into effect on 30 September 2016, countries will not assume any obligations until they accede to that treaty. The accession requirement advanced by developing countries through TRIPS-plus negotiations will therefore enlarge the protection granted to individuals with print disabilities while ensuring that the relevant exceptions be built into national laws.

4.3   Facilitate Mutual Supportiveness with Pro-Development International Agreements

Even if countries fail to incorporate provisions from other international agreements into the negotiating texts, they could still provide the much-needed linkage through the careful drafting of the agreement's preamble or the insertion of mutual supportiveness or non-derogation clauses. A case in point is the ongoing negotiations in the WIPO Intergovernmental Committee on Intellectual Property and Genetic Resources, Traditional Knowledge and Folklore (IGC). Established in September 2000, this committee sought to explore 'the development of an international legal instrument or instruments for the effective protection of traditional cultural expressions and traditional

---

[63]   World Intellectual Property Organization, *Key Questions on Patent Disclosure Requirements for Genetic Resources and Traditional Knowledge* (Geneva: World Intellectual Property Organization 2017).
[64]   Abdel-Latif, fn. 12 *supra*, 624.

knowledge, and to address the intellectual property aspects of access to and benefit-sharing in genetic resources'.[65]

In the area intersecting intellectual property and genetic resources, one of the latest documents issued by the IGC was the *Consolidated Document Relating to Intellectual Property and Genetic Resources.*[66] That document provided the text of the proposed instrument for intellectual property and genetic resources. At the time of writing, the draft preamble includes the following bracketed language:

> [The disclosure of the source would increase mutual trust among the various stakeholders involved in access and benefit sharing. All of these stakeholders may be providers and/or users of genetic resources and [traditional knowledge associated with genetic resources]. Accordingly, disclosing the source would build mutual trust in the North–South relationship. Moreover, it would strengthen the mutual supportiveness between the access and benefit sharing system and the [intellectual property] [patent] system.]
>
> ...
>
> [Reaffirm, in accordance with the Convention *on* Biological Diversity, the sovereign rights of States over their [natural] [biological] resources, and that the authority to determine access to genetic resources rests with the national governments and is subject to national legislation.]

Draft article 2 also includes language that '[e]nsur[es] mutual supportiveness with international agreements relating to the protection of genetic resources and traditional knowledge associated with genetic resources, and those relating to [intellectual property]'.

In addition, draft article 10 covers the instrument's relationship with international agreements. Aiming to foster linkages to other international agreements while preventing the derogation of the rights of indigenous communities, this provision states:

> 10.1   This instrument [shall]/[should] establish a mutually supportive relationship [between [intellectual property] [patent] rights [directly based on] [involving] [the utilization of] genetic resources and [traditional knowledge associated with genetic resources] and] [with] relevant [existing] international agreements and treaties.
>
> ...

---

[65]   Yu, 'Anatomy of Human Rights', fn. 14 *supra*, 84, fn. 193.
[66]   WIPO Intergovernmental Committee on Intellectual Property and Genetic Resources, Traditional Knowledge and Folklore, 'Consolidated Document Relating to Intellectual Property and Genetic Resources', 9 April 2019, WIPO/GRTKF/IC/40/6.

10.2   [This instrument [shall]/[should] complement and is not intended to modify other agreements on related subject matter, and [shall]/[should] support in particular, [the Universal Declaration on Human Rights, and] Article 31 of the UN Declaration on the Rights of Indigenous Peoples.]

10.3   [No provision in this instrument shall be interpreted as harming, or being to the detriment of the rights of indigenous people enshrined in the United Nations declaration on the rights of indigenous people. In the case of a conflict of laws, the rights of indigenous people enshrined in such declaration shall prevail and any interpretation shall be guided by the provisions of such declaration.]

4.4   Ensure a Transparent Process

From ACTA to the TPP to the RCEP, policymakers, commentators and non-governmental organizations have heavily criticized the lack of transparency, accountability and democratic participation in plurilateral intellectual property negotiations. The non-transparent process used to negotiate these agreements has made it highly challenging for policymakers in developing countries – or, for that matter, policymakers in any participating or third countries – to analyse the negotiation text and to anticipate problems brought about by the adoption of new TRIPS-plus standards. That process has also made it difficult for developing countries to secure technical assistance from internal and external experts. As if these challenges were not bad enough, the flawed negotiation process has undermined the longstanding effort to promote transparency and the rule of law.[67] It is indeed highly disturbing that EU and US negotiators wilfully ignore what their governments have preached.

To be sure, both ACTA and the TPP include transparency provisions. Article 18.9 of the TPP Agreement – and, by extension, the CPTPP – specifically requires parties to make available the laws, regulations, procedures and administrative rulings in the intellectual property area, as well as information about related applications, registrations and grants. Nevertheless, the negotiation process for both agreements has been secretive. In the case of the TPP, the lack of transparency in the negotiation process has rendered the transparency provisions in the finalized agreement 'some of the most ironic and hypocritical provisions ever written into a treaty adopted for the Asia-Pacific region'.[68] There is simply no good justification for having a non-transparent, unaccountable and undemocratic process to develop a treaty that calls for transparency.

Moreover, one cannot forget that the preamble of the Declaration on the Right to Development recognizes development as 'a comprehensive economic,

---

[67]   Yu, fn. 22 *supra*, 1050–59.
[68]   Peter K. Yu, 'TPP and Trans-Pacific Perplexities' (2014) 37 *Fordham International Law Journal* 1129, 1175.

social, cultural and political process'.[69] Because development is a cumulative
enterprise, the process may be just as important as the outcome itself. As the
UK Commission on Intellectual Property Rights rightly reminded us, the protection of intellectual property rights should be 'a means to an end, not an end
in itself'.[70] The protection in TRIPS-plus intellectual property chapters should
therefore balance the protection and enforcement of intellectual property rights
against other important, and often more important, goals, including those
relating to the SDGs.

4.5 Introduce Complementary Measures

While most of the intellectual property negotiations have focused on substantive standards, one cannot overlook the possibility for TRIPS-plus trade agreements to include provisions on the development of complementary measures.
In the case of climate change, for instance, developed countries, including
Australia, Japan, South Korea, the United Kingdom and the United States,
have explored ways to expedite the patent examination process concerning
environmentally sound technologies.[71] Proposals have also emerged to employ
differentiated fee structures for initial examination and renewal and to extend
the term of patent protection, perhaps with corresponding commitments to
license the patented technologies to developing countries.[72] Considering that
these complementary measures favour neither developed nor developing countries, the measures could easily be written into TRIPS-plus bilateral, regional
and plurilateral agreements.

In addition, policymakers and commentators could advance proposals
to facilitate the use of alternative innovation models – that is, models that
are not yet enshrined in or supported by the TRIPS Agreement or other
WIPO-administered international intellectual property agreements. Potential
models include grants, subsidies, prizes, reputation gains, open innovation
models and equity-based systems built upon liability rules.[73] To provide the

---

[69]   Bunn, fn. 12 *supra*, 119–21; Rumu Sarkar, *International Development Law: Rule
of Law, Human Rights, and Global Finance* (Oxford: Oxford University Press 2009)
78; Amartya Sen, *Development as Freedom* (New York: Anchor Books 1999) 3; Peter
Uvin, *Human Rights and Development* (Bloomfield: Kumarian Press 2004) 137–9.
[70]   Commission on Intellectual Property Rights, fn. 48 *supra*, 6.
[71]   Keith Maskus, *Differentiated Intellectual Property Regimes for Environmental
and Climate Technologies* (Paris: Organisation for Economic Co-operation and
Development 2010) 23.
[72]   *Ibid* 22–3.
[73]   Frederick M. Abbott, *Innovation and Technology Transfer to Address Climate
Change: Lessons from the Global Debate on Intellectual Property and Public
Health* (Geneva: International Centre for Trade and Sustainable Development 2009)

needed incentives, policymakers and commentators may also want to consider
the following:

- make greater use of buyouts, advance market commitments, patent pools, collective licensing and new models of intellectual property management;
- provide public mapping of [environmentally sound technologies] in the public
  domain;
- facilitate deeper coordination among intellectual property offices and related
  authorities; and
- undertake more skilful deployment of public-private partnerships.[74]

Finally, policymakers and commentators have underscored the importance of
impact studies.[75] In its Development Agenda, WIPO has included 'assessment,
evaluation, and impact studies' among its six clusters of recommendations.
Impact assessments have also been widely used in the fields of biological
diversity, human rights and public health.[76] With respect to the SDGs, impact
assessment will also likely be very important. Although ex ante review is generally considered more effective, ex post review can still provide some useful
information that helps determine what needs to be done to promote and fulfil
the SDGs.

7–8; Matthew Rimmer, *Intellectual Property and Climate Change: Inventing Clean Technologies* (Cheltenham, UK and Northampton, MA, USA: Edward Elgar Publishing 2011) 311–76.

[74] Peter K. Yu, 'Intellectual Property Enforcement and Global Climate Change' in Joshua D. Sarnoff (ed.), *Research Handbook on Intellectual Property and Climate Change* (Cheltenham, UK and Northampton, MA, USA: Edward Elgar Publishing 2016) 116–17.

[75] 'Principles for Intellectual Property Provisions in Bilateral and Regional Agreements' (*Max Planck Institute for Intellectual Property and Competition Law*) paras 16, 22, https://www.ip.mpg.de/fileadmin/ipmpg/content/forschung_aktuell/06 _principles_for_intellectua/principles_for_ip_provisions_in_bilateral_and_regional _agreements_final1.pdf, accessed 23 June 2019; Yu, 'Nonmultilateral Era', fn. 14 *supra*, 1096–8; Yu, fn. 36 *supra*, 901; Peter K. Yu, 'The Strategic and Discursive Contributions of the Max Planck Principles for Intellectual Property Provisions in Bilateral and Regional Agreements' (2014) 62 *Drake Law Review Discourse* 20, 29.

[76] Convention on Biological Diversity art. 14(1)(a), 5 June 1992, 1760 UNTS 143; Committee on Economic, Social and Cultural Rights, fn. 13 *supra*, para. 35; Commission on Intellectual Property Rights, Innovation and Public Health, *Public Health: Innovation and Intellectual Property Rights* (Geneva: Commission on Intellectual Property Rights, Innovation and Public Health 2006) 10.

4.6   Enable Selective Adaptation

Policymakers and commentators tend to develop a kneejerk resistance to high international intellectual property standards. Nevertheless, the technological rise of China, India and other emerging countries – or what I have called the 'middle intellectual property powers'[77] – has called for a pause to rethink appropriate intellectual property norm-setting strategies.

During the TRIPS negotiations, developing countries were repeatedly told that the TRIPS Agreement, along with other commitments in the WTO, would provide the painful medicine they needed to boost economic development.[78] Although it is easy to dismiss the sales pitch of TRIPS advocates and supporters, it is much harder to evaluate whether China, India and other now-emerging countries have in fact benefited from the many economic reforms pushed on them by the WTO Agreement.

Indeed, many policymakers and commentators have taken the view that China would not have been as economically developed and technologically proficient as it is today had it not embraced the reforms required by WTO accession.[79] To be sure, one could still debate whether the improvements actually originated from all the WTO agreements or just the TRIPS Agreement – an important distinction. Nevertheless, the WTO's 'single undertaking' approach has virtually guaranteed this distinction to be a non-issue. Under this approach, any country acceding to the WTO cannot have non-intellectual property reforms and benefits without also implementing TRIPS-based reforms.

Moreover, as China moved from the stage of transplanting foreign laws to the stage of developing indigenous standards,[80] the country has skilfully deployed 'selective adaptation' strategies to ensure the incorporation of only beneficial features from the outside without also transplanting the harmful

---

[77]   Peter K. Yu, 'The Middle Intellectual Property Powers' in Randall Peerenboom and Tom Ginsburg (eds), *Law and Development of Middle-Income Countries: Avoiding the Middle-Income Trap* (New York: Cambridge University Press 2014).

[78]   Gervais, fn. 35 *supra*, 43; Edmund W. Kitch, 'The Patent Policy of Developing Countries' (1994) 13 *UCLA Pacific Basin Law Journal* 166, 166–7.

[79]   Campbell, fn. 26 *supra*, 195; Gordon G. Chang, 'TPP vs. RCEP: America and China Battle for Control of Pacific Trade' *National Interest* 6 October 2015; Peter K. Yu, 'The Rise and Decline of the Intellectual Property Powers' (2012) 34 *Campbell Law Review* 525, 550–51.

[80]   Peter K. Yu, 'Building the Ladder: Three Decades of Development of the Chinese Patent System' (2013) 5 *WIPO Journal* 1, 3–13; Peter K. Yu, 'A Half-Century of Scholarship on the Chinese Intellectual Property System' (2018) 67 *American University Law Review* 1045, 1058–87.

and unsuitable elements.[81] Thus, even though one could continue to debate how much China, India and other emerging countries have benefited from TRIPS-induced intellectual property reforms, it is much harder to deny the positive benefits the TRIPS Agreement has provided to the economic development and technological proficiency in these countries.

In sum, policymakers and commentators should not automatically reject TRIPS and TRIPS-plus standards without thinking about whether they can help promote and fulfil the SDGs. Instead, they should explore how these standards can be selectively adapted to suit the country's needs, interests, conditions and priorities. To respond to climate change, for example, a strong intellectual property system could provide the much-needed incentives to promote and accelerate the development of environmentally sound technologies.[82] Those incentives would be needed whether in developed or developing countries.

5. CONCLUSION

The past two decades have seen developed countries actively pushing for the negotiation of bilateral, regional and plurilateral trade agreements. By including TRIPS-plus standards that do not fit well with the needs, interests, conditions and priorities of developing countries, these agreements have made it highly difficult to promote and fulfil the SDGs. To help alleviate this shortcoming, the present chapter identifies the harms caused by TRIPS-plus intellectual property agreements and negotiations. It further advances six distinct strategies to help developing countries realign their negotiations with the SDGs. It is my hope that such realignment will help facilitate the development of the laws and policies needed to advance the 2030 Agenda for Sustainable Development.

---

[81] Pitman B. Potter, 'China and the International Legal System: Challenges of Participation' in Donald C. Clarke (ed.), *China's Legal System: New Developments, New Challenges* (Cambridge: Cambridge University Press 2008) 147–8; Wu Handong, 'One Hundred Years of Progress: The Development of the Intellectual Property System in China' (2009) 1 *WIPO Journal* 117, 118–19; Peter K. Yu, 'The Transplant and Transformation of Intellectual Property Laws in China' in Nari Lee, Niklas Bruun and Li Mingde (eds), *Governance of Intellectual Property Rights in China and Europe* (Cheltenham, UK and Northampton, MA, USA: Edward Elgar Publishing 2016) 26.

[82] Jon P. Santamauro, 'Failure Is Not an Option: Enhancing the Use of Intellectual Property Tools to Secure Wider and More Equitable Access to Climate Change Technologies' in Abbe E.L. Brown (ed.), *Environmental Technologies, Intellectual Property and Climate Change: Accessing, Obtaining and Protecting* (Cheltenham, UK and Northampton, MA, USA: Edward Elgar Publishing 2013); Yu, fn. 74 *supra*, 116.

4. Disrupted creativity: cultural sustainability in peril[1]

Daniel J. Gervais

1. INTRODUCTION

Sustainability of the environment is essential. We must find ways to make the economy sustainable. This chapter argues that as important and essential as the environment is for humans who inhabit this planet, who should act as its custodians instead of its last owners, the notion of sustainability must include cultural and intellectual facets. To be sustainable, markets must ensure continued production, dissemination and access to information and cultural products.

2. DEFINING AND SITUATING CULTURAL SUSTAINABILITY

The idea that cultural sustainability is essential to human development is not new. David Lempert identified it as a way of translating aspirations contained in the 'Universal Development Goals' into measurable Categories.[2] Indeed, protecting an ecosystem can be defined as including ecological, economic and cultural sustainability.[3] This link between culture and the environment can be pushed much further, however, in that sustainability of the environment and cultural sustainability are coequal normative goals in implementing sustainability.[4] The Sustainable Development Goals (SDGs) also contain several references to culture. To take just a few examples, under Goal 8 (Decent Work and Economic Growth), target 8.3 provides in part that policies should '[p]romote

---

[1] All views expressed, errors and omissions are the author's own.

[2] David Lempert, Measuring 'Progress' and 'Regress' in Human Rights: Why We Need A Set of Social Contract Measures to Replace Indices of Violations and Slogans, (2017) 10 DePaul J. for Soc. Just. 1–58, at 48.

[3] See Keith H. Hirokawa, Disasters and Ecosystem Services Deprivation: From Cuyahoga to the Deepwater Horizon, (2011) 74 Alb. L. Rev. 543–561, at 554.

[4] George Francis, Ecosystem Management, (1993) 33 Nat. Resources J. 315–345, at 324.

development-oriented policies that support productive activities, decent job creation, entrepreneurship, *creativity and innovation*'. Goal 9 (Industries, Innovation and Infrastructure), target 9C is to 'increase access to information and communications technology and strive to provide universal and affordable access to the Internet'. The last goal arguably presupposes that the material available online will help, not hinder, sustainable development. This includes access to quality cultural material, including ideally material that reflects both an Internet user's local culture, and the world's cultural diversity.

Sustainability is a holistic, overarching goal. The World Commission on Environment and Development (WCED) – better known as the Brundtland Commission – noted, first, that there are 'moral, ethical, *cultural*, aesthetic, and purely scientific reasons for conserving wild beings'.[5] That is, environmental sustainability is culturally relevant.[6] Water is vital for both environmental and cultural sustainability.[7] For example, the collapse of wetlands can mean cultural as well as environmental losses.

Another sign of the linkages between cultural and environmental sustainability is the protection of natural and cultural heritage under the same international instrument, namely the *Convention Concerning the Protection of the World Cultural and Natural Heritage*.[8]

The notion of cultural sustainability has emerged directly in several contexts, most notably urban planning and land use. As Sara Gwendolyn Ross notes, cultural sustainability can be a beacon for city development projects that 'aim to establish communities of a mixed-use or mixed-income variety'.[9] In defining policies to promote 'ecotourism', Deborah McLaren argues that the

---

[5]　Report of the World Commission on Environment and Development: Our Common Future (1987), part of UN document A/42/427, available at http://un-documents.net/wced-ocf.htm (accessed 17 July 2020).

[6]　See Richard Haeuber, Setting the Environmental Policy Agenda: The Case of Ecosystem Management, (1996) 36 Natural Resources J. 1–28, at 26.

[7]　See Mark Davis & James Wilkins, A Defining Resource: Louisiana's Place in the Emerging Water Economy, (2011) 57 Loy. L. Rev. 273–298, at 282; and about the cultural relevance of a hydroelectric dam, Report of the Committee Set Up to Examine the Representation Alleging Non-observance by Colombia of the Indigenous and Tribal Peoples Convention, 1989 (No. 169) at paras 58–59, available at https://bit.ly/2qBJTML (accessed 17 July 2020).

[8]　Adopted by the UNESCO General Conference at its seventeenth session Paris, 16 November 1972, available at https://whc.unesco.org/archive/convention-en.pdf (accessed 17 July 2020).

[9]　Sara Gwendolyn Ross, Legislating Tolerance: Article 976 of the Civil Code of Quebec and Its Application to Mixed-Income and Mixed-Use City Redevelopment Projects, (2016) 62 Loyola L. Rev. 749–775, at 753. See also Keith H. Hirokawa, At Home with Nature: Early Reflections on Green Building Laws and the Transformation of the Built Environment, (2009) 39 Environmental L. 507–575, at 536.

objective should encompass both environmental and cultural sustainability.[10] Indeed, cultural sustainability has been described as one of the three pillars of ecotourism.[11]

Several environmental-oriented projects factor in the cultural sustainability of local and indigenous communities as a goal equal to ecosystem conservation.[12] Ana Filipa Vrdoljak argued that 'self-determination, cultural sustainability, and indigenous legal ownership and control of cultural heritage' all form part measures designed to provide restitution to dispossessed indigenous communities.[13] The Brundtland Commission noted in the same vein that many 'groups become dispossessed and marginalized, and their traditional practices disappear. They become the victims of what could be described as *cultural extinction.*'[14] Voices from local communities support this view. The Inuit Circumpolar Council (ICC) position is that sustainable development should include cultural sustainability.[15]

Cultural sustainability is also used to draw the contours of corporate social responsibility. Professor Kamille Wolff Dean, among others, suggested that

Corporations may engage in self-regulation to maintain ethical business practices and standards in developing culturally sensitive land projects in an eco-friendly manner ... The promotion of cultural competency in the corporate development of land could also assist in the just assessment of taxes when these developments serve to dramatically increase the tax basis of the local community. Corporations may

---

[10] Deborah McLaren, Rethinking Tourism and Ecotravel: The Paving of Paradise and What You Can Do To Stop It (West Hartford: Kumarian Press, 1997), at 97–114. See also Carla Gowen McClurg, The International Year of Ecotourism: The Celebration of a New Form of Colonialism, (2002) 34 McGeorge L. Rev. 97–133, at 102.

[11] See Daniel J. Whittle et al., International Tourism and Protection of Cuba's Coastal and Marine Environments, (2003)16 Tulane Environmental L.J. 533–589, at 559.

[12] See Jerry L. Hoffman, Renewing the Great Plains: Towards A Greater Black Hills Wildlife Protected Area, (2001) 5 Great Plains Natural Resources J. 16–24, at 19.

[13] Ana Filipa Vrdoljak, International Law, Museums and the Return of Cultural Objects (Cambridge: Cambridge University Press, 2008). See also Leah Castella, Note, The United States Border: A Barrier to Cultural Survival, (2000) 5 Texas Forum on Civil Liberties & Civil Right 191–194, at 191.

[14] Brundtland Commission, fn. 5 *supra*, para 73.

[15] Jim Stotts, The Inuit Future: Food Security, Economic Development, and U.S. Arctic Policy, (2013) 43 Envtl. L. Rep. News & Analysis 10869–10874, at 10871. For a view from Southeast Asia, see Annette Van den Bosch, Professional Artists in Vietnam: Intellectual Property Rights, Economic and Cultural Sustainability, (2009) 39 J. Arts Management, L. & Society 221, 226; and see generally Zvi Bekerman & Ezra Kopelowitz eds., Cultural Education-Cultural Sustainability (Oxford: Routledge, 2008).

even owe a fiduciary duty to develop community plans that will support economic, environmental, and cultural sustainability.[16]

Cultural sustainability has links to the legal system as well, including how laws are made and applied. Work by Julie Cohen and Jessica Silbey on the cultural situatedness of law is illuminating in this regard. As Professor Silbey noted:

> [T]hese notions, for example, that the community and not the individual is the origin of value and that property by default should be communally held appear to be sea changes in intellectual-property policy. They put cultural sustainability on par with legal precedent. And they remind us that our rights and responsibilities toward each other (our laws) reflect and constitute the erasures, possibilities and power that structure our social relations. There is no way to designate an outside of culture by which to judge the law as separate. Similarly, there is no means outside of the law to assess its neutral effect on cultural production.[17]

Having seen how cultural sustainability forms an integral part of a 'sustainability' plan, can a more formal definition of cultural sustainability be provided? I will adopt (Canadian) Professor George Francis' proposed text for the purposes of this chapter. It reads as follows:

> Cultural sustainability depends upon the ability of a society to claim the loyalty of its adherents through the propagation of a set of values that are acceptable to the populace and through the provision of socio-political institutions that make realizations of these values possible. Sustainability is a normative ethical principle. It has both necessary and desirable characteristics. There is no single version of a sustainable system.[18]

Hence, cultural sustainability is not about imposing a set of values, but rather about the empowerment to develop and propagate values in a given society, including via art, literature and information. This allows a society to build and sustain the institutions necessary for that society to cohere. This implies,

---

[16]   Kamille Wolff Dean, Corporate Social Responsibility and Conservation: The Preservation of Ecology and Culture to Sustain the Sea Islands, (2013) 37 William & Mary Environmental. L. & Policy Rev. 375–423, at 398. See also Mark Starik & Patricia Kanashiro, Toward a Theory of Sustainability Management: Uncovering and Integrating the Nearly Obvious, (2013) 26 Organization & Environment 7–30, at 8; and L. Jane McMillan, Colonial Traditions, Co-Optations, and Mi'kmaq Legal Consciousness, (2011) 36 Law & Social Inquiry 171–200, at 196.

[17]   Jessica Silbey, Comparative Tales of Origins and Access: Intellectual Property and the Rhetoric of Social Change, (2010) 61 Case Western Reserve L. Rev. 195–267, at 235. See also Julie E. Cohen, Network Stories, (2007) 70 Law & Contemporary Problems 91–95, at 91–92.

[18]   Francis, fn. 4 *supra*, at 324.

as I see it, the existence of an effective system to generate and maintain the mimetic and epistemological signal that current generations are sending to the next ones.

3.   CRITIQUES OF CULTURAL SUSTAINABILITY

The notion of cultural sustainability has been the subject of stinging challenges, in some cases arguing the exact opposite of Lempert, namely that the notion is too indeterminate and that 'contemporary assessments of cultural value are notoriously problematic'.[19] Professor Sean Pager, for instance, noted that:

> The notion of cultural sustainability appears, at best, problematic. Sustainability of traditional culture is hardly analogous to fishery management, where empirical models of replenishment can determine responsible limits. Moreover, the idea that we can identify 'normal' development in traditional culture is deeply suspect. It assumes that change can be made to unfold in a gradual, evolutionary fashion and that we can meaningfully evaluate new developments as they arise. Yet there are no extrinsic criteria by which to make such determinations.[20]

Although Professor Pager's point is well taken, much of his critique can be addressed as a matter of semantics. If the notion of cultural sustainability is defined adequately, as an ethical principle, noting, as the chapter does in the definition it adopts above, that there is no single version of sustainability, then the values it enshrines, namely the ability to claim the loyalty of a community's 'adherents through the propagation of a set of values that are acceptable to the populace and through the provision of socio-political institutions that make realizations of these values possible'[21] strikes me as a valid normative proposition.

A second critique is that true sustainability in certain Aboriginal economies is fundamentally incompatible with growth economics even with an emphasis on efficiency, green energy and green jobs.[22] This critique is also on point, but not insurmountable. Economic development within a community should reflect the goals and values of that community, along the lines of the 'multiple version' argument in the previous paragraph. If certain forms of economic development are indeed incompatible with sustainability in that environment,

---

[19]   Sean A. Pager, Folklore 2.0: Preservation through Innovation, (2012) Utah L. Rev. 1835–1895, at 1846.

[20]   *Ibid.*

[21]   Francis, fn. 4, *supra*, at 324.

[22]   John W. Ragsdale Jr., Time Immemorial: Aboriginal Rights in the Valles Caldera, the Public Trust, and the Quest for Constitutional Sustainability, (2018) 86 University of Missouri at Kansas City (UMKC) L. Rev. 869–912, at 889.

then choices must be made. In most cases, one could hope that such adjustments can avoid incompatibility. There is, however, little doubt that maximizing economic growth is hardly the way to a sustainable future, whether as a strictly environmental matter or an economic one. To take a simple example, letting strict market rules dominate the production and dissemination of cultural products may well lead to homogenization or cultural products available through major dissemination channels, including film, book and music.[23] This is the 'culturally homogenizing effect of cultural trade'.[24] This risk explains why, by a vote of 148 to 2 (Israel and the United States), on 20 October 2005 the United Nations Educational, Scientific and Cultural Organization (UNESCO) adopted the *Convention on the Protection and Promotion of the Diversity of Cultural Expressions.*[25] The Convention reaffirms the 'sovereign right to maintain, adopt and implement policies and measures that they deem appropriate for the protection and promotion of the diversity of cultural expressions on their territory'.[26] One of the aims of cultural diversity instruments is to allow local cultures to be protected, a crucial part of self-determination.[27]

A third critique is that when cultural sustainability goals inform environmental policies, they tend to focus on aesthetically pleasing ecosystems and leave less striking ones at risk.[28] This is probably correct but can be mitigated by applying the necessary measures to raise awareness about this unintended consequence. Moreover, this risk is arguably inherent in almost any type of policymaking.[29]

---

[23]   See A Review of Canadian Feature Film Policy, Discussion Paper, Department of Canadian Heritage, (1998) 19:9 Entertainment L. Rep. 5–9.

[24]   Alex Khachaturian, The New Cultural Diversity Convention and Its Implications on the WTO International Trade Regime: A Critical Comparative Analysis, (2006) 42 Texas International L. J. 191–209, at 206.

[25]   Convention on the Protection and Promotion of the Diversity of Cultural Expressions, Oct. 20, 2005, UNESCO Doc. No. CLT-2005, available at unesdoc.unesco .org/images/0014/001429/142919e.pdf (accessed 17 July 2020). The Convention entered into force on 18 March 2007.

[26]   *Ibid.*, art 1. See also *ibid.*, arts 5 and 20; and Christopher M. Bruner, Culture, Sovereignty, and Hollywood: UNESCO and the Future of Trade in Cultural Products, (2008) 40 New York Univ. J. International L. & Policy 351–436.

[27]   See fn. 13, *supra*; and Michael J. Glennon, Self-Determination and Cultural Diversity, (2003) 27 Fletcher Forum World Affairs 75–82.

[28]   See Joan Iverson Nassauer, Cultural Sustainability: Aligning Aesthetics and Ecology, in Joan Nassauer, ed., Placing Nature (Washington, DC: Island Press, 1997), at 67–68; and Kimberley W. Smith Mere Taste: Democracy and the Politics of Beauty, (2000) 7 Wisconsin Environmental L.J. 151–195, at 159.

[29]   See Daniel J. Gervais, The Regulation of Inchoate Technologies, (2010) 47 Houston L. Rev. 665–705, at 684–88.

4.   PROFESSIONALS AS THE MAIN VECTORS OF CULTURAL SUSTAINABILITY

As mentioned above, cultural sustainability is not about imposing a set of values or a dominant culture, quite the opposite. It is about the empowerment to develop and propagate values in a given society, including via art, litera-ture and information. This is not a particularly hard sell in Europe. Europe traditionally likes to stand as a global beacon for free press, democracy and human culture.[30] The creation, distribution, use, integration and manipulation of information is a significant economic, political, and cultural activity that acts as a cornerstone of the EU 'information society'.[31] Norway is no stranger to these ideas, where I believe they resonate loud and clear.

Two very visible vehicles that can move the information society forward, not backward, are, first, literary and artistic creation and, second, journalistic information, by which I mean both news generation (fact-finding and report-ing) and analysis.[32] The continued role of those two vehicles is in serious peril; their very existence depends on factors wrongly taken for granted. These factors are the existence of professional creators, including journalists, on the one hand, and of organizations that support them such as publishers and news organizations, on the other hand.[33] Professional creators need income to support their craft and hone their skills.[34] Being a professional creator gener-ally implies 'using copyright more consistently than amateur production',[35] in part because amateur content is often not produced with a view to generating (significant) income, and possibly with less attention paid by the amateur author to the possible reuse or adaptation of the content. Put differently, the assumption that these key architects of the information society will continue to exist is in serious doubt – for the first time on such a scale – due to the shift

---

[30]   For a comparison of the Israeli, EU and US approaches, see Hillel Nossek & Yehiel Limor, Fifty Years in A 'Marriage of Convenience': News Media and Military Censorship in Israel, (2001) 6 Communications L. & Policy 1–35, at 12.

[31]   See Directive 2001/29/EC of the European Parliament and of the Council of 22 May 2001 on the harmonisation of certain aspects of copyright and related rights in the information society, O.J. L 167, 22/06/2001 P. 0010 – 0019, recital 8.

[32]   See *ibid.*, recitals 11 and 12 and 34; and Goodwin v. United Kingdom (No. 7), 1996-II Eur. Ct. H.R. 483.

[33]   See Daniel J. Gervais, Restructuring Copyright (Cheltenham: Edward Elgar, 2017), at 158–175.

[34]   See Martin Kretschmer, Copyright and Contract Law: Regulating Creator Contracts: The State of the Art and A Research Agenda, (2010) 18 J. Intellectual Property L. 141–172, at 146–148.

[35]   Aram Sinnreich et. al., Copyright Givers and Takers: Mutuality, Altruism and Instrumentalism in Open Licensing, (2018) 23 Comm. L. & Policy 197–220, at 207.

of professionally created art and journalistic information to an online environment where they must compete with non-professional or amateur 'content' and where revenue is often a function of search rank results on Google.[36] This has dramatically eroded financial flows to many types of creators and professional news sources in a way that impedes forms of creation that depend on the existence of viable markets and the work of journalists and professional news organizations.

Major digital platforms whose aim is to maximize both the amount of available 'content' and the amount of time each person spends on their platform play a leading role in the filtering of access to news and many forms of art and information. The resulting capture of financial flows to creators and professional news organizations combined with a cost-saving push to maximize the use of amateur reporting is detrimental to the ability of professional creators, cultural industries and news outlets to contribute to cultural development, information flows and democratic processes.[37] While the platforms have allowed some new creators and forms of creation to emerge, they have caused massive amounts of damage to cultural creation in many sectors, essentially by syphoning off very large chunks of revenue.

On the positive side, global platforms like Facebook have made many forms of content more accessible, opened up popular participation in some democratic processes (but negatively influenced others), and stimulated innovative ways of producing news. On the negative side, impacts on resources available to news organizations have put in question the viability of the business model of legacy news organizations, namely the sale of copies/access and advertising. The revenue streams are shifting from legacy media with high content production costs to platforms with little or no content production costs.[38]

The Socially Responsible News (SRN) ideal of journalism has been a dominant professional paradigm.[39] This tradition emphasizes journalism as a trustee of the polity that aims to look after the varied information needs of the public in an independent way.[40] It celebrates the idea of the press as a 'fourth estate'

---

[36] See Julia Cagé, Saving the Media Capitalism, Crowdfunding, and Democracy (Cambridge, MA: Belknap Press, 2016), at 31–35; and Larry E. Ribstein, From Bricks to Pajamas: The Law and Economics of Amateur Journalism, (2006) 48 William & Mary L. Rev. 185–249, at 204.

[37] See Mike Pride, Turn the Newsroom Inside Out, (2012) 66:1 Nieman Reports 13–15.

[38] Rasmus K. Nielsen, The Business of News (Los Angeles: Sage, 2016).

[39] C. Edwin Baker, Media, Markets, and Democracy (Cambridge: Cambridge University Press, 2001).

[40] Clifford G. Christians, Theodore L. Glasser, Denis McQuail, Kaarle Nordenstreng & Robert A White, Normative Theories of the Media: Journalism in Democratic Societies (Urbana, IL: University of Illinois Press, 2010).

operating as a check and balance on the legislature, executive and judiciary branches of public governance. Global platforms such as Facebook use the current regulatory environment to defend their position as 'platforms', not media companies. As such, they do not share the same social responsibilities as news organizations, but they are de facto slipping into the role of a fourth estate, but one animated not by a societal mandate, only a desire to generate income. The idea that basic fact-checking, for example, may be subordinated to the need to generate more revenue seems hard to reconcile with the notion of SRN, although some platforms have recently begun to take steps to verify accuracy.[41] Put simply, for global digital platforms generating or providing access to information that meets journalistic standards is unimportant and, in some cases, squarely unproductive, as it may drive a user away from their site or platform (stepping out of the comfort of the echo chamber may require a greater mental effort and the user might click away to avoid it).

It is not an overstatement to say that without professional and independent journalists and news organizations, democratic systems may no longer function correctly: 'Journalism is responding to larger changes in society as much as it is driving those changes.'[42] As Anderson et al. noted:

> We might ... envision a world in which the majority of citizens know very little about politics and care about politics even less, a world where interest groups and politically passionate actors provide not only the normative orientation for news production but also the economic means of sustaining it.[43]

Citizens' agency is also under assault. People gain access more and more to material pushed towards them by secret, advertising-maximizing algorithms that use past behaviour as guide and thus provide 'more of the same' instead of challenging Internet users. The COVID-19 pandemic made matters worse for many creators who tried to maintain markets not controlled by the digital platforms, such as live music concerts and other performances, sales at art galleries and many other vectors. The pandemic may thus accelerate the demise of artistic creation caused by the growth of the role of digital platforms.

Although some amateur content (such as video feeds of live events created often using a mobile phone) undoubtedly has value, a considerable proportion

---

[41] Jack Andersen & Sille Obelitz Søe, Communicative Actions We Live By: The Problem with Fact-checking, Tagging or Flagging Fake News – The Case of Facebook, (2020) 35:2 European J. of Communication 126–139.

[42] See Chris W. Anderson, Leonard Downie Jr. & Michael Schudson, The News Media (Oxford: Oxford University Press, 2016), at 162.

[43] *Ibid.* at 163.

of high-quality creations and information depends on professional creators.[44] It is also true that what professionals produce does not always constitute SRN or otherwise make a significant artistic or literary contribution. From the tabloid press and its multiple fake scandals to commercially motivated, short-lived pop music, examples abound.[45] Yet a very high proportion of SRN and cultural products that contribute to human progress (as a shortcut for this purpose I will assume two ways to measure this are whether they last and whether they generate new forms or waves of creation) are created by professionals. Without professional artists, creators, journalists, publishers and news organizations (press), the future of the information society is in doubt. If the funding and dissemination of art and journalistic information is left to Internet platforms whose aim is not to create quality art or provide quality journalistic information but to maximize contacts between Internet users and any type of content that will get those users to stay online, the future of SRN and some forms of creativity that are likely essential for human progress are at risk. Enfeebled information and weakened culture, in turn, leads to poorer interactions among the polity and a deterioration of democratic processes. Artistic productions that meet the above description are key indicia of a vibrant information society, one which values culture and those who create it.

Factors that affect the output include training of the creators; experience of the creators, which implies an ability to gain such experience; and available financial and other resources. In the case of journalism, experience and resources will in turn affect available sources, the ability to be on location (e.g., the '*grand reporters*'), and the depth of the analysis.

5.   CONSEQUENCES FOR COPYRIGHT POLICY

The entire copyright-based system of production of entertainment and informational works is in disarray. Yet it remains a system that, properly structured, can be a very effective incentive to generate, disseminate and even maintain culture. Copyright is agnostic as to the values embedded in cultural production (whether art, literature or information). Hence, a 'rethink' of copyright is very much called for to maintain cultural sustainability. Many scholars have heeded the call from the numerous articles and books (including mine) and the Wittem

---

[44]   Amateur content can be anonymous and fill gaps in the professionally produced news. See *ibid.*

[45]   See Morten Skovsgaard, A Tabloid Mind? Professional Values and Organizational Pressures as Explanations of Tabloid Journalism, (2014) 36:2 Media, Culture & Society 200–218.

group that produced the draft European Copyright Code.[46] My own view is that copyright is poorly structured (one can always try to impose a structure ex post). The inadequacy or absence of the structure of the current copyright system is due to two main factors, both of which are linked to the transition of almost everything to the digital realm.

First, copyright evolved from a system mostly meant to control certain uses of physical products to a primary regulatory vector for the online environment. It was created for, and traded by and between, professionals (authors, publishers, producers, various distributors etc.), who could typically afford greater transaction costs, including understanding sometimes arcane copyright rules. This also afforded policymakers the 'luxury of expediency' in defining copyright rights not in terms of actual market or other impacts but by focusing on the technical nature of the use made of a protected work (reproduction, adaptation, performance in public, communication to a public at a distance etc.). In the 'bricks and mortar' environment, the poor structure of copyright was often remedied in contracts among copyright 'professionals'. Hence, private ordering stepped in to compensate structural deficiencies in areas where the law created unnecessary complexity or did not map well into actual uses of protected material. As a practical matter, this remedial posture is often no longer available. The shift from a professional or 'one-to-many' distribution infrastructure in which copyright was managed mostly by professionals to a 'many-to-many' infrastructure means that individual users are at once authors, users and reusers of material and hence often in the crosshairs of copyright. Contractual patches no longer work well or make matters worse, such as lengthy End User Licensing Agreements (EULAs), those contracts of adhesion in which users are often asked to give up the right to use statutory flexibilities.[47]

Second, the size and might of online intermediaries (right holders and/or users) pulling policy decisions in their direction without any obvious desire to compromise has eclipsed many options for discussions focusing on actual

---

[46] See The Wittem Project: European Copyright Code, available at https://www.ivir.nl/publicaties/download/Wittem_European_copyright_code_21_april_2010.pdf (accessed 17 July 2020). For the book referred to here, see fn. 51 *infra*.

[47] This is the case in several jurisdictions and may be subject to consumer protection laws. In the United States, as a federal court explained, 'A contract or clause is procedurally unconscionable if it is a contract of adhesion'. A contract of adhesion, in turn, is a 'standardized contract, which, imposed and drafted by the party of superior bargaining strength, relegates to the subscribing party only the opportunity to adhere to the contract or reject it'. Comb v. PayPal, Inc., 218 F. Supp. 2d 1165, 1172 (N.D. Cal. 2002) (citations and internal quotation omitted). The doctrinal details of what constitutes a contract of adhesion vary from state to state. See Bryan T. Camp, The Play's the Thing: A Theory of Taxing Virtual Worlds, (2007) 59 Hastings L.J. 1–70, at 52–60.

authors and users of copyright material. The result is an increasing distance between authors, individual users and copyright policy. Imogen Heap, the well-known British singer-songwriter, said it well:

> More and more third parties jump on board to help the artists, or labels, navigate and collect feedback or money, but it just adds to the noise and confusion, further widening the gap between fan and artist and the journey of their music. I feel digitally torn apart; and in the data-driven era, the movement of music, money and feedback should be frictionless.[48]

All of these profound shifts are making it harder to see – and thus a fortiori for many users to accept – a justification for copyright. Yet, a justification for copyright, properly recast, does exist and should inform appropriately structured policy choices.

Let us avoid the trap of seeking perfection when a significant improvement is possible. I do not believe that there is a perfect copyright law somewhere outside a platonic policy cave. Policy is imperfect and contingent. Changes in technological tools and the social norms that develop around them make optimal policy design a moving target. Indeed that 'movement' (of the target) is best viewed as part of the equation, thus favouring a (more) dynamic copyright system. That said, dynamism and discombobulation are not synonyms. Copyright should always strive to achieve normative equilibrium. In this sense, one can agree with Plato's direction to the legislator to bring about a result that is the closest possible to the 'most noble and most true'.[49] I can hardly think of anything nobler and truer than humans fostering human creativity.

6.   A PATH TOWARDS REFORM

A comprehensive international reform is not only necessary to ensure that copyright meets its needs in the future. It is also a far better alternative than the current path to a patchwork of regional and bilateral trade agreements, sometimes not compatible with one another, evolving in parallel with myriad new multilateral copyright treaties often ratified only by a fairly small number of countries, and then only years after the treaty's adoption.

Copyright should not be structured around two 'sides' as most debates are now framed, namely authors and users. Yet that is the way most laws and national treaties read: a series of exclusive rights on the one hand, and a series

---

[48]   Jamie Bartlett, Imogen Heap: Saviour of the Music Industry?, The Guardian (London, 6 September 2015), http://www.theguardian.com/music/2015/sep/06/imogen-heap-saviour-of-music-industry (accessed 17 July 2020).
[49]   Plato, Laws, V 746 (New York: Basic Books, 1980), at 134.

of exceptions and limitations, on the other. My proposal is to rebalance the expression of the right itself to align it with its purpose, therefore reducing the perceived need to fight the right, including by introducing more and more exceptions and limitations.

The economic component of copyright should be *a right to prohibit uses that demonstrably interfere with actual or predictable commercial exploitation*. This would be subject to limitations and exceptions, but the objective is to build intrinsic limits in the scope of the right itself and make it independent of the technical nature of the use made (copy, performance, etc.).[50] In my book *Restructuring Copyright*,[51] I suggested a partial new draft of the Berne Convention – still today the most important copyright treaty (at least in terms of global membership, with 179 member states as of April 2021) – that remains compatible with the obligations undertaken by Members of the World Trade Organization (WTO) under the Agreement.[52]

The current paradigmatic separation of rights, limitations and exceptions, and enforcement fundamentally – and incorrectly – skews outcomes. While using a creator–user dialogic approach can facilitate the analysis, rights, exceptions and remedies must be viewed in a 'systemic' light.

The task at hand is to balance the protection of authors of 'works', on the one hand, and 'access' to such works by users and reusers of copyrighted material, on the other hand. This is how sustainability is achieved. While efforts to seek a balanced level of protection are not new, translating this high-level balancing act into a structured approach and deriving actual policy objectives, levers and decisions have thus far proven elusive.

Reform should be based on the public interest, which is best served neither by over-production nor by under-protection. Achieving sustainability implies finding the right balance. In short, the level, mode and type of enforceability of copyright must all be rebalanced to achieve systemic protection at equilibrium.

---

[50]   To comply with international norms, the right should be interpreted by defining 'use' to encompass current technical uses (reproduction, performance, communication). This would be subject, however, to the commercial exploitation test, based on the three-step test. On the interpretation of the test, see Christophe Geiger et. al., The Three-Step Test Revisited: How to Use the Test's Flexibility in National Copyright Law, (2014) 29 American Univ. Intl. L. Rev. 581–626.

[51]   Daniel J. Gervais, Restructuring Copyright: A Comprehensive Path to International Copyright Reform, Revised edition (Cheltenham: Edward Elgar, 2019).

[52]   Berne Convention for the Protection of Literary and Artistic Works, Sept. 9, 1886, as revised at Paris, July 24, 1971, 828 UNTS 221; Agreement on Trade-Related Aspects of Intellectual Property Rights, Apr. 15, 1994, Marrakesh Agreement Establishing the World Trade Organization, Annex 1C.

Current copyright law is a 'one-size-fits-all', yet at the same time highly fragmented, regime.[53] This means that every copyright holder gets more or less the same package of 'right fragments' (reproduction, performance, adaptation, etc.), which can then be split by country, language, etc. But then copyright protects one thing, and one thing only, namely 'works', it provides a single set of rights and exceptions and the term of protection is typically the same for all works. Copyright, simply put, is both highly fragmented and unstructured. The current system rests on the assumption that a single set of rights, limitations and exceptions works optimally to serve the interests of authors and those of the people who use and reuse their works. That is simply not so.

The most common legal metaphor to describe a balancing process is probably that of a scale with two pans. In copyright policy terms, the scale weighs the interests of authors, in one pan, and those of users, in the other, without tipping the normative scale unfairly in one direction. It is worth noting that this approach reflects human rights norms: Article 27 of the Universal Declaration on Human Rights (UDHR) protects both the rights of authors (to the protection of the moral and material interests resulting from any scientific, literary or artistic production) and the rights of users (freely to participate in the cultural life of the community, to enjoy the arts and to share in scientific advancement and its benefits).[54]

It should be self-evident that not all 'authors' are in the same situation. The harder and more interesting inquiry is whether one can push the analysis beyond merely acknowledging the existence of this diversity. Structuring sustainable copyright implies abandoning the fiction of homogeneity of authorship that pervades current policy and derives a taxonomy of authorship, with direct policy effects.

7.   AN EVOLVING NOTION OF AUTHORSHIP

The notion of authorship itself has evolved throughout the twentieth century and has now been replaced with that of a 'twenty-first century author'. This 'new' author, who could be referred to as 'post post-modern',[55] is often happy

---

[53]   See Michael W. Carroll, One Size Does Not Fit All: A Framework for Tailoring Intellectual Property Rights, (2009) 70 Ohio St. L.J. 1361–1434.

[54]   Universal Declaration of Human Rights, General Assembly Res No 217 A (III), UN Doc A/810 at 71 (1948), available at http://www.un.org/en/documents/udhr/index .shtml#a2 (accessed 17 July 2020). See Mary W. S. Wong, Toward an Alternative Normative Framework for Copyright: From Private Property to Human Rights, (2009) 26 Cardozo Arts & Entertainment L.J. 775–843, at 808–811.

[55]   See Kyle Serilla, 'What's in A Name? A Parody by Any Other Name Would Smell As Sweet': A Dueling Case Study and Comment, (2017) 99 J. Patent & Trademark Office Society 460–480, at 461–462.

to reuse pre-existing material and to cooperate with others, but also insists on attribution (that is, recognition of their authorship).[56] Of those authors who seek protection of their interests, some, not all, also expect financial returns when their works are used in commerce. For those who do not, it is often because they are otherwise compensated (academics and scientists, for example).

Authors are increasingly supported by technology, and AI engines create more and more literary and artistic content, from brief news articles to weather reports and even loose forms of poetry.[57] One question I leave aside for now is whether AI-produced works could or should get copyright protection. I discussed it in detail elsewhere.[58] Back to humans. Unlike distributors and commercial entities that aggregate rights and content, most authors (whether or not they seek financial gain) have a limited interest in trying to control the dissemination of their works. Simply put, most authors want attribution and wide dissemination, at least once a work has been made publicly available. Some want payment, but very few want (or think they can or should exert) control over what individual non-professional users do. This matters in policy analysis because, while the major commercial intermediaries who often own copyright and who do want (some) control over dissemination networks are an increasingly small part of the copyright picture, copyright policy often seems entirely articulated around their interests. The current system provides protection without intentionality. A vast amount of material is protected by copyright by default due to the absence of formalities. This issue is ripe for a fresh debate.[59]

The other pan of the scale weighs the interests of users. Users can make mere consumptive uses of commercial copyrighted material, such as watching a movie or reading a book. They can do more, however. They can add comments (and social media 'likes'). They may want to re-disseminate the material with these 'additions'. Some users will go beyond this. They will copy or derive from pre-existing works and sometimes genuinely transform and

---

[56] This is the ace, for example, with Creative Commons licenses. See Ashley West, Little Victories: Promoting Artistic Progress Through the Enforcement of Creative Commons Attribution and Share-Alike Licenses, (2009) 36 Florida State Univ. L. Rev. 903–929, at 906–908.

[57] See Amanda Levendowski, How Copyright Law Can Fix Artificial Intelligence's Implicit Bias Problem, (2018) 93 Washington L. Rev. 579–630.

[58] See Daniel J. Gervais, The Machine As Author, (2020) 105 Iowa L. Rev. 2053–2106.

[59] See Daniel J. Gervais & Dashiell Renaud, The Future of United States Copyright Formalities: Why We Should Prioritize Recordation, and How to Do It, (2013) 28 Berkeley Technology L.J. 1459–1496.

re-contextualize them, and become authors in their own right.[60] Others may only be looking for ideas or information contained in copyrighted material, for example as part of a research project (here defined very broadly). For them, searching, accessing and being able to quote from existing texts is essential to their ability to engage with the material.

In sum, a comprehensive reform is not only necessary to ensure that copyright meets its needs in the future. It is also a far better alternative than the current path to a patchwork of regional and bilateral trade agreements, sometimes not compatible with one another, evolving in parallel with myriad new multilateral copyright treaties often ratified only by a fairly small number of countries, and then only years after the treaty's adoption.

8.   A WORD ABOUT THE BLOCKCHAIN

Copyright as a means of creating scarcity (mostly of physical copies) of books, sheet music and other works of art and literature emerged by most accounts in the UK in the Statute of Anne (1709–1710).[61] Blockchain technologies can be used to re-introduce a form of 'scarcity' to the digital world.[62] This promise of technology-based digital scarcity has led to the emergence of multiple startups aiming to revolutionize the digital distribution of creative works and the remuneration of creators. The plan roughly looks like this: authors publish their works on blockchain creating a quasi-immutable record of initial ownership, and create smart contracts to automate the control of who has access under what conditions. Remuneration can then happen on the same technological platform as the distribution of works, where so-called smart contracts reside. In theory, such a setup allows for the complete private ordering of the domain currently under copyright law: with sufficiently detailed smart contracts, a substantial share of possible commercial exploitation in terms of volume and value can be covered and automated.[63]

---

[60]   See Joseph P. Fishman, Creating Around Copyright, (2015) 128 Harvard L. Rev. 1333–1404; and Daniel J. Gervais, The Derivative Right, or Why Copyright Law Protects Foxes Better Than Hedgehogs, (2013) 15 Vanderbilt J. Entertainment & Technology L. 785–855.
[61]   See Jeffrey M. Gaba, Copyrighting Shakespeare: Jacob Tonson, Eighteenth Century English Copyright, and the Birth of Shakespeare Scholarship, (2011) 19 J. Intellectual Property L. 21–63, at 26–30.
[62]   See Balázs Bodó, Daniel J. Gervais & João Pedro Quintais, Blockchain and Smart Contracts: The Missing Link in Copyright Licensing?, (2018) 26:4 Int. J. of L. & Information Technology 311–336, available at https://academic.oup.com/ijlit/article/26/4/311/5106727 (accessed 17 July 2020).
[63]   *Ibid.*

Would it really be this easy? Let us take a look at some of the potential issues by trying to imagine how smart contract-based licensing could work. First, it may not be easy to map those smart contracts onto individual uses. Moreover, some of those individual uses may not need to be licensed because they may amount to private or fair use, for example, and finding a definitive legal answer to which use requires a copyright licence in theory requires going to court case by case. This amounts to insurmountably high transaction costs. Finally, why would smart contracts be bound or limited by the 'fake scarcity' that copyright aims to create in the online environment? In other words, what is to prevent a smart contract from coding a level of exclusivity beyond that allowed under the copyright regime?

At a slightly higher level of abstraction, why would a blockchain contract need to map onto *any* of the exclusive rights contained in the copyright bundle, or exceptions and limitations thereto? If it does, in which jurisdiction?

Even if blockchain contracts are seen as a form of private ordering *not tied to a particular jurisdiction*, international copyright law has a problem. In effect, the problem is this: although it is not inaccurate to speak of international copyright *law* (as contained, for example, in the Berne Convention, TRIPS and the WCT[64]), there is no such thing as an international copyright *right*. The treaties create a right to protection of a copyright right in multiple jurisdictions but based on the law of each jurisdiction. If I create a literary work in Norway, that work must be protected under the copyright laws of all other 178 member countries of the Berne Union, but according to the law of each one.

It gets worse. Each of those copyright *rights* can be sliced and diced. For example, the author of a literary work may license or transfer to a third party only the right to translate the work in a different language and then only for, say, the Russian market. In other words, each right in the copyright bundle can be owned and exploited separately – as far as the Berne Convention goes – 179 times.

It gets worse still. Each country is free to choose which form of 'exhaustion' rule it will apply, as this matter is yet to be settled at the international level.

Does the blockchain have to reflect all the layers and facts of this legal complexity? The answer we suggest to this question is this: if a use of a work was *allowed* under a smart contract in a territory but not by the correct right holder (of the relevant right fragment) in that territory, the user might still face infringement proceedings.

---

[64]   For the Berne Convention and TRIPS Agreement, see above n. 51 The WCT is the WIPO Copyright Treaty, 20 December 1996. For Berne Convention membership, see http://www.wipo.int/treaties/en/ShowResults.jsp?lang=en&treaty_id=15 (accessed 17 July 2020).

This suggests that the way to exploit the potential of smart contracts is to *decouple* them from international copyright's 179 national bundles of rights. But how? Absent an internationally recognized mechanism for authors to permanently dedicate a work to the public domain (the Creative Commons CC0 license is perhaps the closest we have come[65]) and thus 'get rid' of copyright for at least works so dedicated, a world in which smart contracts put in place a form of private ordering *to replace copyright* that would then be enforced technologically, while technically feasible, seems a very distant goal indeed.

9.   CONCLUSION

To quote the Brundtland report again,

> Perceived needs are socially and culturally determined, and sustainable development requires the promotion of values that encourage consumption standards that are within the bounds of the ecological possible and to which all can reasonably aspire.[66]

For this reason alone, culture and the environment cannot be separated. The logical next step is to state that a stronger culture will make it easier to design better rules, technologies, methods and patterns of consumption for environmental sustainability. Cultural and environmental policy can and should cross-fertilize one another.

One of the main policy levers to create incentives for and sustain the production of cultural (and informational) goods has been copyright. Copyright is deficient in several ways, owing in significant part to technological developments. Policy changes are necessary. Indeed, they are urgent if we want to ensure that professional journalists and creators can continue to exist. This is crucial because historically professional authors have been the source of a vast amount of cultural and informational flows, those that actually educate and inform the deliberations of the polity.

---

[65]   See CC0: 'No Rights Reserved', available at https://creativecommons.org/share -your-work/public-domain/cc0/ (accessed 11 November 2018).
[66]   See fn. 5 *supra*, chapter 2 part IV.

5. Repairing and re-using from an exclusive rights perspective: towards sustainable lifespan as part of a new normal?

Taina Pihlajarinne

1. INTRODUCTION

Many environmental problems are associated with increased consumption of products, especially those with a short lifespan. Repair markets and markets where recycled products are used are crucial parts of sustainable markets, with IPRs having a remarkable impact on those markets. From a sustainability standpoint, repairing and using recycled products as material for new products results in energy savings and reduction of waste, and should therefore be promoted.[1] Technological advances, such as 3D printing, might create new possibilities for repairing activities.[2] However, right holders frequently have business strategies that create incentives for invoking patent or trade mark rights to restrict recycling that they deem unwelcome. Problems might emerge in secondary markets as well as in markets for products beyond those offered by intellectual property (IP) owners.

Since mass products are often delivered across vast geographical areas, the only realistic way to promote their circulation is to open markets for

---

[1]   On those impacts in detail, see B Liu, 'Towards a Patent Exhaustion Regime for Sustainable Development' (2014) 32 Berkeley J Int'l L 330, 336–337. In addition to environmental impact, repair activities may promote general knowledge of technology in developing countries and thus social sustainability (Liu 2014, 334–335).

[2]   If a 3D printer can use material suitable for making a spare part, it is possible to print perfect copies of spare parts by 3D printers. In that case, the problem of making or repairing in patent law might become even more relevant if 3D printers become the mainstream technique used by households. See, e.g., M Norrgård, RM Ballardini and MM Kasi, 'Intellectual Property Rights in the Era of 3D Printing' in RM Ballardini, M Norrgård and J Partanen (eds), *3D Printing, Intellectual Property and Innovation* (Kluwer Law International 2017) 63, 69.

repair services and other recycling activities. There are several problems in this context. For instance, patenting tools and methods for re-using materials might be problematic. Exclusive rights targeted at spare parts might restrict the freedom to offer them.[3] In addition for instance, a secondary market actor might need to use another's trade mark to indicate compatibility with the main product or the fact that it provides a repair service targeting products originating from a trade mark holder.[4] A general relationship between competition law and sustainability is not straightforward. For instance, competition law can promote sustainability by restricting such anti-competitive IPR strategies that would hinder more sustainable technological development. On the other hand, competition law might impede sustainability since sustainability arguments cannot override harms to competition, for instance when co-operation between firms is considered. However, some of the problems relating to spare parts can be addressed by using competition law mechanisms.[5] Further, end user licence agreements (EULAs) can be used by IP rights holders in software industries to restrain repair activities by non-authorized repairers, and the legal status of EULAs remains unclear.[6]

This chapter examines repair activities and the use of recycled materials from European patent and trade mark law perspectives. Due to the wide scope of the theme, the assessment is not comprehensive. Instead, it focuses on two examples demonstrating a strong property right impact on recycling efforts. The first is the consideration of normal lifespan in the repair or reconstruction dichotomy in the patent context, and the second a possibility to use trade

---

[3]   For instance, in a Norwegian Supreme Court judgment, HR-2020-1142-A (Apple), the Supreme Court concluded that it was a trade mark infringement to import mobile screens intended to be used as spare parts. See further *Chapter 6 in this volume.*

[4]   The Trademark Directive (Art 14.1(c)) provides a limitation for using a trade mark to indicate the intended purpose of goods or services. See, e.g., CJEU Case C-228/03 *The Gillette Company, Gillette Group Finland Oy v LA-Laboratories Ltd Oy* [2005] ECR I-02337. Even though this situation falls beyond the scope of this chapter, the interests are to some extent similar: it is a question of access to spare parts markets connected to the circular economy on the one hand, and trade mark holders' interest in preventing confusion of origin and free-riding on the signs' goodwill on the other hand.

[5]   Refusal to supply spare parts can, in certain situations, be considered an abuse of a dominant position. See, e.g., Judgment of the General Court in Case T-712/14 *CEAHR v European Commission* EU:T:2017:748. Additional sector-specific mechanisms concerning supply of spare parts include, e.g., the Automotive Block Exemption Regulation (EU) 461/2010.

[6]   On EULAs as impediments for repair activities both from the European and US perspectives, see S Svensson, L Richter, E Maitre-Ekern, T Pihlajarinne, M Aline and C Dalhammar, 'The Emerging "Right to Repair" Legislation in the EU and the U.S.' (Conference paper for the Going Green – Care Innovation 2018).

marks in so-called upcycling[7] activities. The chapter assesses the structures and interpretations of exclusive rights conferred by patent law and trade mark law as impediments for the circular economy in achieving its full potential in terms of repairing products or re-using materials. When considering repairing activities and how IPRs might impede them, the doctrine of exhaustion is the most essential.[8] While contractual mechanisms, such as EULAs, might also have significant importance for possibilities as to repairing activities, they fall beyond the scope of this chapter.

A fundamental structural problem is that a repair business must resort to exceptions and limitations, such as the doctrine of exhaustion. Instead of integrating sustainability into only exceptions and limitations, revisiting exclusive rights themselves might be needed to incorporate sustainability comprehensively in IPRs.

2. CIRCULAR ECONOMY, SUSTAINABILITY AND IPRS

The concept of 'sustainable development' originates from the Report of the World Commission on Environment and Development (WCED) of 1987, where it was defined as 'development that meets the needs of the present without compromising the ability of future generations to meet their own needs'. Since then, the concept has been widely used.[9]

Sustainability is usually defined through interconnected pillars that include environmental, economic and social issues. These pillars represent a wide range of issues, for instance the environmental pillar refers to protection of environmental resources for present and future generations.[10] Environmental sustainability is also defined as the social foundation for humanity within

---

[7]   On the definition of upcycling, see Section 3.2, *infra*.

[8]   Previous research supports this assumption: e.g., Liu concludes that 'the current exhaustion doctrine, when applied to the refurbishing industry, fails to balance its mandate of promoting technological progress with the broader program of sustainable development and is therefore unsuitable for countries on the modernization path'. Liu, fn. 1, *supra*, 332.

[9]   In the WCED, it was also stated that sustainable development is 'the process of change in which the exploitation of resources, the direction of investments, the orientation of technological development and institutional change are all in harmony'. See D McGoldrick, 'Sustainable Development and Human Rights: An Integrated Conception' (1996) 45 ICLQ 796, 796.

[10]   E Rodrigues, *The General Exception Clauses of the TRIPS Agreement. Promoting Sustainable Development* (CUP 2012) 1–2.

'planetary boundaries'.[11] Two of them – climate change and biosphere integrity – could be described as being core planetary boundaries, which the circular economy might have great potential to affect. Moreover, a division has recently arisen between 'weak' and 'strong' sustainability. Weak sustainability brings environmental concerns into existing business structures and systems, while strong sustainability aims at integrating business into environmental systems by challenging existing structures so that industrial activities would fit within the capacity of the planet.[12]

Sustainability as a policy or legal principle[13] has connections to fundamental rights and human rights. Although direct mentions of sustainability or environmental issues in international human rights instruments are relatively infrequent, there has been a gradual development where sustainability has gained a position in human rights discussion and the issue of a 'human right to the environment' has been discussed.[14]

A provision on sustainable development appears in the Treaty on the Functioning of the European Union (TFEU). According to Article 3(3) TFEU, the EU shall work for the sustainable development of Europe, which specifically includes a high level of protection and improvement of the quality of the environment. Article 11 of the TFEU states that environmental

---

[11]   See, e.g., J Rockström, 'Planetary Boundaries: Exploring the Safe Operating Space for Humanity' [2009] 14 Ecology and Society; B Sjåfjell, J Mähönen, A Johnston and J Cullen, *Obstacles to Sustainable Global Business. Towards EU Policy Coherence for Sustainable Development*. SMART Project, 2018, 16–18 (on file with the authors).

[12]   N Roome, 'Looking Back, Thinking Forward: Distinguishing Between Weak and Strong Sustainability' *The Oxford Handbook of Business and the Natural Environment* (Online book, 2012).

[13]   See C Voigt, 'Article 11 TFEU in the Light of the Principle of Sustainable Development in International Law' in B Sjåfjell and A Wiesbrock (eds), *The Greening of European Business under EU Law. Taking Article 11 TFEU Seriously* (Online book, Routledge 2014).

[14]   E.g., the Rio Declaration (1992) states that human beings are at the centre of concerns for sustainable development and they have a right to a healthy and productive life in harmony with nature. That standpoint was affirmed in the Johannesburg Declaration in 2002. See more J Glazebrook, 'Human rights and the Environment' (2009) 40 Vict U Wellington L Rev 293, 294–298. Some countries, such as Switzerland, have explicitly incorporated the concept of environmentally sustainable development into their constitutions. See MD Khalid, F Jalil and BM Mazlin, 'Environmental Sustainability as a Human Right' in V Mauerhofer (ed), *Legal Aspects of Sustainable Development. Horizontal and Sectorial Policy Issues* (Springer 2016) 79, 83–84. However, several issues in this regard have raised discussion. These include the individualistic nature of the human rights-based approach, which does not correspond well with the value of the environment; the uneasiness of defining the qualitative level of environment that could be guaranteed by the human rights approach; and the possibility to impose obligations on individuals. See McGoldrick, fn. 9, *supra*, 811–812.

protection requirements must be integrated into the definition and implementation of Union policies and activities, in particular with a view to promoting sustainable development. The Charter of Fundamental Rights (Article 37) includes a similar provision: 'A high level of environmental protection and the improvement of the quality of the environment must be integrated into the policies of the Union and ensured in accordance with the principle of sustainable development.' This provision requires the promotion of environmental protection in EU policies. In addition, EU law should be interpreted by taking the environmental objectives of TFEU Article 11 into consideration in issues beyond those that are directly environmental.[15] Hence, the environmental integration obligation is not only one of the oldest integration clauses in EU law; it also holds enormous potential as a means of steering the interpretation and application of EU legal instruments that – in one way or the other – affect the environment. This objective must be balanced with protection of property and IP protection referred to in TFEU Articles 36 and 118. In IP issues, the CJEU should balance the objectives of IPR protection and Article 11.[16] On the other hand, Member States have a duty of loyalty (TFEU Article 4.3), which means they must follow the principle of sustainable development when applying EU law.[17]

Even though sustainability must be promoted whenever possible, nevertheless, both in formulation and application of EU intellectual property regulation, the relationship between IPRs and environmental sustainability is not straightforward. There are several cross points, of which, for instance, the role of IPRs in development, deployment and access to green technology innovations[18] and the relationship between the circular economy and IPRs are among the most relevant.

---

[15] B Sjåfjell and A Wiesbrock, 'The Importance of Article 11 TFEU for Regulating Business in the EU: Securing the Very Basis of Our Existence' in B Sjåfjell and A Wiesbrock (eds), *The Greening of European Business under EU Law. Taking Article 11 TFEU Seriously* (Online book, Routledge 2014).

[16] Sjåfjell uses Case C-513/99 Concordia Bus Finland [2002] ECR I-07213 as an example of cases where the court has, in a traditionally economic area, stressed the objective of environmental protection by referring to the environmental integration rule. B Sjåflell, 'The Legal Significance of Article 11 TFEU for EU Institutions and Member States' in B Sjåfjell and A Wiesbrock (eds), The Greening of European Business under EU law. Taking Article 11 TFEU Seriously (Online book, Routledge 2014).

[17] Sjåfjell, fn. 16, *supra.*

[18] See, e.g., M Rimmer, *Intellectual Property and Climate Change: Inventing Clean Technologies* (EE 2011) and A Brown, *Environmental Technologies, Intellectual Property and Climate Change* (EE 2013). On the interplay between climate change and IPRs, see also J Sarnoff (ed), *Research Handbook on Intellectual Property and Climate Change* (EE 2016).

The circular economy is a term that describes a new industrial model that aims to reduce waste and optimize the use of resources. As opposed to a linear model of consumption 'take, make, waste' the aim is to base it on 'reuse, repair, recycle, functional economy, eco-design, industrial ecology, sustainable supply and responsible consumption'.[19] The transition to the circular economy has been described as entailing four fundamental building blocks: (1) materials and product design (2) new business models (3) global reverse networks and (4) enabling conditions. It depends, however, on decisions by policymakers and on business entities introducing circularity into their business models.[20] At the same time, short-term oriented legal systems often support linear models of consumption, which are not necessarily in line with the requirements of the circular economy.[21]

The current structures of IP rights systems mainly reflect a need for weighing and balancing between the aims of exclusive rights and general arguments on free competition and efficient markets but not sustainability. However, sustainability interests are often intertwined with competitive issues of the recycling industry since competition arguments also cover competition by sustainable business models. From a broader perspective, the aim of IP rights is – by encouraging innovations and creative work and reducing search costs – to foster scientific, technical and social progress, that is to say, sustainable welfare.[22]

Due to the stated objective, in some singular cases fine-tuning the system might be enough. From a strong sustainability perspective, a more fundamental change is needed to direct incentives in a way that fosters sustainability. A strong property rights approach to IP can create incentives for original manufacturers, but it fails in terms of creating incentives for sustainable business models. Environmental arguments should, however, have a standalone position instead of having only indirect, implicit relevance through arguments relating to competition. In the case of having only implicit relevance, it might

---

[19] D Gaullard and L Blandine, *Circular Economy, Industrial Ecology and Short Supply Chain: Towards Sustainable Territories* (John Wiley & Sons 2016) 1, 3–4.

[20] M Lewandowski, 'Designing the Business Models for Circular Economy – Towards the Conceptual Framework' (2016) 8 Sustainability 1, available at http://www.mdpi.com/2071-1050/8/1/43.

[21] J Mähönen, 'Financing Sustainable Market Actors in Circular Economy' (26 October 2018) University of Oslo Faculty of Law Research Paper No 2018-28. Available at SSRN: https://ssrn.com/abstract=3273263.

[22] From the patent perspective, see G van Overwalle, 'Smart Innovation and Inclusive Patents for Sustainable Food and Health Care: Redefining the Europe 2020 Objectives' in Christopher Geiger, *Constructing European Intellectual Property. Achievements and New Perspectives* (EE 2013) 231–254, 250.

be difficult for sustainability arguments to override strong utilitarian justifications for IPRs in their traditional understandings.[23]

Incorporating sustainability in terms of exceptions and limitations to the exclusive rights is not sufficient as such. From a perspective of implementing strong sustainability into IPR regulation, sustainability cannot have a role only in levels of exceptions and limitations, that is to say, as an exception to the main rule of IP rights as strong property rights. This is because – due to a strong property rights perspective having often been followed in Europe – new exceptions and limitations are difficult to implement, while existing ones are in many traditions interpreted narrowly. Conceiving sustainability as only an exception to strong property rights as a main rule, namely, seeing sustainability as a negative variable, does not enable the ambitious goals of a 'strong' sustainability approach. A balance between sustainability and IP rights as property-related arguments requires sustainability to be embedded into IP rights regulation as a general principle.

3.   TWO EXAMPLES OF THE NEGATIVE EFFECTS OF A STRONG PROPERTY RIGHTS APPROACH ON THE CIRCULAR ECONOMY

3.1   Repairing Activities and Patents: The Outdated Idea of 'Normal' Lifespan?

The rights conferred by patent are wide, and these provisions do not usually provide much flexibility.[24] Therefore, repair business' activities targeted at patented products are easily considered as prima facie infringements and exhaustion as limitation turns out to be of utmost importance. The basic idea under the doctrine of exhaustion is that, once sold, a product can be used and

---

[23]   However, the ultimate problem – even if sustainability were fully recognized by the IPR system – is the priority of legitimate interests. As Voigt (see fn. 13, *supra*) points out, if other interests are considered as having importance enough, interests relating to environmental protection 'can simply be "balanced away"'.

[24]   Patent infringements in European countries are of two types: direct and indirect, e.g., such acts as making, using, selling and importing a patented invention without permission are direct infringements. Indirect infringement refers typically to secondary liability on the basis of supplying means that relate to an essential element of a patented product to a person with the knowledge that such means will be used in an infringing product. See more detail, RM Ballardini, M Norrgård and T Minssen, 'Enforcing Patents in the Era of 3D Printing' (2015) 10(11) Journal of Intellectual Property Law & Practice 850, 852–862. E.g., Arts 25 and 26 of the Unified Patent Court Convention include detailed and broadly formulated provisions on the direct and indirect use of patents as infringements.

repaired within its normal lifespan. After the first sale or, to be more precise, first marketing, the patent has fulfilled its purpose and the patentee received compensation.

In Europe, Josef Kohler developed the theory of exhaustion at the end of the 19th century. In his theory, the doctrine of exhaustion regarding patents was developed out of the implied licence construction, since Kohler discussed firstly the implied licence doctrine and after that expanded his view into a general doctrine of exhaustion that could be applied outside of the contractual relationship.[25] A purchaser is allowed to use a product within its 'intended use', and repair within the 'normal lifespan of products' is also possible.[26]

The scope of exhaustion is not, however, internationally harmonized but left to the discretion of national courts instead (for instance, TRIPS Article 6). The fact that exhaustion might be national, regional and international (the scope of exhaustion is defined by a national territory or a region such as the EU or it concerns the entire world) might create barriers for repair activities.[27] Interpretations of what kind of activities constitute making a new product might differ between jurisdictions; additionally, a lack of clear rules results in lack of uniformity inside jurisdictions. Moreover, some of these practices might stand in fundamental contradiction to the modern circular economy.

The principle of exhaustion is closely linked to single market policies since a broad interpretation of exhaustion is supported by the free movement of goods. The CJEU has stated that patent law must be compatible with those policies.[28] The Convention on the Grant of European Patents (EPO) allows an

---

[25] See G Westkamp, 'Exhaustion and the Internet as a Distribution Channel: the Relationship Between Intellectual Property and European Law in Search of Clarification' in I Calboli and E Lee (eds), *Research Handbook on Intellectual Property Exhaustion and Parallel Imports* (EE 2016) 498–499 referring to J Kohler: *Deutches Patentrecht* (1878) 157–161.

[26] J Kohler, *Handbuch des deutschen Patentrechts* (Mannheim 1900) 452–456, available at http://dlib-pr.mpier.mpg.de/m/kleioc/0010/exec/books/%22161848%22.

[27] The EU applies regional exhaustion to sales in the European Economic Area. The USA applied national exhaustion before US Supreme Court decision 30.6.2017 *Impression Products Inc. v Lexmark International* according to which foreign sales also exhaust US-based patent rights, meaning that the doctrine of international exhaustion applies. Japan and China apply international exhaustion as well.

[28] In *Merck & Co. Inc. v Stephar BV and Petrus Stephanus Exler* (C-187/80) the CJEU stressed that the 'substance of a patent right lies essentially in according the inventor an exclusive right of first placing the product on the market'. After that, the right is exhausted. The CJEU has stated that Art 36 TJEU allows exceptions to the free movement of goods only to the extent to which such exceptions are necessary for the purpose of safeguarding rights that constitute the specific subject matter of the type of intellectual property in question (Case C-10/89 *SA CNL-SUCAL NV v HAG GF AG*). Therefore, first marketing can be seen as a specific subject matter. See S Enchelmaier,

applicant to acquire a bundle of national patents by a single application, but the Convention does not include much harmonization. Article 29 of the Agreement of the Unified Patent Court (UPC) includes a provision on exhaustion.[29] The big picture regarding exhaustion will not be changed: once products have been put in markets anywhere in the internal markets, they can subsequently be sold everywhere in the internal markets. It is possible that the details of exhaustion will be harmonized in the practice of the UPC. However, this is only a partial solution due to the fact that defendants might still face claims for infringement of national patents.

From the circular economy perspective, the most essential feature in the exhaustion doctrine is drawing a line between repair and reconstruction. While repairing a patented product is permissible, construction of a new product is not. Claims of both direct and indirect infringements can be assessed under the exhaustion doctrine.[30] An impermissible reconstruction might constitute a direct patent infringement. In addition, sale of an unpatented replacement part can be counted as indirect infringement, as facilitating direct patent infringement.

The limits between repair and reconstruction are not clear. For instance, in the UK exhaustion is partially based on an implied licence construction.[31] Exhaustion provision can be found in UK law only to the extent that it is required due to the EC Treaty. Under domestic law, the concept of an implied licence is still to some extent decisive.[32] A principal weakness from the sus-

---

'A Competition Law Perspective I: Competition Law Aspects of European Patents with Unitary Effect' in J Pila and C Wadlow (eds), *The Unitary EU Patent System* (Hart 2017) 111, 114–115.

[29] According to the article, there is an exhaustion of the patent after the product has been placed on the market in the EU by the patent holder, unless there are 'legitimate grounds for the patent proprietor to oppose further commercialisation of the product'.

[30] On direct and indirect infringements, see fn. 24, *supra.*

[31] The situation is similar in the USA. Eg, *Anton/Bauer, Inc. v PAG Ltd.* (Fed Cir 2003) illustrates well the position of the implied licence doctrine in connection with repair activities. See more about the case in Amber Hatfield Rovner, 'Practical Guide to Application of (or Defense Against) Product-Based Infringement Immunities Under the Doctrines of Patent Exhaustion and Implied License' (2004) 12 Tex Intell Prop LJ 227, 248–249.

[32] E.g., in an early decision, *Solar Thomson Engineering Co. Ltd. and Another v Barton*, High Court of Justice, Civ Div, 17 March 1977, the court stressed that there was an implied licence to repair a patented product, but not for making new products. E.g., *United Wire v Screen Repair Services* (Scotland 2000) concerned screens for filtering machines used in oil exploration. There were patents relating to filter meshes and their frames. The defendant supplied new meshes at the correct tension. The Court of Appeal stated that genuine repair did not infringe the patent. However, although a patentee exhausted his patent rights on sale, allowing the owner to make repairs, this did

tainability standpoint lies in setting the recycling business dependent on the right holder's declaration of will-type acts, which might strengthen the right holder's possibilities to set conditions on subsequent use of a product. In *Schütz v Werit*[33] the Supreme Court concluded that the division between repair and reconstruction depends on various factors, for instance the life expectancy of the part and whether the part embodies the inventive concept of the patent.

In Germany, there is a tradition of stressing the 'essential element of invention' and 'inventive function'.[34] The Supreme Court has applied a test according to which the line between repair and reconstruction is drawn by assessing whether replacement of the components can usually be expected during the working life of the device, that is to say, how the product's lifespan is seen in the trade. If replacement of a component can be expected, then replacement is not per se infringement, but then it must be assessed whether the technical effect of the invention is reflected in replaced components. If the answer is affirmative, then the use constitutes reconstruction and counts as a patent infringement (BGH: *Palettenbehälter II, Pallet Container II* and *Trommeleinheit, Drum Unit*). As a comparison, in the USA, the main principle is that unpatented consumable parts are free to be replaced, while in Germany a broad interpretation of indirect infringement is applied – a wide interpretation of an essential element of an invention might impede secondary market actors.[35]

---

not mean that the owner also had an implied licence to make a product. The court concluded that there was a patent infringement.

[33]   *Schütz v Werit* [2013] UKSC 16.

[34]   E.g., the German Reich Supreme Court, 4 October 1938, Case No. I 233/37, *Gerbsäure*; Federal Supreme Court, 12 June 1951, Case No. I ZR, *Tauchpumpensatz*; Federal Supreme Court, 10 December 1981, Case No. X ZR 70/80, *Rigg*. In the German Reich Supreme Court, 25 October 1924, Case No. I 521/23, 1926 GRUR 163 – *Schraubstöpselsicherung*, the court stated that the replaced part, a 'cartridge', was an important part of the invention and embodied the inventive function. About these cases, see M Mohri, '*Patents, Repair and Recycling from a Comparative Perspective*' (IIC 2010) 41(7) 779, 791–792.

[35]   See Federal Supreme Court, 4 May 2004, Case No. X ZR 48/03, *Flügelradzähler*. The case concerned a flow meter comprising housing and removable measuring capsules. The measuring capsule was intended to be replaced during the lifespan of the product. The plaintiff sold flow meters and replaceable measuring capsules. The housing part was the 'novel' part. The defendant sold measuring capsules. The court concluded that this was an indirect patent infringement of the Patent Act section 10 since they were 'means relating to an essential element of the invention'. The court stated that means relates to an essential element of the invention if it is capable of cooperating functionally with that element in the implementation of the protected inventive concept. The defendant's measuring capsules were designed in accordance with a feature of the patented product and were suitable and intended to interact with the housing. Replacement of the part during the expected working life of a machine did

The first problem is that unpredictability due to lack of harmonization both at the international and European level as such is a risk for recycling activities. Secondly, the threshold of 'normal' lifespan, that a product can be used and repaired within the normal lifespan of a product, involves problems. Assessment should be made on the basis of whether the product has fulfilled its function: is life at an end? The normal lifespan of a product has been assessed on the basis of 'common understanding in society',[36] but not without criticism.

---

not constitute a new making of the product. However, if that part embodies essential elements of the invention, the patent holder has not already drawn the technical or commercial benefits as a result of the first putting into circulation of the device as a whole. The case has been criticized as favouring patent holders, since every element of the patent claim could be an 'essential' element of the invention. Mohri, fn. 34, *supra*, 788–789. Additionally, in the Düsseldorf High Court case, 17 November 2005, *Kaffee-Filterpads*, a patent on a coffee machine consisted of a filter holder and filter pads. The court concluded that selling filter pads that were compatible with the machine was an indirect infringement, since the coffee pads were compatible with the filter holder, both of which performed an inventive function. The means of putting a new coffee pad into the machine was described in the patent specification. The court stated that the patentee had not yet capitalized on its invention by selling coffee machines that have such a combination and therefore replacing the pad was considered as a reconstruction of the patented invention. In the USA, the approach has instead been open for replacements. In *Aro Mfg. Co. v Convertible Top Replacement Co.*, 365 U.S. 336 (1961) and *Aro Mfg. Co. v Convertible Top Replacement Co.*, 377 U.S. 476 (1964) the patent holder owned a patent on a convertible top. The defendant sold fabric components that replaced portions of worn-out fabric, which required replacement after three years of use. The court stated that the combination patent covered the totality of the elements in the claim, and there was no legally recognizable or protected 'essential' element, 'gist' or 'heart' of the invention in a combination patent. The court stated that a purchaser cannot reconstruct or make a totally new patented product after a product sold as a whole has become spent, but 'mere replacement of individual unpatented parts, one at a time, whether of the same parts repeatedly or different parts successively, is no more than the lawful right of the owner to repair his property'.

[36]   The reasoning adopted by the German Supreme Court in BGH, 17 July 2012, X ZR 97/11 (Palettenbehälter II) offers a good example of such argumentation. The patent covered a pallet container, consisting of an inner container, flat pallets and bars of metal in the shape of a basket. The defendant sold and exchanged the inner containers in containers originally sold by the plaintiff. The court stated that in drawing the line between repair and reconstruction, it is important to assess whether the technical effect of the patented invention resides in the part exchanged. However, if consumers and trade circles believe that a replacement constitutes a remanufacture of the patented product, the action constitutes a patent infringement, in spite of the estimation of whether the replacement reflects the technical aspects of the innovation. Therefore, consumers' perceptions of the product – the assumptions of its use value as well as exchange value – are relevant. However, the meaning of repair in common language and in the IPR context can sometimes be remarkably different. For instance, as stated in *United Wire*: 'repair' refers to remedial actions that might not involve replacement of parts or involve

The concept of a normal lifespan under a common understanding in society can lead to imbalanced results since the way the public perceive a product's lifespan very much depends on the patent holder's guidance. In addition, a normal lifespan does not necessarily reflect the core interests that are aimed to be protected by IPRs. To illustrate, a sold product as the public perceive it does not necessarily correspond to the invention. For instance, both single-use or durable products can be based on the same invention.

The patent holder's way of marketing and presenting a product has an impact on how the public perceive its lifespan.[37] Potentially, a patent holder can choose to create or to not create an assumption that a product's normal lifespan includes changes of replacement parts by, for instance, selling replacement parts separately. Additionally, it is relevant what kind of implicit or explicit information they give on the lifespan of the product; for instance, on its use value or exchange value. From the sustainability viewpoint, right holders' possible tendency to see a product's lifespan as shorter than it could potentially be might be problematic.

A third problem is that, in general, traditional property right perspectives seem to guide the courts towards the tendency to follow old traditions rather than opening their argumentation for sustainability. It seems that the courts are not inclined to use arguments relating to sustainability in their interpretations of repair and reconstruction.[38] A traditional, property rights attitude for courts is highly problematic in Europe from the perspective of Article 11 TFEU.

3.2   Upcycling: Trade Marks as Right Holder's Property, Badge of Origin or an Indicator on Recycling?

From the perspective of the reuse of trade marked products, trade marks might serve several purposes. In some cases, a trade mark is affixed to a product that is reused and it is impossible or difficult or expensive to remove – if a trade mark right prohibits its presence on the product, it constitutes a direct obstacle for recycling. A trade mark as a sign might be irrelevant as such.

---

extensive replacement of parts. The latter might infringe the patentee's rights while the former does not (*United Wire v Screen Repair Services*, House of Lords (UK), judgment of 20 July 2000).

[37]   C Heath and M Mōri, 'Ending is Better than Mending – Recent Japanese Case Law on Repair, Refill and Recycling' (2006) 37 International Review of Intellectual Property and Competition Law 856 863. In addition, Heath and Mori suggest that the concept of the normal lifespan is too vague and thus creates legal uncertainty as to the markets for repair.

[38]   Similarly, from the perspective of the USA and Japan. MS Hashiguchi, 'Recycling Efforts and Patent Rights Protection in the United States and Japan' (2008) 33 Colum J Envtl L 169, 180–185.

Secondly, a secondary market actor might have an interest in using a trade mark in a product or in its package as an indication of the origin of raw material.[39] From several potential situations, the example of so-called 'upcycling' (or 'trashion') cases is used here to demonstrate problems of a strong property rights approach from the trade mark perspective. The concept of upcycling is used to describe the creation of objects, such as bags, jewellery and home-decorative items, from used products.[40] In these cases, beyond the markets of trade marked products, a trade mark might be a key feature of a product for the consumer. With regard to a product used as raw material and a new product, the product categories and the functionality of products are, surprisingly, completely different. For instance, in a lamp made from Coca-Cola cans the Coca-Cola trade mark is a crucial feature. It is an element that makes it attractive for consumers. In these cases, a trade mark serves as an indication of recycling. However, this kind of (new) function of trade marks is a reflection of the origin function of the product used as raw material. When a trade mark has changed as a badge of recycling, the risk of confusion might be low despite the fact that the trade mark might form a prominent feature of the product.[41]

In general, trade mark law has on the one hand been demonstrated as being rather flexible when facing challenges such as digitalization. This is due to flexible building blocks such as the principle of confusion and the commercial

---

[39]   The Trademark Directive 14 1b limitation could be applied to such situations since when a trade mark's purpose is to indicate the origin of raw material, it directly tells something about the goods offered, and it can be permitted if it is in accordance with honest practices in industrial or commercial matters. In Germany, the right to use a trade mark indicating the origin of a raw material has traditionally been assessed by paying special attention to the degree of alteration of the original product. See G Riehle, 'Trade Mark Rights and Remanufacturing in the European Community. With Special Emphasis on the Rebuilding of Automotive Parts'. Max Planck Institute for Intellectual Property, Competition and Tax Law (Munich 2003) 91–92. In the case Bundegerichtshof (GRUR 1998) 687 *Venus Multi*, the German Supreme Court stated that it was irrelevant in these situations whether a raw material's trade mark had been left untouched on the new product or re-affixed there.

[40]   See, e.g., A Anderson, 'Trash or Treasure? Controlling your Brand in the Age of Upcycling' (2009) July/August(129) Trademark 1, 1.

[41]   However, right holders might be suspicious of their trade mark being utilized, e.g., see Anderson, fn. 40, *supra*, 1–2 who argues the importance of reacting to this kind of use, e.g., stating that in the case of a bag constructed only from cookie wrappers originating from a single trade mark holder, the prominent nature of the trade mark would lead a reasonable consumer to assume that the bag was produced by the trade mark holder or under its supervision. However, Anderson recognizes that aggression towards this kind of trade mark utilization might also result in ill-will associated with the trade mark holder, as the trade mark holder could be seen as having little concern about the environmental impact of its products.

use criterion.[42] In upcycling cases, trade mark infringements under Article 10.2(a) (so-called double identity rule) and (b) (confusing similarity rule) are not probable since the goods are typically different from the ones for which the trade mark is registered.[43] However, the requirements set by Article 10.2(c) for protection of trade marks with a reputation could be fulfilled; among others, on the basis that the use means free-riding (use 'takes unfair advantage of the distinctive character of repute' of the trade mark) or tarnishing the trade mark's reputation (use is 'detrimental to repute' of the trade mark).[44]

If trade mark owners' interests dominate the interpretation of Articles 10.2(a)–(c) and upcycling is deemed as being a prima facie infringement, the next step is to consider the exceptions and limitations. Exhaustion of a trade mark is harmonized in the EU. There is relatively little case law from the CJEU on exhaustion in the contexts of recycling and re-using materials. However, one possible interpretation is that the exhaustion doctrine might cover only repairing a product to its original condition. It might not be applied, instead, to a recycled product bearing an original product's trade mark in a case where, due to a stage of alteration, the identity of the product has turned into a new,

---

[42]   See T Pihlajarinne, 'Non-traditional Trademark Infringement in the 3D Printing Context' in RM Ballardini, M Norrgård and J Partanen (eds), *3D Printing, Intellectual Property and Innovation* (Kluwer International 2017) 303–316, 305–308.

[43]   However, the so called double identity rule (Art 10.2(a), Dir (EU) 2015/2436), which requires both trade marks and goods to be identical, could be applied in such exceptional cases where a trade mark proprietor has registered the mark for the same goods that are produced by used materials. It is possible that that the requirements set by CJEU would be considered to be fulfilled – for instance, that use is detrimental for the investment function of trade mark. The CJEU has stressed that only use that is detrimental to the functions of a trade mark, especially to the origin function, is an infringement under the double identity rule, e.g., the following judgments of the ECJ: *Arsenal Football Club plc v Reed*, C-206/01; *Anheuser-Busch v Budéjovicky Budvar*, C-245/02; *Adam Opel AG v Autec Ag.*, C-48/05. Such a use is not, however, necessary, since the CJEU has stated that use that is detrimental to the investment function could also be infringing under this rule. See Cases C-487/07 *L'Oréal SA, Lancome parfums et beauté & Cie SNC and Laboratoire Garnier & Cie v Bellure NV, Malaika Investments Ltd and Starion International Ltd* and C-323/09 *Interflora Inc. Interflora British Unit v Marks & Spencer et al.*

[44]   The CJEU has stated that free riding refers to use where a user seeks 'to ride on the coat-tails of the mark with a reputation in order to benefit from the power of attraction, the reputation and the prestige of that mark and to exploit, without paying any financial compensation, the marketing effort expended by the proprietor of the mark in order to create and maintain the mark's image'. The CJEU has defined tarnishing as use that reduces the trade mark's power of attraction. In particular the characteristic or quality of the goods might have a negative impact on the image of the mark (C-487/07 *L'Oréal SA, Lancome parfums et beauté & Cie SNC and Laboratoire Garnier & Cie v Bellure NV, Malaika Investments Ltd and Starion International Ltd*).

independent product. In that case, the product is not the same as was originally put on the market, since arguably the essence of the exhaustion doctrine is to define the limits of a trade mark right on a product originating from the trade mark owner. If the identity of a product has essentially changed, the product originates from recycling businesses, not from the trade mark owner. However, when it is applied, a trade mark holder might additionally prevent further commercialization of the product in the case of a 'legitimate reason' as meant in Article 15.2 of the Trade Mark Directive, 'especially where the condition of the goods is changed or impaired after they have been put on the market'.[45] Assessment of whether there is substantial material alteration does

---

[45]   This problem was considered by the CJEU in Case C-46/10 *Viking Gas A/S v Kosan Gas A/S*. The plaintiff sold so-called composite bottles with carbon dioxide, as the holder of an exclusive licence of three-dimensional trade marks (the shape of bottles and containers for liquid fuels). A consumer purchased a bottle from the plaintiff, paying for the gas as well as for the bottle. After this sale, a buyer could exchange the bottle for a new one filled by the plaintiff, paying only for the gas. The defendant offered a possibility for consumers to exchange an existing composite bottle in return for a full one, affixing its name and logo thereto, adding information on gas filling stations. The name of the plaintiff was also visible. The CJEU pointed out that composite bottles to be re-used a number of times are not mere packaging of the original product but have an independent economic value and must be considered as goods. A balance must be found between the legitimate interests relating to a licensee profiting from the trade marks and the legitimate interests of purchasers of those bottles, in particular the interest in fully enjoying their property rights in those bottles, and the general interest in maintaining undistorted competition. The court concluded that the right holder could not prevent this without a proper reason for the purposes of Art 7.2 of Dir 89/104. Therefore, the exhaustion doctrine was applicable, but with the restrictions set by Art 7.2 of the Trademark Directive. The use of the word 'especially' in Art 7.2 of the Directive indicates that alteration or impairment of the condition of goods bearing a mark is given only as an example of what may constitute legitimate reasons. A legitimate reason also exists when use by a third party of a sign identical with, or similar to, a trade mark seriously damages the reputation of that mark or when that use is carried out in such a way as to give the impression that there is a commercial connection between the trade mark proprietor and that third party, and in particular that the third party is affiliated to the proprietor's distribution network or that there is a special relationship between those two persons. The labelling of the composite bottles and the circumstances in which they are exchanged must not lead the average consumer who is reasonably well informed and reasonably observant and circumspect to consider that there is a connection between the two undertakings at issue in the main proceedings or that the gas used to refill those bottles comes from Kosan Gas. In order to assess whether such an erroneous impression is precluded, it is necessary to take into account the practices in that sector and, in particular, whether consumers are accustomed to gas being filled by other dealers. The Court stated that it is reasonable to assume that a consumer who goes directly to Viking Gas might be more able to be aware that there is no connection between Viking Gas and Kosan Gas. Interestingly, the Court also stated that 'as regards the fact that the composite bottles bear word and figurative marks made

not necessarily reflect the legitimate interest of trade mark protection. In many upcycling cases there certainly is substantial material alteration but no risk of confusion or damaging the reputation of trade mark.

In EU trade mark law, the general idea of whether use harms trade mark functions, such as an original function or an investment function, is at the core of finding infringements and therefore is likely to be reflected in the interpretation of exhaustion.[46] The CJEU view in *Copad SA v Christian Dior Couture SA and Others*[47] indicates a rather extensive protection for brand owners from damaging the luxury image in connection with exhaustion.

However, the Trade Mark Directive (Article 14.1(b)) limitation might also be applicable in cases where, due to a stage of alteration, the end product has turned into a new, independent product.[48] In upcycling cases, one could argue that the trade mark serves as an indication of the characteristics of a good, that is to say, an indication of the origin of the raw material used. To be permitted, the use must be 'in accordance with honest practice in industrial or commercial matters'. However, the CJEU offered guidance in *Adam Opel AG v Autec AG* and *Adidas AG et al. v Marca Mode CV*, whereby only such use that indicates the characteristics of the products of the third party using a trade mark falls within the scope of the limitation. A trade mark as an indication must directly relate to the characteristics of the goods marketed. More specifically, the CJEU

---

up of the name and logo of Kosan Gas which remain, according to the findings of the national court, visible in spite of the labelling affixed by Viking Gas to those bottles, it must be pointed out that this constitutes a relevant factor in so far as it seems to rule out that labelling from altering the condition of the bottles by masking their origin'.

[46]   See fn. 43, *supra*, from the perspective of Art 10.2(a). In the context of exhaustion, the previous case law on repacking pharmaceuticals has been based on the 'special rights constituting specific subject matter of trademark' test. In its case law, the court has developed rules on which forms of repacking and using a trade mark can negatively impact either on how consumers perceive the origin referred to by the trade mark, or on the trade mark's reputation, and therefore can constitute a legitimate reason for a trade mark owner to object to the use of the trade mark. See, e.g., cases C-102/77 *Hoffmann-La Roche & Co. AG v Centrafarm Vertriebsgesellschaft Pharmazeutischer Erzeugnisse mbH.*, C-427/93 *Bristol-Myers Squibb v Paranova A/S*, and C-429/93 *C H Boehringer Sohn, Boehringer Ingelheim KG and Boehringer Ingelheim A/S v Paranova A/S* and C-436/93 *Bayer Aktiengesellschaft and Bayer Danmark A/S v Paranova A/S*, C-143/00 *Boehringer Ingelheim KG, et al. v Swingward Ltd*, C-348/04 *Boehringer Ingelheim KG et al. v Swingward Ltd et al.*

[47]   Case C-59/08 *Copad SA v Christian Dior couture SA and Others* [2009] ECR I-03421.

[48]   According to this limitation, it is permitted to use signs or indications that are not distinctive or that concern the kind, quality, quantity, intended purpose, value, geographical origin, the time of production of goods or of rendering the service, or other characteristics of goods or services; on condition that the use by a third party is in accordance with honest practices in industrial or commercial matters.

explicitly stated in *Adidas* that exploitation of a trade mark in a purely decorative purpose does not amount to such use.[49] These strict interpretations do not give much room for trade mark usage in connection to recycling. Division between usage of (a) a trade mark as a characteristic *itself* of a good offered by the recycling industry or (b) a trade mark as an *indication* of the characteristics of a product offered by the recycling industry is not easy or even feasible.[50]

Upcycling cases belong to a grey area. On the one hand, trade marks serve as decorations that are very attractive to consumers. On the other hand, a trade mark indicates the origin of raw material and, therefore, it might genuinely be perceived as an indication of recycling. In that case, use of the trade mark could refer to recycling as a characteristic of a good. There is no certainty on how the CJEU would interpret these contradictory roles of trade marks. The assessment is further complicated by the 'honest practices' requirement.

The ultimate problem lies in the way the limitations are formulated: the purpose of use covered by limitations is defined narrowly and the content of limitations fails to meet the interests of the circular economy. Innovative ways to utilize recycled products, such as manufacturing products by utilizing raw materials from completely different product categories, should be encouraged in this respect. For an environmentally conscious consumer, an original trade mark left affixed to such a product might serve as an important indication of the origin of its raw material. However, trade mark law fails to recognize such interest. An additional difficulty might be unpredictability due to the very limited amount of case law in the recycling context in Europe.

3.3   Possible Remedies

A general-level problem is fundamental: the basic structures of IP rights do not offer enough support for sustainability. Since sustainability arguments are often intertwined with competition arguments, and since the fundamental aim of IP rights is to contribute to the welfare of society, there should not exist enormous difficulties in promoting sustainability by regulation of intellectual property rights. A strong property rights approach, however, might in some situations hinder sustainability arguments, and a balance between sustainability and the interests of right owners requires sustainability to be embedded

---

[49]   See Case C-48/05 *Adam Opel AG v Autec AG* [2007] ECR I-01017; Case C-102/07 *Adidas AG et al. v Marca Mode CV* [2008] ECR I-02439.

[50]   For instance Kur criticizes the division between using a trade mark as an element of a good or an element that indicates something on the good. A Kur, 'Small Cars, Big Problems? – An analysis of the ECJ's Opel / Autec Decision and its consequences' in A Bakardjieva Engelbrekt, U Bernitz, B Domeij, A Kur and PJ Nordell (eds), *Festskrift till Marianne Levin* (Norsteds Juridik, Stockholm 2008) 329–352, 343.

more explicitly into IP rights regulation. In the IP rights context, sustainability should serve as a general principle with limiting effects on IP rights, directing the incentives set by IP rights in a way that fosters sustainability and sustainable competition.

As such, the fact that the repair business must resort to exceptions and limitations is a structural problem that leads to sustainability being easily overridden by right holders' interests. The awareness of a need for comprehensive changes in consumption models should be reflected in weighing between sustainability and protection of property rights. In this assessment, sustainability cannot be seen as less valuable in society than protection of property rights. From that perspective, the best alternative would be to embed sustainability and the right to repair perspective directly in the provisions conferring exclusive rights as such. Exclusive rights should be formulated so that they are limited within the sustainable lifespan idea. This would mean that the scope of infringing acts should be re-defined in a way that only acts beyond the genuine purpose of maximizing the lifespan of a product or material would be infringing acts. In that case, property rights would be seen in a realistic way in relationship with planetary boundaries as enforced in the limits set by sustainability.

A second general problem is legal uncertainty, as such, as a remarkable risk for repair activities. In many areas of the repair business, there is no great profit expectation.[51] Therefore, risks of court proceedings are too great in relation to profit expectations. This in turn reduces incentives for the repairing business. The UPC will offer only limited harmonization in many respects, and international harmonization is needed for dismantling these barriers.

A first aid solution, beyond correcting structural bias, might be to update Kohler's ideas to the era of the modern circular economy. In fact, it seems that Kohler's ideas as such are not problematic, but rather the way the 'normal lifespan' of a product is perceived in society. The problem is exacerbated by the civil law tradition of the courts' strong respect for the will of the legislator and a sceptical attitude towards court-made rules.[52] Therefore, the courts have a tendency towards dogmatic and traditional viewpoints instead of opening their argumentation for issues beyond the traditional doctrinal basis.

The way that the public perceives a product's lifespan is crucial in assessing repairs in the patent context. General attitudes towards 'take, make, waste' consumption models as well as consumption models adopted by the circular economy all impact on this. However, patent holders' business models and

---

[51]   Liu, fn. 1, *supra*, 332.

[52]   See more, e.g., J Husa, K Nuotio and H Pihlajamäki, 'Nordic Law – Between Tradition and Dynamism' in J Husa, K Nuotio and H Pihlajamäki (eds), *Nordic Law – Between Tradition and Dynamism* (Intersentia 2007) 1, 9.

marketing acts might have a fundamental impact. In case they have incentives to apply linear, short-term consumption models, consumers might see the lifespan of the product as short. Therefore, general attitudes in society towards sustainability are crucial.

One option would be to embed the incentive for the circular economy into the repair and reconstruction dichotomy by reassessing the 'normal lifespan of the product' idea. Instead of the 'normal lifespan', which is often perceived as, following the 'take, make and waste' consumption models, excluding an obligation for sustainable lifespan, we could apply, for instance, a threshold of a 'normal, sustainable lifespan for that particular category of product', or an 'environmentally friendly lifespan'.

This would mean a transformation from the idea of what the lifespan of a product *is* to an idea of what it *should* be, that is, how long the product should work in a sustainable-based society. That would include, for instance, assessing the feasibility of selling changeable parts for such products. What kind of consequences would there be if such an approach were adopted? It would create incentives for the circular economy and sustainable products, but a drawback might be more uncertainty. To avoid this, more detailed guidelines for assessing sustainable lifespan should be adopted. However, the difficulty is that there must be a certain level of flexibility in thresholds relating to repair and reconstruction. The threshold for assessing originality or innovative step must depend on circumstances and technology, for example. Therefore, a certain level of unpredictability is present since it is not possible to create detailed guidelines.

Harmonization efforts should be taken under the idea of sustainable lifespan. Since international harmonization might not be a realistic option as being arduous to achieve, a faster and more flexible mechanism could be to set the guidelines of sustainable lifespan by soft law mechanisms. For instance, guidelines could be set by WIPO recommendations.

A tendency to consider non-typical uses of a trade mark where a trade mark is perceived as something else than a badge of origin, as prima facie trade mark infringements, reflects a strong property right perspective. A vice-versa assumption should be applied: in cases where the ultimate focus of trade mark use is not on the badge of origin type of purpose and the use is considered feasible from the sustainable business model point of view, it should be out of the scope of trade mark rights. For instance, if a new item is made by using recycled materials representing a completely different product category, and the trade marks of the raw material are visible in a new product, the presumption could be applied. Flexibilities under the rules conferring rights (Article 10.2(a)–(c)) should be used not only to adapt trade mark rights to new use environments but also to foster innovative ways to recycle. After that, sustainable business would more easily avoid the traps of narrow interpretations offered by trade mark exceptions and limitations. In principle, it would be relatively easy for the CJEU to revisit the interpretations of Article 10.2(a)–(c) and genuinely put Article 11 of TFEU into effect in EU trade mark law.

4.   CONCLUSIONS

Genuine integration of sustainability into the IP rights system would require a fundamental change in how the relationship is perceived between IP as property rights and interests relating, for instance, to the circular economy. As long as a possibility to radically extend the lifespan of patented products and their materials is perceived as an exception to a strong property right, sustainability does not serve as a strong argument in the context of repairing and recycling. The same concerns arise when creating attractive and innovative recycled products for consumers through the use of a raw-material trade mark as an indication of recycling, which might contribute to improving attitudes towards recycling.

A first aid type of solution to the two key problems described in this chapter would be to integrate the sustainable lifespan threshold into the exceptions and limitations, such as into the exhaustion doctrine. However, structural bias should primarily be corrected by formulating exclusive rights so that sustainable lifespan defines the scope of exclusive rights themselves. IP rights should cover only acts beyond those whose genuine purpose is to maximize the lifespan of a product or material. This might restrain perceiving sustainability only as an exception and would apply to all situations where IP rights and circular economy interests collide in the context of IP rights infringements.

6. Revisiting the concept of 'trade mark piracy' in light of sustainable development goals: a discussion of the Norwegian 'Apple Case'

Ole-Andreas Rognstad

1. INTRODUCTION

Following the direction of Pihlajarinne's contribution in the previous chapter about the need to reform IP law in the circular economy,[1] I will discuss a recent decision from the Norwegian Supreme Court regarding the de-branding and importation of spare parts of iPhones for repair purposes.[2] Here, the Court came to the conclusion that importation of mobile phone screens from Hong Kong to Norway infringed Apple's trade mark rights in a situation where Apple logos on the screens that were affixed without Apple's consent were concealed by a marker prior to the importation. The case, and the decision, have caused strong reactions among public opinion in Norway from a sustainability point of view.[3] The discussion is indeed relevant to the concept of sustainable markets.

For the average IP lawyer, however, the case might look like an ordinary 'piracy case' and the Supreme Court treated it that way.[4] The Court's final statement to address the sustainability issue that was raised by the defendant is illustrative, as the Court remarked that (competition and) sustainability concerns were not relevant to the case since the case was not about the importation

---

[1] *Chapter 5 in this volume.*

[2] Case HR-2020-1142-A, see *Chapter 5, fn. 3, supra*. An English translation provided by the Supreme Court is found here, https://www.domstol.no/globalassets/ upload/hret/decisions-in-english-translation/hr-2020-1142-a.pdf (accessed 29 October 2020). Quotations from the decision in this chapter are taken from this translation.

[3] See, for example, Maja van der Velden, 'Apple Uses Trade Marks to Strengthen its Monopoly on Repair' (Blog post 7 July 2020), see https://www.jus.uio.no/english/ research/areas/companies/blog/companies-markets-and-sustainability/velden--apple -uses-trademark-law.html (accessed 29 October 2020).

[4] See further Sections 2 and 3, *infra*.

of the spare parts but about use of the trade marks affixed to the spare parts.[5] Thus, the Court emphasized that trade mark law 'does not prevent a Norwegian mobile phone repairer from importing screens that are compatible with Apple's smartphones, as long as the imported screens do not have trade marks unlawfully affixed to them'.[6] That statement is, however, no more than a postulate, since the sustainability argument raised by the defendant was meant to support his challenging the notion of what *is* an unlawful use of a trade mark. We will return to this issue later in the chapter. The allegation here is that the argument was definitely relevant to the case, and even targeted the very core of it. If the Court had taken the argument seriously, but still had chosen to uphold its position that the importation constituted an unlawful use of the trade mark, it should have rejected the argument on the ground that sustainability concerns cannot override the trade mark rights in cases like that at hand. That is the reality of the decision, no matter how the Court phrased it.

In this contribution, I will try to take the sustainability argument seriously, not necessarily to attack the *result* of the Supreme Court decision on the facts of the case, but to raise the question whether current trade mark law rules and notions are unnecessarily strict, or prejudicial, in light of sustainability arguments.

2.   THE NORWEGIAN APPLE CASE: FACTS AND FINDINGS

The case concerned the owner of the one-person enterprise PCKompaniet, whose activities included repair of Apple smartphones and replacement of broken iPhone screens without authorization or any business relation with Apple. In March 2017, Oslo District Court had issued a general interim measure upon Apple's request requiring the customs service 'to seek to disclose and keep from release all articles with trade marks or figure marks belonging to Apple Inc'. Pursuant to this decision, the customs service at Oslo airport later that year seized a package of 63 mobile phone screens sent from Hong Kong to PCKompaniet, the reason being that the screens were provided with Apple logos concealed by a marker. Following the seizure, Apple demanded destruction of the screens before Oslo District Court, without success, as the Court held that the owner of PCKompaniet had not 'used' the trade marks. Upon appeal however, the Borgarting Appellate Court came to the opposite conclusion and demanded destruction of the screens.

---

[5]   Para. 39 of the judgment.
[6]   *Ibid.*

The Supreme Court upheld the Appellate Court decision and dismissed the further appeal. One important feature of the Supreme Court's judgment is that the leave to appeal before the Court was limited to the application of the law and did not include the assessment of the facts.[7] This meant, inter alia, that the Supreme Court had to rely on the Appellate Court's findings 'that the imported screens [were] not original products, that the affixed logos [were] identical to Apple's registered figure mark, that the logos [had] not been affixed by Apple, and that they [had] been covered with a removable marker'.[8] Moreover, the Supreme Court asserted as undisputed that the:

> concealed logos were on the part of the screen that will be hidden once the screen is fitted into the phone ... that the mark [was] used on such products for which it is protected [and] ... that [the owner of PCKompaniet] had not obtained Apple's consent to use the company's registered trade mark, and that the import took place for commercial purposes.[9]

Against this background, the Supreme Court considered whether the import of the mobile phone screens infringed Apple's trade marks under section 4 of the Norwegian Trade Mark Act (NTMA), which at the time of the judgment implemented Article 5 of Directive 2008/95/EC (later amended as to implement Directive (EU) 2015/2436).[10] The provision includes the so-called double identity clause, implying that use of signs identical with the trade mark and for the same goods or services, without the consent of the right holder, is prohibited (section 4, first paragraph, litra a). At the same time, import of goods under the trade mark is considered as use (section 4, third paragraph, litra c). As to the question whether the import of the screens with the Apple trade mark concealed by a marker represented 'use' of the trade mark, the Court started by referring to its earlier case HR-2018-110-A (Ensilox).[11] In this case, a trader selling a preservative to the fishing industry had affixed labels showing a trade mark, belonging to a different supplier than the supplier of the product, but with a notice indicating the name of the producer. The Supreme Court emphasized the significance of trade mark functions in interpreting section 4 NTMA and found it sufficient to show a 'clear possibility' that the guarantee of the

---

[7] See judgment para. 19.
[8] Para. 20.
[9] Para. 21.
[10] Act 8/2010 of 26 March 2010 and act 67/2020 of 12 June 2020 respectively.
[11] English translation by the Court available here, https://www.domstol.no/globalassets/upload/hret/decisions-in-english-translation/hr-2018-110-a.pdf (accessed 29 October 2020).

trade mark's origin would be affected.[12] The Court found that there was a risk that the trade mark's functions were affected where the trade mark was affixed to a different supplier's products even beyond the sale situation. In Apple, the Supreme Court cited its holding in Ensilox that:

> although the goods were delivered to a fixed circle of customers who are normally end-users, such mis-labelling generally creates a risk of affecting the proprietor's interests in the trade mark's functions. And while the intention was not to resell the goods, it cannot be excluded that tradesmen borrow or buy from each other.[13]

Furthermore, the Supreme Court referred to the CJEU ruling in case C-129/17 (Mitsubishi). Here, a company (Duma) had purchased original Mitsubishi forklifts outside the EEA and parallel imported them into the EEA (Belgium).[14] Before putting the goods on the market in Belgium, the importer removed all of Mitsubishi's trade marks and replaced them with his own. The Norwegian Supreme Court emphasized that the CJEU in this case found trade mark infringement on the ground that the removal of the trade mark affected the essential functions of the trade mark, notably the function of indicating origin and the functions of investment and advertising, and was considered contrary to the objective of ensuring undistorted competition. According to the Supreme Court the Mitsubishi judgment:

> shows that the protection of the trademark extends beyond the trademark's function as a guarantee of origin and quality. Furthermore, the judgment shows that use must be demonstrated based on a complex assessment that also absorbs the marketing function of a trade mark.[15]

Consequently, the Supreme Court defined the 'central issue in the case at hand ... [to be] whether the trade mark's functions may be harmed in connection with import and a possible continued sale when the trade marks are covered'.

---

[12] See HR-2020-1142-A (Apple) para. 31, with reference to HR-2018-110-A (Ensilox), paras. 59–60 and the CJEU judgment in case C-206/01, *Arsenal Football Club plc v Matthew Reed*, EU:C:2002:651, para. 57.

[13] Para. 33, cf. HR-2018-110-A (Ensilox), para. 73.

[14] Paras. 34–36, with reference to case C-129/17, *Mitsubishi Shoji Kaisha Ltd and Mitsubishi Caterpillar Forklift Europe BV v Duma Forklifts NV and G.S. International BVBA*, EU:C:2018:594.

[15] Para. 34, cf. paras. 44, 46 and 47 of case C-129/17 (Mitsubishi), fn. 14, *supra*.

Furthermore, it cited the Court of Appeal's description of the covering of the Apple logo on the imported screens:

> [T]he logos were covered with ink that could be removed without difficulty. It is easy to see that the pen marks are added later and are not an integrated part of the screen. If the ink is removed, the copy of Apple's trade mark becomes visible.

The Supreme Court observed that contrary to the Mitsubishi case, the case at hand dealt with the covering of logos unlawfully affixed to unoriginal reserve parts and that the covering alone did not eliminate the risk of harm to the trade mark's functions, since the marker might be removed. The Court remarked that at the outset trade mark protection could not be weaker in such a case than where the original trade mark has been permanently removed.[16]

The Court then returned to its finding in the Ensilox case and concluded that even though the import of the goods was the use in question, one should not disregard the risk of harm in a post-sale situation. Hence, it observed that if the importer, subsequent retail links or others who receive the screens removed the marker, the screens would look like original Apple screens, and that one could not generally rule out the risk that anyone getting hold of the screens might remove the marker covering the trade marks. On the contrary, the Court held, in a sales situation, both towards other repairers or retailers and end customers, the seller might have a wish to remove the marker to obtain a higher price.[17]

Furthermore, the Supreme Court opined that the trade mark's origin function was harmed even if the marker was not removed, since the screens appeared identical to Apple's original screens, and the marker was added exactly where the logo was placed on the original screens. The visible covering, thus, according to the Court, might create confusion as to the product's origin. For the average consumer it would be unclear whether the screen was an original or a copy, and such confusion – the Court held – was sufficient to establish a risk of harm to the trade mark's function.[18]

Ignoring the sustainability argument – as pointed out in the introduction – on the ground that the screens were not the issue in the case,[19] the Supreme Court dismissed the appeal on the ground that the import of the mobile phone screens affixed with Apple's trade mark covered with the marker amounted to a trade mark infringement.

---

[16] Para. 36.
[17] Para. 37.
[18] Para. 38.
[19] Para. 39.

3. SOME CRITICAL REMARKS FROM A TRADE MARK LAW PERSPECTIVE

When reading the decision from the Norwegian Supreme Court, it appears obvious that the Court considers this a 'piracy case', and that the concealment of the trade mark with a removable marker is unacceptable. Although the origin of the screens was not known, the *Court of Appeal* supported its findings of the facts on a statement by an expert witness, who summarized his analysis of 13 samples of the screens as follows:

> 12 of the screens (exhibit 2–13) carry poor quality counterfeit Apple trade marks that falsely suggest that these are genuine Apple products. The Apple trade mark and QR-code on the screens is not printed by Apple. 1 screen ... did not carry any trade mark and is simply a look-alike copy of an Apple screen.

All of the screens have serial numbers and none of these serial numbers are valid Apple serial numbers.

All genuine Apple serial numbers are unique and are never applied on more than 1 device. 6 of these devices carry the same identical serial numbers, showing that the producer has simply re-applied the same non-unique serial number on 6 of the 13 devices.

None of the 13 iPhone screens were produced by Apple.[20]

The Court of Appeal concluded on the basis of the expert witness statement that it was sufficiently proven that the screens were counterfeits, and dismissed inter alia the importer's arguments that Apple had not investigated a representative selection of the imported screens. Since the leave to appeal before the Supreme Court was limited to the applicability of the law, these were the facts on which the Supreme Court's decision was based. Nevertheless, the reasons given by the Court for why the import of the screens, with Apple's logo concealed by a removable marker, was a trade mark infringement, is not entirely convincing on their merits.

First, the Court's observation that trade mark protection cannot be weaker in a case where the trade mark is concealed by a removable marker than where the original trade mark has been permanently removed, with reference to the CJEU ruling in Mitsubishi, is too general to stand scrutiny. The facts of the case in Mitsubishi were quite different from those of the case at hand. In Mitsubishi, the traders removed the trade mark from the goods themselves, which was considered as a *use* of a trade mark by the CJEU. In Apple, the trade mark was concealed before entering the EEA. Moreover, the Mitsubishi case

[20] Borgarting Court of Appeal, judgment of 21 June 2019, in case 18-06235ASD-BORG/03.

concerned lawfully made products imported by the defendants from outside the EEA. Here, the CJEU put much weight on the trade mark proprietor's interest in controlling the first placing of goods *bearing the trade mark* on the market in the EEA. Both the origin function and other functions, like quality guarantee, investment and advertising, were linked to that right.[21] In contrast, the Apple case concerned concealment of unlawfully placed trade marks on spare part products meant to be incorporated in another product. The interests of the trade mark holder here are different. In contrast to the Mitsubishi case, the trade mark functions were not linked to the interest to place the goods on the market in the EEA *with* the trade mark applied. The antithesis, namely, *revealing* the trade mark, would in this situation conflict with the origin function and other functions. Thus, the situations are more or less opposite, and the reasons given in the Mitsubishi case for damage to the trade mark functions are not applicable in the Apple case. This is not to exclude the argument that trade mark functions may suffer damage in cases such as this, rather the Mitsubishi analogy is not pertinent on this point.

Finally, the CJEU in Mitsubishi admits the relevance of the fact that the products in question – the forklift trucks – would be recognized by the consumers as Mitsubishi products despite the removal of the trade mark. Even if the Court stated that the essential function of the trade mark might be harmed irrespective of this fact, it was nevertheless 'likely to accentuate the effects of such harm'.[22] As we shall see, the Norwegian Supreme Court's decision is ambiguous as to the relevance of a corresponding argument in the Apple case, and in any event it is disputable in that context.

In sum, the 'greater subsumes the lesser' argument of the Norwegian Supreme Court – that trade mark protection cannot be weaker in a case where the trade mark is concealed by a removable marker than where the original trade mark is permanently removed – is off track as far as the comparison with the CJEU ruling in Mitsubishi is concerned. Besides the fact that the situations in the two cases are quite different, the Mitsubishi decision is in itself controversial,[23] and cannot in any case be considered as expressing as a general rule that de-branding constitutes trade mark infringement.

Second, the Supreme Court's assertions that 'one cannot generally rule out the risk that anyone getting hold of the screens may remove the marker covering the trade marks' and that 'the seller may wish to remove it to obtain

---

[21]   See case C-129/17 (Mitsubishi), fn. 14, *supra*, paras. 44–46.

[22]   Para. 45.

[23]   See Annette Kur, 'Trademark Functions in European Union Law', in Irene Calboli and Jane C. Ginsburg (eds), *The Cambridge Handbook for International and Comparative Trademark Law* (Cambridge UK: Cambridge University Press 2020) 162–177, 175–176.

a higher price'[24] are unsubstantiated. It is far from given that this is even
a theoretical possibility, and in this matter, the decision of the Court of Appeal
does not provide any guidance as to the relevant facts. Since the trade marks in
question are not visible for the end user, it is possible to question which interest
a repairer would have in removing the marker and whether this would have any
effect at all on prices in the repair market. As far as repairers are concerned,
they will know that the seller is not an authorized Apple dealer, and will hardly
have any expectation that the screens are genuine Apple products.[25] As long as
the Court bases its reasoning on risk assessments it should at least have some
sort of factual basis for the assessment and not only make a general statement
of this kind.

Third, there are at least two problems with the Supreme Court's allusion
to the risk of harm to the trade mark functions even if the marker were not
removed.[26] One problem is that it is holding that 'the screens appear identical
to Apple's original screens, and the marker is added exactly where the logo
is placed on the original screen … [and] … may create confusion as to the
product's origin', which is ambiguous and partly inconsistent. The ambiguity
and inconsistency flow from the Court's statement cited in the introduction of
this chapter that 'the screens are not the issue …, but the use of the trade marks
on them'.[27] If the screens as such are creating, or contributing to creating, confusion as to the product's origin, it must be because of the screen's own trade
mark function, which the Court implicitly denies when rejecting the relevance
of the sustainability argument.

The other problem is that the Court's assertion, that 'to the relevant circle
of trade, it may be unclear whether it is an original screen or a copy',[28] is also
a mere postulate without any further discussion. The Court had concluded that
'[r]epairers and professional retail links are at the centre of the circle trading
in spare parts to be fitted into ready products'.[29] In other words, these were the
average core consumers. As pointed out above, however, it may be discussed
whether professional repairers or retail links at all would be likely to perceive
the screens as original, given the presumably high level of attention of this
group of traders, and the fact that they are outside the network of authorized
Apple product distributors. One would at least have appreciated a discussion

---

[24]   HR-2020-1142-A (Apple), para. 37.
[25]   This viewpoint is also expressed in Ole-Andreas Rognstad and Inger Berg
Ørstavik, 'Inngrep i varemerke. Høyesteretts dom 2. Juni 2020, HR 2020-1142-A,
APPLE', *Nytt i privatretten* 3/2020, 29–31.
[26]   Para. 38.
[27]   Para. 39.
[28]   Para. 38.
[29]   Para. 30.

of this instead of a postulate.[30] It is also possible to question the general observation that the origin function is harmed in the post-sale situation with reference to the Supreme Court's previous ruling in the Ensilox case as the situation in that case was quite different from that at hand. Moreover, the fact that the logos and the marker were not visible to the end user should also be of relevance here, in light of the case law of the CJEU, which shows that end users are part of the relevant public even if the concrete sale situation concerns prior sales links.[31]

There is much to say about the express reasoning of the Norwegian Supreme Court's decision in the Apple case. The underlying rationale, however, seems to be that the screens were 'piracy products', which harm trade mark functions *per se* irrespective of the fact that the trade marks are concealed by a marker. Even though the Court puts some weight on the proven fact that the marker was removable, it is highly conceivable that the Court would have reached the same result had the marker been fixed and unable to be removed. The Court's finding that the origin function is harmed even if the marker is not removed points in that direction.

4.   SUSTAINABILITY CONCERNS AND THEIR RELEVANCE TO TRADE MARK LAW

Considering the Apple case as a 'piracy' case, the resulting decision is given from a trade mark perspective. A possible justification for this approach is that a different result could create incentives for production of trade mark-infringing products. Products with trade marks affixed without the consent of the right holder could be produced and sold in the exporting country and then be 'laundered' by putting on a concealer before exporting the product to a different country or region. The Norwegian Supreme Court's decision is understandable from that point of view.

---

[30]   Compare case C-257/07, *Intel Corporation Inc. v CPM United Kingdom Ltd.*, EU:C:2008:655, para 77, where the Court emphasized that proof that the use of a trade mark would be detrimental to the distinctive character of the (earlier) trade mark, requires evidence of a change in the economic behaviour of the average consumer or a serious likelihood that such a change will occur in the future.

[31]   See case C-412/05, *Alcon Inc. v European Union Intellectual Property Office* (TRAVATAN), paras. 52–57. Cf. also Rognstad and Ørstavik, fn. 25, *supra*.

From the sustainability point of view, however, electronic and electric equipment is one of the fastest growing waste streams in Europe. To quote the Circular Economy Action Plan of the EU Commission:

> Value is lost when fully or partially functional products are discarded because they are not reparable, the battery cannot be replaced, the software is no longer supported, or materials incorporated in devices are not recovered. About two in three Europeans would like to keep using their current digital devices for longer, provided performance is not significantly affected.[32]

It goes without saying that the producer and trade mark holder will at least have split incentives regarding the repair of used products as the repair will affect sales of new products. It is also a fact that authorized repairs are expensive for the consumer, and prices are a determinative factor in the choice between purchasing new products and repairing the old ones. Hence, as pointed out by Pihlajarinne in the previous chapter, competition and sustainability concerns are often intertwined in the recycling industry.[33] Concentrating here on sustainability, the question is whether sustainability and environmental concerns can, and should, be taken into consideration in trade mark infringement cases. In the Apple case, the importer had argued that such concerns had to be taken into consideration when interpreting the term 'use' of a trade mark in section 4 of the NTMA (corresponding to Article 5(1) of Directive 2008/95/EC and Article 10(2) of Directive (EU) 2015/2436). The Court did not directly respond to this allegation, but rejected the relevance of the argument on the ground that the Trade Mark Act does not prevent the importation of screens that 'do not have trade marks unlawfully affixed to them'. In the case, however, the importer had argued that he did not have access to screens of sufficient quality through other channels than those used. The court of first instance (Oslo District Court) concluded that his status as a market actor to a large extent depended on the importation of the screens with concealed logos.[34] This is not an undisputable fact, but neither is the Supreme Court's allusion that (competition and) sustainability concerns are secured through the liberty to import screens that were not originally provided with Apple's trade mark. The Court of Appeal did not address this question since this court found that the import constituted a trade mark infringement *per se*, on the ground that the screens were counterfeits.

---

[32]   EU Commission, 'Circular Economy Action Plan. For a Cleaner and More Competitive Europe', 11 March 2020, 10.

[33]   *Chapter 5, Section 2, supra.*

[34]   Note, however, that the District Court made certain reservations in this respect due to the lack of information provided by the importer.

Nevertheless, the Supreme Court's rejection of the relevance of (competition and) sustainability arguments was based on unconvincing grounds.

By rejecting the argument's relevance, the Court failed to confront the interpretation issue inherent in the defendant's argument by postulating that the defendant *had used* the trade marks in the case at hand. The real question, which the Court failed to address, is what impact sustainability concerns should have on the interpretation of the trade mark rules? As emphasized in Pihlajarinne's contribution, the relevance of sustainability and environmental concerns in an EU context, even in trade mark law, follows from Article 3(3) and Article 11 TFEU.[35] Corresponding provisions are not found in the EEA Agreement, on which Norway's relationship to the EU acquis is based, but Article 73(1) of that agreement, corresponding to Article 191(1) TFEU, which confirms that action by the Contracting Parties (the EU and the EFTA states) shall have the objective of preserving, protecting and improving the environment. Given also the fundamental goal of the agreement, to achieve homogenous rules related to the single market in the entire EEA, it is possible to argue that any development on the trade mark sustainability relationship on the EU level is relevant also in an EEA context.

Perhaps a more substantial concern from a Norwegian point of view, and indeed relevant in the discussion of the Apple case, is section 112 in the Norwegian Constitution, which gives 'every person ... the right to an environment that is conducive to health and to a natural environment whose productivity and diversity are maintained'. In the discussion about the concrete impact of the provision, the function of the word 'right' may imply legal positions that can be invoked on an individual level. In the lawsuit based on section 112 against the Norwegian state with claims for invalidation of decisions granting licences to petroleum extraction in the Barents Sea, the Supreme Court – although dismissing the claims – confirmed that the constitutional provision provides for individual rights and is 'undoubtedly relevant with regard to interpretation of laws'.[36] Hence, there is a possible legal basis for the relevance of a sustainability argument in Norwegian trade mark law, which was ignored by the Supreme Court in the Apple case. Given that constitutional provisions take precedence over other provisions, it is at least a bit surprising that the sustainability issue was rejected as irrelevant in this case.

If taken as a point of departure that sustainability is a relevant factor, both in EU/EEA law and in domestic Norwegian law, the question is how the Supreme Court should, and could, have dealt with the argument when deciding on whether the import of the iPhone screens constituted a 'use' of the trade

---

[35]   *Chapter 5, Sections 2 and 3.3, supra.*
[36]   HR-2020-2472-P, judgment of 22 December 2020, paras. 88, 89 and 138.

mark pursuant to section 4 NTMA. One possible solution, compatible with the Court's own approach based on the case law of the CJEU, would be to require further evidence and substantiation of the allegation that trade mark functions are harmed in such situations.

Indeed, the Supreme Court's reasoning in the Apple case shows that there is potential for taking sustainability concerns into consideration in trade mark law if a fact-based less dogmatic approach is taken to trade mark infringement. The overarching question in this case was whether trade mark functions *were* damaged in situations where repairers import spare parts containing trade marks that are concealed to the repairer and other retailers and not visible to the end user. The Supreme Court – in contrast to the Court of Appeal – asked many of the right questions, but based the answers on mere postulates, obviously influenced by the one-sided property protection perspective that often dominates IP law. With a less dogmatic and more open approach, where the sustainability and environmental aspects inherent in Articles 3(3) and 11 TEUF (cf. Article 73 EEA and section 112 in the Norwegian Constitution) is considered relevant,[37] one could discuss the basic questions raised by the Court in a less prejudicial way: (i) *is* there a risk of confusion about the products' origin in the post-sale situation?; (ii) is there a risk of damage to the trade mark holder's reputation and quality and investment functions? In line with the case law of the CJEU, only if these questions are answered in the affirmative is there a 'use' of the trade mark that conflicts with the exclusive rights.[38]

I am not totally convinced that these answers should be affirmative given the facts of the case, but they would require further investigation of the factual basis, not merely theoretical, abstract and hypothetical second-guessing.[39] The fact that the supplies of the importer of good quality screens could be hampered if the screens were seized should, in this context, be relevant due to the sustainability concerns and require a deeper analysis of the damage of the trade mark functions. Adopting this approach, one could achieve a balanced assessment of trade mark interests and sustainability concerns, in the sense that the former only have priority if there is a *concrete*, and not only an abstract

[37]   Compare Pihlajarinne's observation that 'it would be relatively easy for the CJEU to revisit the interpretations of Article 10.2(a)–(c) [Trade Mark Directive] and genuinely put Article 11 of TFEU into effect in EU trademark law', see *Chapter 5, Section 3.3, supra.*
[38]   Cf. joined cases C-236/08 and C-238/08, *Google France SARL and Google Inc. v Luis Vuitton Malettier SA et al.*, EU:C:2010:159, paras. 75 et seq. See further Kur, 'Trademark Functions in European Law', fn. 23, *supra*, 165–174.
[39]   Cf. case C-257/07 (Intel), see fn. 30, *supra.*

and hypothetical, risk of harm to the trade mark functions in the case at hand.[40] Dogmatic concepts, such as once a 'piracy product' always a 'piracy product', are not sufficiently justified from a functional point of view. This is not to say that the Norwegian Supreme Court in the Apple case should necessarily have reached a different result under this approach, but it is difficult to say since the factual basis for the Court's assessment of the relevant question was more or less absent.[41] The fact that the ruling of the Court of Appeal was based on said dogmatic concept is an explanatory factor here, since it implied that many of the relevant circumstances discussed by the first instance court were not addressed. Given that the Supreme Court's leave to appeal exclusively was limited to legal, and not factual, assessments, the factual context for the function assessments that the Court embarked upon was consequently rather thin.

5.   CONCLUSION

IP protection of spare parts has a long history of discussion, not least in the design field. Although there is a development towards a certain liberalization of IP law in this respect,[42] for competition law purposes, the sustainability aspects have until now been more or less absent in the discussion. This has to change, given the enormous waste problems we are facing globally, not least in the electronics sector. The legal basis for taking sustainability concerns into consideration are present both in EU law and domestic Norwegian law. A revisiting of traditional IP concepts, even that of 'piracy', is a good way to start. The Norwegian Supreme Court had the chance to set an example, at least

---

[40]   The approach is held to be compatible with the case law of the CJEU on trade mark functions. However, in line with what was pointed out in Section 3, *supra*, the Supreme Court's analogy to the CJEU ruling in case C-129/17 (Mitsubishi) is misleading because the facts of that case were quite different from those in the Apple case and sustainability concerns not specifically relevant.

[41]   See Section 3, *supra*.

[42]   See Dani Beldiman, Consantin Blanke-Roeser and Anna Tischner, 'Spare Parts and Design Protection – Different Approaches to a Common Problem. Recent Developments from the EU and the US Perspective', 69 *GRUR Int.* (2020) 673–692, 677–680, regarding EU design law. In light of the development in the design field, the authors hold that the development (i.e. the repair clause in the Design Regulation) may have changed market behaviour in the aftermarket, and that this also 'should be taken into account in assessing the adverse effect on the functions of the trademark and especially the risk of confusion' (682). For a thorough analysis of the possible effect of the repair clause for trade mark law, see Anna Tischner, 'Chopping off Hydra's Heads: Spare Parts in EU Design and Trade Mark Law', in Niklas Bruun, Grahame B. Dinwoodie, Marianne Levin and Ansgar Ohly (eds), *Transition and Coherence in Intellectual Property Law. Essays in Honour of Annette Kur* (Cambridge UK: Cambridge University Press 2021) 392–403, 397–402.

by addressing the problem and highlighting sustainability concerns. Instead, it chose to reject the relevance of the sustainability argument in the case. This approach is not only disappointing, but also problematic in light of section 112 of the Norwegian Constitution. Nonetheless, as demonstrated here, the case, and the functional approach adopted by the Court and the CJEU to trade mark law, provides an opportunity to take the discussion further.

7. A modern role for intellectual property rights in sustainable finance, prudential banking and capital adequacy regulation

Janice Denoncourt

1. INTRODUCTION

Technological innovation and capitalism have rapidly transformed our planet, raising our living standards while degrading the environment. The most striking impact of the advance of human-created technological progress on the natural environment is climate change.[1] The planet will only be sustainable if it can continue to exist indefinitely into the future. Sustainability is broadly understood to comprise development that meets the needs of the present while safeguarding Earth's life-support system as set out in the United Nations 2030 Sustainable Development Agenda.[2] There is an urgent need for a wide variety of innovations to solve problems on a global scale. One of the multi-faceted aspects of sustainable development in a market-based context is the role that intellectual property rights (IPRs) play in incentivizing new knowledge and fiscal regulatory policy. How banks provide innovation firms with credit, while mitigating their own risk, is an ongoing challenge with both short- and long-term implications.[3] With new insights regarding the role of prudential financial regulation treatment of intangibles and IPRs, this chapter aims to

---

[1]   For research and data about climate change, see the Intergovernmental Panel on Climate Change, at https://www.ipcc.ch/ accessed on 27 February 2020. The human cause and the reality of climate change are accepted in the scientific community.

[2]   See https://www.un.org/sustainabledevelopment/ accessed on 3 March 2020.

[3]   'COVID-19: How Global Trade Finance is Being Disrupted and Redefined' (webcast, 3 June 2020) Ernst and Young Global Limited, available at https://www.ey.com/en_gl/webcasts/2020/05/covid-19-how-global-trade-finance-is-being-disrupted-and-redefined accessed on 5 June 2020.

make an original contribution to the interdisciplinary literature[4] regarding Sustainable Development Goal 9 (SDG 9)[5] to promote inclusive and sustainable industrialization while fostering innovation.[6]

In terms of the impact of climate change, to avoid adverse impacts on financial infrastructure, the World Bank estimates that global warming needs to be limited to no more than 2 degrees Celsius.[7] Many in the finance sector are concluding that traditional tangible loan security, notably land and buildings, is under threat from climate change. For example, nearly 12% of land in England is adjacent to a river or a stream with increased vulnerability to flooding[8] due to climate change, posing a considerable financial risk to the UK financial sector and the mortgage market. At a global level, the impact of climate change is currently being studied by 50 of the world's central banks (including the Bank of England) through the Network for Greening the Financial System.[9] In May 2020 the Network published its status report on financial institutions' practices with respect to risk differential between green, non-green and brown financial assets and a potential risk differential.[10] The *Financing for Sustainable Development Report 2020*[11] provides policy guidance and states that a key

---

[4]   *Facilitating Interdisciplinary Research* (2004) Committee on Facilitating Interdisciplinary Research, Committee of Science, Engineering and Public Policy, National Academic Press, Washington.

[5]   The United Nations Sustainable Development Agenda, available at https://www .un.org/sustainabledevelopment/development-agenda/ accessed on November 2019.

[6]   *Ibid.*

[7]   'Climate Change' The World Bank, available at https://www.worldbank.org/en/ topic/climatechange accessed on 18 June 2020.

[8]   According to the UK National Planning Policy Framework, 'flood risk' is a combination of the probability and the potential consequences of flooding from all sources – including from rivers and the sea, directly from rainfall on the ground surface and rising groundwater, overwhelmed sewers and drainage systems, and from reservoirs, canals and lakes and other artificial sources, see https://www.gov.uk/guidance/flood-risk-and -coastal-change accessed on 13 June 2020.

[9]   In 2017 at the Paris 'One Planet Summit' eight central banks and supervisors established the Network of Central Banks and Supervisors for Greening the Financial System (NGFS). Since then the NGFS has grown to include central banks from five continents. The NGFS aims to enhance the role of the financial system to manage risks and to mobilize capital for green and low-carbon investments in the broader context of environmentally sustainable development, see https://www.ngfs.net/en accessed on 14 June 2020.

[10]   *A Status Report on Financial Institutions' Experiences from Working with Green, Non-green and Brown Financial Assets and a Potential Risk Differential* (May 2020) NGFS / *Banque de France*, available at https://www.ngfs.net/sites/default/files/ medias/documents/ngfs_status_report.pdf accessed on 13 June 2020.

[11]   Inter-agency Task Force on Financing for Development, *Financing for Sustainable Development Report 2020* (2020) United Nations, New York, available from: https://developmentfinance.un.org/fsdr2020 accessed on 30 April 2020.

action needed is to 'accelerate long-term investment in resilient infrastructure for sustainable development through public investment and incentives for the private sector'. Sir Roger Gifford, Chair of the Green Finance Institute and Senior Banker, *Skandinaviska Enskilda Banken* (SEB) warns, 'It is critical that financial markets and policymakers collaborate to create the solutions to move the global economy towards a more sustainable future'.[12] One solution, to be explored in sections 2–4 below, may be for prudential banking regulation policymakers to revise their approach to bank asset credit risk and intangible registered granted IPRs.

An independent report commissioned by the UK Intellectual Property Office found that intangible investment in the UK was 9% greater than tangible investment in 2014 at £133bn and £121bn respectively.[13] IPRs are designed to work as legal instruments within an environment comprising other legal mechanisms and have proven to be robust against time and societal development. However, prudential banking regulation has yet to fully consider the modern role of intangible assets and IPRs in business and the economy and as bank assets. Founded in 1974, the Basel Committee on Banking Supervision (BCBS) is an international forum where members cooperate on banking supervision matters to enhance financial stability through voluntary regulations, known as accords. The Basel I–IV Accords set out a framework for how banks and depository institutions must calculate their capital adequacy ratios (CARs) when lending against all types of loan security.

According to the BCBS, the minimum capital ratio framework has been introduced in member countries and across the globe in virtually all countries with active international banks.[14] The Basel I Accord was issued in 1988, introducing a clear focus on the capital adequacy of financial institutions, creating a classification system for assets. While the IPR legal framework has significantly evolved since 1988, the capital adequacy regulation applied to intangibles assets (a class that includes unregistered and registered IPRs) has not altered. The increase in economic investment in intangibles in the UK, in

---

[12] Established in 2019, the Green Finance Institute is an independent, UK-based, commercially focused organization, supported by seed funding from HM Treasury (UK), the Department of Business, Energy and Industrial Strategy and the City of London Corporation.

[13] P. Goodridge, J. Haskell and G. Wallace, 'UK Intangible Investment and Growth: New Measures of UK Investment in Knowledge Assets and Intellectual Property Rights' (September 2016). Research commissioned by the Intellectual property Office, available at https://assets.publishing.service.gov.uk/government/uploads/system/uploads/attachment_data/file/554480/Investment-in-Intangibles.pdf accessed on 30 May 2020.

[14] J. Chen, 'Basel I' (8 March 2020), available at https://www.investopedia.com/terms/b/basel_i.asp accessed on 18 June 2020.

the author's view, supports a re-think on the relationship between banking CAR buffers and their impact on intangibles and IPRs as loan security as an important component of sustainable innovation finance (see sections 2.1 and 2.2 below).

Within the class of intangibles, the subset of registered granted patents, for example, may provide a more resilient and legally certain store of value/capital for the purpose of secured business loans and banking capital adequacy requirements than previously thought (see section 2.3 below). However, in terms of banking prudential regulation, while registered granted IPRs are legally constructed and state-sanctioned monopoly rights, they are currently treated the same as other more nebulous intangibles such as goodwill and other unregistered intangibles such as know-how, confidential information and trade secrets. In the author's view, it is timely to consider unbundling this wide asset class to provide an improved categorization of intangibles. The wider class of intangibles could be refined and better classified so that it more accurately reflects improvements in the modern IPR legal framework, the global commercial reality of corporate IPR investment and bank credit risk. In this chapter, we will explore the level of risk assigned to granted patents and other granted IPRs for CAR purposes with a view to designing sustainable finance in support of SDG 9. We aim to make out a case and found the basis for a recommendation that central banking regulators review their prudential capital regulation approach to intangible registered granted IPRs assets (patents, designs and trade marks) as loan security and re-consider the risk weighting assigned to this class within a class of intangible bank assets.

The remainder of this chapter contemplates designing a sustainable innovation finance system that will better support inventors, patent owners and SME operating companies, beyond the venture capital milestone. One component of the sustainable innovation finance design that has yet to receive significant attention in the academic literature is banking CAR risk-weighting requirements and their impact on approval of intangible and innovation finance. In earlier academic research I introduced the issue.[15] This chapter provides an opportunity for a more in-depth exploration of the Basel Accords I–IV[16] and

---

[15]   See J. Denoncourt, *Intellectual Property, Finance and Corporate Governance* (2018) Routledge Taylor Francis, Research in Intellectual Property Series, Chapter 3, section 3.5 Basel III Banking Capital Adequacy Requirements: An Adverse Impact on IP Finance, 76–78; partially derived from J. Denoncourt, *Patent-backed Debt Finance: Should Company Law Take the Lead to Provide a 'True and Fair' View of SME Patent Assets* (2015) PhD Thesis, University of Nottingham.

[16]   The second, third and fourth of the Basel Accords issued by the Basel Committee on Banking Supervision.

developments in the IPR framework, with a focus on patent law by way of illustration.

The finance sector is a complex area. Recognizing that sustainable development is a global responsibility and there are indeed problems concerned with seeking global solutions to the IPR/banking regulation interface, this original analysis introduces and explores, from an interdisciplinary IP and banking law perspective, the adverse impact of prudential regulation on innovation finance as it currently applies to loan transactions secured by intangibles. In short, the BCBS regulatory adjustment to Common Equity Tier 1 regulatory capital requires that goodwill and *all other intangibles* (including IPRs) must be deducted in the calculation of Common Equity. This regulation makes the loan pricing or interest rate offered more expensive. As such, lending against intangibles and IPRs is less attractive as they are not considered assets realizable on default. As such, there is potential for cooperation between policymakers in the fields of IPR and banking regulation to work together at both the international and national level.

The structure of this chapter is as follows. In the next section, in order to provide a foundation for our interdisciplinary study of how CARs apply to intangible IPR loan security and could be reformed, a brief primer on banking and capital adequacy requirements is provided.

In section 2.4 we analyse the implications of Basel III and IV for IPRs and hypothesize that the security potential of modern registered IPRs such as granted patent, trade mark and design monopolies is underestimated. Intangibles are a wide asset class, it will be argued, that could be unbundled and better categorized to more accurately assign risk in a prudential lending context.

In section 3, we undertake a qualitative non-doctrinal analysis of statements and thinking on the topic of monetary policy and intangibles as published in the speeches of various high-level central bank professionals. The speeches qualitatively reviewed include those given by: Mr Muhammad bin Ibrahim, Deputy Governor of the Central Bank of Malaysia (Bank Negar Malaysia); Mr Mario Drago, President of the European Central Bank (ECB); Mr Philip R. Lane, ECB Executive Board Member; and Professor Jonathan Haskel, External Member of the Bank of England Monetary Policy Committee. The critical discussion sheds light on the unique commercial monopoly advantages provided by modern registered IPRs and builds a rationale for arguing they should be 'carved out' of the intangibles asset class or be considered a distinct subset thereof.

Finally, section 4 considers the impact of climate change and flood risk on the quality of residential mortgages in the UK as security. We further elaborate the case for treating registered IPRs differently to the wider class of intangible assets (e.g. goodwill and unregistered IPRs) in view of the modern IPR framework and valuation methodologies. Final conclusions and recommendations are set out in section 5.

2.   COMMERCIAL BANKS AND BANKING CAPITAL ADEQUACY RATIOS

This section provides context, explaining the relevance of CARs for intangible assets used as loan security and how banking regulation interrelates with IP rights. We introduce the national and international monetary policy institutions responsible for the banking monetary policy and the capital regulation framework. In essence, a commercial bank is a financial intermediary, an institution that accepts deposits from savers, extends loans to borrowers and provides a range of other financial services to its customers.[17] The largest portion of the funds raised by the bank is used to grant loans to individuals or businesses, generating a future stream of interest payments from borrowers to the bank.[18] The difference between the bank's total assets and its liabilities, in the form of funds raised from depositors and investors, is the bank's capital (also known as equity or net worth). For a bank to remain solvent, the value of its assets must always exceed the value of its liabilities.[19] Goddard and Wilson explain that most commercial banks are privately owned by shareholders who seek to earn a profit.[20] By acting as a financial intermediary, a bank takes on many risks,[21] one of which is credit risk – the risk that a borrower will fail to repay the loan. If there is no prospect of the borrower repaying, the bank must reduce the value of the assets shown on its balance sheet.

An equivalent reduction must also be shown on the liabilities side of the balance sheet, by reducing the bank's capital. The bank's capital therefore provides a buffer or cushion, enabling it to absorb losses on its loans or other investments. If the bank's capital is wiped out altogether by losses on loans or other investments, the bank becomes insolvent. A useful measure of a bank's loss-absorbing capacity is the capital-to-assets ratio known as the CAR, defined as the ratio of the bank's capital to its total assets.[22] Leverage or gearing is measured by the reciprocal of the CAR: total assets divided by capital. A bank with a capital ratio of 5 (the bank's total assets are 10 times its

---

[17]   J. Goddard and J.O.S. Wilson, *Banking: A Very Short Introduction* (2016) Oxford University Press, 1.
[18]   *Ibid*, 11.
[19]   *Ibid*.
[20]   *Ibid*.
[21]   Other important risks include liquidity, operational, settlement, currency, and sovereign or political risk.
[22]   See fn. 17, *supra*.

capital) could potentially absorb a 5% drop in the value of its assets and still be solvent. The higher the leverage, the smaller the capital buffer or cushion and the greater the risk of insolvency.[23, 24] The bank's executive management team often face a conflict between the competing objectives of maximizing the bank's profitability and minimizing the risk of insolvency; at these times they are guided in their decision making by monetary policy and banking regulation.[25]

2.1 The Banks of England, a Central Bank and Monetary Policymaker

The Bank of England is the UK government's bank and since 2012 has been responsible for the regulation and supervision of banks and other financial institutions in the UK.[26] It is the country's central bank that manages money supply,[27] interest rates and commercial bank CARs, the latter via the Prudential Regulation Authority (PRA).[28] Prudential regulation rules require financial firms to maintain sufficient capital and have adequate risk controls in place.[29] The Capital Requirements Directive IV (CRD IV) is an EU legislative package covering prudential rules for banks, building societies and investment firms.[30] The principle of independence means that the Bank of England's Monetary Policy Committee should take decisions that cannot be overridden or reversed by politicians.[31]

---

[23] See fn. 17, *supra*.
[24] The implications of credit risk can be explored by running a stress test, essentially hypothesizing losses and the impact of same on the bank's capital base.
[25] See fn. 17, *supra*.
[26] The European Central Bank is the central bank to the Eurozone; the US has 12 Federal Reserve Banks, the most important of which is the Federal Reserve Bank of New York.
[27] Commercial banks borrow from the Bank of England, which services the UK's banking system.
[28] The Bank of England's PRA is responsible for this prudential regulation and supervision of around 1,500 banks, building societies, credit unions, insurers and major investment firms, see https://www.bankofengland.co.uk/prudential-regulation accessed on 14 April 2020.
[29] *Ibid.*
[30] Until the UK exits the EU on 31 December 2020, EU law will continue to apply. The new legal and regulatory capital framework will be updated thereafter.
[31] See fn. 17, *supra*.

122 Intellectual property and sustainable markets

2.2 Supervision of the Banking Industry and Capital Adequacy Regulation Post-2008

In 2008, following the global financial crisis,[32] after writing off delinquent loans or writing down the value of other assets, commercial banks seeking to restore their capital-to-assets ratios cut back aggressively on their lending to small businesses and other borrowers. Banking capital regulation requires that a sufficient fraction of the bank's investments or assets be funded by un-borrowed money.[33] As noted in section 2 above, the difference between total assets and total liabilities is a key indicator of solvency of a bank.[34] The legally mandated banking CARs were made higher under Basel III banking rules (see section 2.2 below) to ensure a stronger buffer and ability to absorb shocks in the long term by increasing the size of capital reserves that a bank must hold against losses.[35] As commercial banks use bank deposits (liquid liabilities) to finance bank loans (illiquid assets) and only hold a small proportion of their assets as reserves (capital), together with leverage, this makes banks inherently precarious entities.[36] Further, one distressed bank can cause a loss of confidence in the others and in the banking system as a whole, a formidable justification for the supervision and regulation of individual banks.[37] As a result, a suite of banking capital regulations was introduced in 1988 by the BCBS at the Bank for International Settlements (BIS) based in Switzerland.

2.3 The Basel Committee on Banking Supervision (BCBS)

Banks have been through difficult times in recent decades with dampened demand for banking services, unusually low interest rates and flat yield curves.[38] The BCBS was established in 1974 following acute disturbances in the international currency and banking markets. It has since responded to the deficiencies in banking regulation that emerged during the 2007–2008 global

---

[32]   *The Run on the Rock: Fifth Report of Session 2007–2008, Vol. 1* (2008) House of Commons Treasury Committee, House of Commons, The Stationery Office Ltd, London, 4–20.

[33]   See fn. 15, *supra*, 76.

[34]   See fn. 17, *supra.*

[35]   'International Regulatory Framework for Banks (Basel III): Capital' (June 2011) Basel Committee for Banking Supervision, Bank for International Settlements.

[36]   See fn. 17, *supra*, 72.

[37]   See fn. 17, *supra*, 72.

[38]   B. Bogdanova, I. Fendr and E. Takats, 'The ABCs of PBRs: What Drives Price-to-Book Ratios' (11 March 2018) BIS, at https://www.bis.org/publ/qtrpdf/r _qt1803h.htm accessed on 13 April 2020.

financial crisis.[39] At the international level, the BCBS is the primary global standard-setter for the prudential regulation of banks and provides a forum for regular cooperation on banking supervisory matters.[40] Its 45 members comprise central banks and bank supervisors from 28 jurisdictions including the UK.[41] The EU Capital Requirements Directive IV (CRD IV) applies to the EU member states.[42] The BCBS mandate is to strengthen the regulation, supervision and practices of banks worldwide with the purpose of enhancing financial stability.[43] It also provides a forum for cooperation on banking supervisory matters in relation to risk management of the global banking sector.[44] While the BCBS does not possess any formal legal supranational authority and its decisions do not have legal force, the Committee's decisions and guidance are highly regarded and rely on their members' voluntary commitments and responsibilities.[45] The EU CRD IV implements the Basel III Accord in the EU and comprises the: (1) Capital Requirements Directive (2013/36/EU) (CRD), which must be implemented through national law; and (2) Capital Requirements Regulation (575/2013) (CRR), which is directly applicable to firms across the EU.

2.4   Background to the Basel I, II and III Accords Package of Regulatory Reforms: EU CRD IV and Intangibles

The BCBS has published banking regulations, known as the Basel Accords since 1998. The Accords provide recommendations on banking regulations with respect to capital, market and operational risk with a view to ensuring that financial institutions have adequate capital on account to meet obligations and absorb unexpected losses. Tiers of bank capital (setting the quality and amount of capital a bank must hold) for large financial institutions originated with Basel I. We briefly summarize the developments introduced by the Basel regime below.

---

[39]   See fn. 32, *supra.*
[40]   See the BCBS Overview section, at https://www.bis.org/bcbs/ accessed on 5 January 2020.
[41]   *Ibid.*
[42]   The EU text was formally published in the Official Journal of the EU on 27 June 2013 (as amended). The bulk of the rules contained in the legislation are applicable from 1 January 2014.
[43]   The BCBS Charter, at https://www.bis.org/bcbs/charter.htm accessed on 5 January 2020.
[44]   *Ibid.*
[45]   See fn. 43, *supra*, section 5.

2.4.1 The first Basel Accord: the Capital Accord

Focusing on mitigating underlying credit risk, Basel I required international banks to maintain a minimum amount (8%) of capital, based on a per cent of risk-weighted assets.[46] Basel I classified a bank's assets into five risk categories ranging from 0% (no risk, e.g. cash, central bank and government debt), 10%, 20%, 50% through to 100% risk, based on the nature of the debtor.[47] For example, risk classification is elastic and public sector debt can be placed between 20% and 50%, depending on the debtor. A residential mortgage is placed in the 50% to 100% risk category.[48] The 100% bank asset risk category applies to real estate, plant and equipment and capital instruments issued at other banks (e.g., government debt, development bank debt, private-sector debt etc.).[49] A degree of variability in risk-weighted assets already exists in practice.[50] Generally, a bank with a high capital adequacy ratio is considered safe and likely to meet its financial obligations.[51]

2.4.2 The second Basel Accord: the new capital framework

Basel II was published by the BCBS in 2009 following the 2008 financial crisis. It focused on minimum capital requirements (CARs) and on regulatory supervision and market discipline. Basel II highlighted the division of eligible regulatory capital of a bank into three tiers. According to BIS, the components of regulatory capital include Common Tier 1 capital, the core capital of a bank, which includes equity capital and disclosed reserves. This type of capital absorbs losses without requiring the bank to cease its operations; Tier 2 capital is used to absorb losses in the event of a liquidation.[52] Common Tier 1 capital is intended to measure a bank's financial health; a bank uses Tier 1 capital, the highest quality of regulatory capital, to absorb losses immediately as they occur without ceasing business operations. Tier 2 capital is supplementary (e.g., less reliable than Tier 1 capital.) A bank's total capital is calculated as a sum of its Tier 1 and Tier 2 capital. Regulators use the capital ratio to determine and rank a bank's capital adequacy. Tier 3 capital consists of Tier 2

---

[46]   M.A. Elbannan, 'The Financial Crisis, Basel Accords and Bank Regulations: An Overview' (December 2017) 7(2) *International Journal of accounting and Financial Reporting*, 225.

[47]   *Ibid.*

[48]   *Ibid.*

[49]   *History of the Basel Committee*, at https://www.bis.org/bcbs/history.htm accessed on 21 June 2020.

[50]   *Ibid.*

[51]   B. Beers, 'What Does a High Capital Adequacy Ratio Indicate?' (30 July 2019), at https://www.investopedia.com/ask/answers/040115/what-does-it-mean-when -company-has-high-capital-adequacy-ratio.asp accessed on 13 April 2020.

[52]   *Ibid.*

capital plus short-term subordinated loans – it is tertiary capital, which many banks hold to support their market risk, commodities risk and foreign currency risk. Tier 3 capital includes a greater variety of debt than Tier 1 and Tier 2 capital. Each tier has a specific set of criteria that capital instruments must meet before their inclusion in the respective tiers.[53]

2.4.3   The Third Basel Accord: responding to the 2007–2009 crisis

Basel III builds on the structure of Basel II but imposes high quality and higher levels of capital and liquidity, thereby increasing oversight and risk management of the banking sector.[54] High quality capital is stated to be predominantly in the form of shares and retained earnings that can absorb losses.[55] Basel III mandates the current capital adequacy requirements with which banks need to comply when lending against intangibles.[56] Before Basel III the solvency ratio was only 2%. Under the 2011 reforms, banks had to progressively reach a higher minimum solvency ratio of 7% (calculated by dividing regulatory capital by risk-weighted capital) by 2019.[57] In my earlier research, I identified that Basel Accord CARs have an adverse impact on the use of IPRs as a form of loan security and thus engagement with IPR-backed debt finance.[58] This chapter adopts an interdisciplinary approach to provide a deeper examination of this barrier to sustainable innovation finance as a component of the sustainable development debate.[59]

In the banking, finance and accounting domain, IPRs form part of the wider asset class of intangibles, nonphysical assets with potential benefit in the long term in contrast with tangible assets such as current assets (usually used within a year) and fixed assets (used for over a year) and are subject to International Accounting Standard (IAS) 38 Intangibles.[60] Under Basel III, all intangibles are treated as low quality security. As an asset class, all types of intangibles are

---

[53]   'Definition of Capital in Basel: Executive Summary' The Bank for International Settlements (BIS), at https://www.bis.org/fsi/fsisummaries/defcap_b3.htm accessed on 13 April 2020. BIS is owned by 62 central banks representing countries that together account for about 95% of world GDP.

[54]   In 2009, the Basel Committee issued the 'Principles for Sound Liquidity Risk Management and Supervision' guidance.

[55]   See fn. 53, *supra*.

[56]   See fn. 53, *supra*.

[57]   'Basel III: A Global Regulatory Framework for more Resilient Banks and Banking Systems' (December 2010, Revised June 2011) BCBS, Bank for International Settlements, 6–23.

[58]   See Denoncourt (2018), fn. 15, *supra*, chapter 3, section 3.5, 76–78.

[59]   M. Bezant, 'The Use of Intellectual Property as Security for Debt Finance' (2003) 1(3) *Journal of Knowledge Management*, 237–263.

[60]   See Denoncourt (2018), fn. 15, *supra*, chapter 4, sections 4.1–4.2, 92–105.

rated as riskier types of assets (e.g. even registered granted patents, trade marks and designs). The definition of 'capital' in a banking context means that intangibles, including registered, granted, state-sanctioned IPRs, must be deducted from the bank's regulatory capital. As such, registered patents, registered trade marks and other IPRs (registered and unregistered) cannot generally be counted towards the loan's security[61] as regulatory capital assets as they are considered too difficult to value.[62] This rationale is arguably outdated and is the friction point where capital regulation meets IP, particularly in developed countries. While IPR valuation is a specialist field, there are methodologies for valuing IPRs for a variety of purposes, including credit risk. An IPR portfolio valuation is comprehensive and considers legal dynamics from a qualitative and accounting perspective. Established IPR valuation methodologies have continued to evolve, are widely used in the private sector and will be discussed in section 2.4.

With respect to goodwill and other intangibles, according to the BCBS, the regulatory adjustment (italicized for emphasis) to be applied to Common Equity Tier 1 regulatory capital must be applied as follows:

Goodwill and other intangibles (except for mortgage servicing rights)
67. Goodwill and all other intangibles *must be deducted in the calculation of Common Equity Tier 1 capital*, including any goodwill included in the valuation of significant investments in the capital banking, financial and insurance entities that are outside the scope of regulatory consolidation. With the exception of mortgage servicing rights, *the full amount is to be deducted* net of any associated deferred tax liability that would be extinguished if the intangible assets become impaired or derecognized under the relevant accounting standards.[63]

In regulation 67 above, IPRs are not specifically mentioned either as part of the goodwill and intangibles asset class, nor are they treated elsewhere differently to goodwill and other intangibles. All intangibles are considered from a one-size-fits-all approach. In the author's view it is timely to unbundle this wide asset class. The wider class of intangibles could be refined to more accurately reflect the modern commercial reality of corporate IPR ownership (especially registered granted IPRs, which are legally constructed and

---

[61] Security (or collateral) is an asset that a borrower pledges to a lender as security for a loan. If the borrower is unable to repay the loan payments as they fall due, the lender can take ownership of the asset.
[62] B. Masters, 'Banks Eye Intangible Assets as Collateral' (11 June 2020) *The Times*, available at https://www.ft.com/content/80c23e56-b08f-11e1-8b36 -00144feabdc0 accessed on 15 March 2021.
[63] 'International Regulatory Framework for Banks (Basel III): Capital', fn. 35, *supra*, 21–22.

state-sanctioned monopoly rights) and revise or relax the level of risk they attract for CAR purposes. Corporate investment in acquiring and exploiting IPRs continues to increase across the world[64] and is a core aspect of business strategy and economic productivity. Earlier in this chapter we recognized that financing innovation is paramount to promote and fulfil SDG 9. IP rights alone will not support innovation, rather sustainable development will benefit from other relevant policies including financial regulation.

2.5 Implications of Basel III and IV for IPRs as Loan Security

The implications of Basel III for intangibles and IPRs as loan security is the higher level of 'risk-weighting' that applies to intangible asset security (collateral) in contrast with other forms of assets such as cash or currency that are considered zero risk. The term 'intangibles' refers to the type of capital that one cannot easily touch or measure, for example investments in software, databases, research and organizational processes, as opposed to tangible investment in items such as hardware, machines and equipment.[65] If loans are secured against intangibles such as patents and trade marks, the bank is legally obliged to make appropriate capital adequacy provision.

Basel III provides for a comprehensive list of regulatory adjustments and deductions from regulatory capital. These deductions typically address the high degree of uncertainty to be applied to the whole category of intangibles, which are thought to lack positive realizable value (illiquid) in periods of stress and are mostly applied to Common Tier 1 capital. We saw that in the Basel III definition of capital at section 67, important deductions are goodwill and other intangible assets (including registered and unregistered IPRs, deferred tax assets and investments in other financial entities).[66] Essentially, this makes the loan pricing or interest rate offered more expensive and lending against intangibles simply less attractive, but not unlawful, so long as the bank meets or exceeds the required CAR.

---

[64] See 'Innovation and Growth Report 2018–19' UKIPO, 3, available at https://assets.publishing.service.gov.uk/government/uploads/system/uploads/attachment_data/file/829730/innovation-and-growth-report-2018-19.pdf accessed on 13 March 2021.

[65] Capital can be defined in several ways. 'Working capital' refers not to an asset, but to a firm's cash. A non-business capital asset would be a family home (a non-business building). Personal savings are financial assets, not capital assets.

[66] 'Definition of Capital in Basel: Executive Summary' The Bank for International Settlements (BIS), at https://www.bis.org/fsi/fsisummaries/defcap_b3.htm accessed on 13 April 2020.

Basically, Basel III regards the whole class of intangible assets when applied as loan security as 'high risk' assets that should be treated carefully[67] and regulatory adjustment made, i.e. not included in the bank's capital for CAR purposes. Brassell explains that intangible assets do not exhibit the same behaviour as tangible assets, which can be traded on transparent and liquid markets, the sale price generally predicted with a degree of confidence.[68] The IPR market landscape is evolving, however, and there are now increasing numbers of alternative IPR platforms from which to derive pricing data to assist regulators and individual banks with IP-rich clients to risk rate IPRs with confidence. Other developments in the IPR system, relevant to IPR risk rating, will be discussed further below.

Meanwhile, the BCBS expects full implementation of its standards by BCBS members and their internationally active banks[69] into local legal frameworks through each jurisdiction's rule-making process within the pre-defined time-frame established by the Committee. BCBS Guidelines elaborate the standards in areas where they are considered desirable for the prudential regulation and supervision of banks, especially internationally active banks. 'Sound practice' bulletins generally describe actual observed practices, with the goal of promoting common understanding and improving supervisory or banking practices.[70]

In summary, the Basel I–IV regulatory framework includes a global, *voluntary* regulatory standard on capital adequacy regulation to make banks better placed to absorb financial shocks in the long term, by increasing the size of capital reserves a bank must hold against losses.[71] To date, Basel III capital adequacy regulatory ratios have been perceived by banks as a major barrier to the development of sustainable innovation finance secured by IPRs and intangibles.[72] Richard McCarthy, UK Head of Banking at KPMG, said, 'We have to remember that banking requires risk-taking, yet in the rush to clean up the past,

---

[67] Definition of Basel III *Financial Times Lexicon*, at http://lexcion.ft.com//term?term=basel-iii.

[68] M. Brassell, 'Unlocking Bank Finance for Intangible Assets: New Models of Support' (9 June 2017) NESTA, available at https://www.nesta.org.uk/blog/unlocking-bank-finance-for-intangible-assets-new-models-of-support/ accessed on 1 June 2018.

[69] BCBS standards constitute minimum requirements and BCBS members may decide to go beyond them.

[70] See 'Principles for the Sound Management of Operational Risk' (30 June 2011), at https://www.bis.org/publ/bcbs195.htm accessed on 15 April 2020.

[71] 'International Regulatory Framework for Banks (Basel III): Capital', fn. 35, *supra*.

[72] See B. Amable, J.B. Chatelain and K. Ralf, 'Patents as Collateral' (2010) 34 *Journal of Economic Dynamics & Control*, 1092–1104; W.J. Brian, 'Using Intellectual Property to Secure Financing after the Worst Financial Crisis Since the Great Depression' (2010) 15 *Intellectual Property L. Rev.* 449.

both banks and regulators have lost sight of this'.[73] In other words, in addition to resilience, banks must have a degree of risk-tolerance and, arguably, treat certain types of intangibles such as expertly examined, state-sanctioned, registered IPRs more favourably as a form of capital. Unbundling the definition of intangibles and carving out registered granted IPRs could be a potential financial solution to supporting sustainable finance. According to Brassell and King, 'The more visible it [IP] becomes in the public accounts, the easier its value becomes to realize. This will lead to greater opportunities for lenders – and higher risks of inaction.'[74] Similarly, the more visible IPRs are as a subset or separate category of intangible loan security, the easier its value as potential loan security will be to realize. With the goal of sustainable development in mind, it would be helpful to consider the interaction between the banking regulatory ecosystems, IPRs and innovation finance and to encourage greater dialogue and understanding of the impacts and constraints the former has on the latter. A high-level expert working group could be tasked by the BCBS with producing an IP Finance Guideline to support sustainable innovation finance, especially for adoption in developed countries. The next section reviews the literature on banking regulation, intangibles and IPRs from the perspective of central banks, beginning with an analysis of extracts from published speeches by central bank personnel since 2014.

3.   QUALITATIVE ANALYSIS OF HIGH-LEVEL PUBLISHED STATEMENTS CONCERNING INTANGIBLES, IPRS AND INNOVATION BY CENTRAL BANK PERSONNEL

For this section, the literature review involved examining high-level speeches published by EU and UK central bank personnel since 2014 with a view to capturing relevant statements regarding intangibles and IPRs as an aspect of capital adequacy regulation. Interdisciplinarity, in the academic sense used here, involves new thinking across the fields of prudential banking regulation, intangible property as security for lending and the intellectual property law framework. The purpose was to identify, document, enumerate and critically evaluate the references that shed light on what central bank thought leaders and policymakers are publishing on this contemporary issue. Presenting the views and attitudes of senior officials from central banks on the thorny issue

---

[73]   L. Eccles, 'How Bank Lending Fell by £365 Billion in Five Years' (7 September 2014) *Daily Mail*.
[74]   M. Brassell and K. King, *Banking on IP? The Role of Intellectual Property and Intangible Assets in Facilitating Business Finance Final Report* (6 November 2013) Independent report commissioned by the UK Intellectual Property Office, 15.

of intangibles and IPRs as part of monetary policy may demonstrate support for more research and/or a formal review of the prudential capital regulation approach to IPRs as loan security. In the author's view the extracts from the speeches below demonstrate a keen awareness of the financial barriers to innovation finance, a key step that will move central banks to actively explore potential guidance, solutions and wider reforms. In the paragraphs to follow, extracts from speeches published on the official webpages of the EU central bank and BIS, specifically referencing monetary policy, intangibles and IPRs, are set out and critically discussed.

3.1   Muhammad bin Ibrahim, Deputy Governor of the Central Banks of Malaysia (2014)

In his speech on 24 September 2014, Mr Muhammad bin Ibrahim, Deputy Governor of the Central Bank of Malaysia (Bank Negar Malaysia), stated that:

> Greater recognition of IP as a relevant factor in financing decisions is a proven concept. Different financial players harness the potential of IP in different ways. The varying business models and risk appetites within the financing ecosystem will determine how IP fits into financing considerations. For example, banks have to prioritize depositors' interests and would not be expected to finance ventures with high risks. However, this is not true in all cases. SMEs with proven track records should be within banks' sights, in such cases the value-add of IP should be more effectively leveraged. Indeed, in other emerging economies, progress has been evident. The Thai SME Bank, Chinese Bank of Communications and the Federal Development Bank of Brazil already take IP into consideration for financing ... Therefore, it is an opportune time that the boards and senior management of the financial service fraternity in Malaysia to begin to actively explore pragmatic approaches to assimilate IP into existing financing considerations.[75]

The Deputy Governor of the Central Bank of Malaysia asserts and acknowledges the important role of the asset class of intangibles, innovation and IPRs for sustainable innovation finance. He recommends that the 'value-add' of IPRs should be more effectively leveraged and notes that three other important state lenders already take IPRs into consideration when approving finance.

---

[75]   *Muhammad bin Ibrahim: Issues Surrounding Intellectual Property* (24 September 2014) IP Financing Conference published by BIS, at https://www.bis.org/review/r141024f.htm accessed on 13 April 2020.

3.2 Mr Mario Drago, President of the European Central Bank (ECB) (2017)

In his 2017 speech entitled, 'Fostering Innovation and Entrepreneurship in the Euro area' Mr Drago, ECB President, thoughtfully raised the issue of innovation (which may be patent-protected) and entrepreneurship, linking it to economic productivity growth:[76]

> This might at first glance seem an unusual topic for a central bank conference, since monetary policy principally operates through the demand side of the economy. But the long-term supply picture evidently also affects our ability to deliver on our mandate. Much of the debate today about the true level of the real equilibrium interest rate, for example, is a debate about the outlook for productivity growth, which of course depends in large part on innovation and entrepreneurship. Higher productivity growth is also vital to safeguard Europe's economic model of high wages and social protection, and hence to counter the sense of economic insecurity that is currently prevalent in several advanced economies.
>
> Consider, for example, the persistent gap between R&D spending in Europe and other major advanced economies. According to the World Economic Forum's Global Competitiveness Indicator, only three euro area countries are in the world's top ten for innovation. So, if, as the world's second-largest economic area, we were to dismantle barriers to innovative activity in the euro area, it would clearly give a boost to global innovation. I will not go into detail here about what policies this might entail, but clearly government support for innovation matters: in Europe differences in innovative capacity between countries are closely related to public spending on R&D, particularly in basic research.[77]

Mr Drago clearly states that one aim of monetary policy is to 'dismantle the barriers to innovative activity'. Next, he proceeds to address the topic of intangibles and IPRs directly, confirming:

> Numerous studies have shown that firms which invest more in intangibles are in a better position to understand and benefit from new technologies.[78] Such investment

---

[76] *Mario Draghi: Moving to the Frontier – Promoting the Diffusion of Innovation* (13 March 2017) Joint ECB and MIT Lab for Innovation, Science and Policy Conference in Frankfurt am Main, Germany, available at https://www.ecb.europa.eu/press/key/date/2017/html/sp170313_1.en.html accessed on 1 March 2021.

[77] *Ibid.*

[78] *Ibid*, 6. See D.T. Coe, E. Helpman and A.W. Hoffmaister, 'North-South R&D Spillovers' (1997) 107 *Economic Journal*, 134–149, H. Engebrecht, 'International R&D Spill Overs, Human Capital and Productivity in OECD economies: An Empirical Investigation' (August 1997) 41(8) *European Economic Review*, 1479–1488, D. Frantzen, 'R&D, Human Capital and International Technology Spillovers: A Cross-country Analysis' (17 December 2000) 102(1) *The Scandinavian Journal of Economics*, 57–75 and R. Griffith, S. Redding and J. van Reenen, 'Mapping the Two

includes conducting their own R&D and developing their own intellectual property, as well as investment in branding, software and databases. Investment in intangibles also appears low in the euro area compared with a number of other advanced economies, although it has been on an upward trend. The aggregate number also masks a wide country-level disparity, with the lack of intangibles investment particularly acute in some countries. Increasing the resources devoted to R&D would improve the ability of euro area firms to absorb more innovation.[79]

Mr Drago concludes his speech advising that it is a 'priority today in the euro area to address weak productivity growth'.[80] However, he does not identify capital regulation specifically as a barrier to innovation finance.

3.3 Philip R Lane, European Central Bank (ECB) Executive Board Member (2019)

Mr Philip R Lane, ECB Executive Board member, addressing the 'Challenges in the digital age' in a speech delivered to the recent 2019 ECB, supports more attention by central banks on new digital business models, the foundation of which is software, an intangible that is largely protected by copyright, an unregistered form of IPR:

A distinctive feature of digital technologies is their reliance on intangible capital. For instance, according to national accounts data, the share of investment devoted to intellectual property has almost doubled over the past two decades. This measure, however, is bound to underestimate the actual importance of intangible capital, since many of its components are not included in the national accounts.[81] There is some evidence that the weakness of physical capital investment over the past few years, if not longer, can to a large extent be explained by intangibles.[82] ... Financing

---

Faces of R&D: Productivity Growth in a Panel of OECD Industries' (2004) 86(4) *The Review of Economics and Statistics*, 883–895.

[79] See fn. 76, *supra*, 6.
[80] See fn. 76, *supra*, 9.
[81] *Philip R. Lane: Welcome Address – Challenges in the Digital Age* (4 July 2019) ECB conference on Challenges in the Digital Age, 1, Frankfurt am Main, Germany, at https://www.bis.org/review/r190715g.pdf accessed on 14 April 2020. See also M. Andersson and L. Saiz, 'Investment in Intangible Assets in the Euro Area' (November 2018) Economic Bulletin, Issue 7, ECB; and *L. De Guindos: Opening Remarks – Investment, Technological Transformation and Skills* (28 November 2018) Conference on Investment, Technological Transformation and Skills, Luxembourg, at https://www.ecb.europa.eu/pub/conferences/html/20181128_investment_technological_transformation_and_skills.en.html accessed on 13 March 2021.
[82] *Philip R. Lane*, fn. 81, *supra*. See also N. Crouzet and J. Eberly, 'Understanding Weak Capital Investment in the Role of Market Concentration and Intangibles' (August 2018) prepared for the Jackson Hole Economic Policy Symposium, Federal Reserve Bank of Kansas, USA.

is one factor that may hold back R&D in the European digital sector. For instance, intangible investment is difficult to collateralise and therefore harder to finance in a conventional bank-centred financial system like the one prevailing in continental Europe.

3.3.1   Critical discussion and new insights to drive CAR reform

Mr Lane acknowledges that the conventional bank-centred financial system prevailing in Europe makes intangible investment difficult to collateralize and therefore harder to finance. His statement helpfully puts the financial barrier faced by intangibles as loan security front and centre for central bank policymakers to acknowledge, reflect upon and contemplate further. This is an important step in the Kübler-Ross cycle of change management.[83] The stages of change management are denial, resistance, exploration and acceptance. This chapter encapsulates stage three, namely exploration. Central banks cannot ignore or fight change, rather they need to actively explore and manage the change affecting the quality of loan security available as it is and not as they wish it to be, i.e. traditional tangible assets.

In the author's view, the extracts from the speeches above demonstrate solid awareness of the financial barriers to innovation finance in an economic sense, a key step that will move central banks to actively explore potential solutions and reforms, but less so on the point of CARs and prudential regulation. The author suggests central banks may be receptive to the argument that there is scope to introduce reforms to ease the negative impact of CAR requirements in respect of intangible loan security such as registered granted IPRs. Carving out registered granted IPRs from the requirement to be deducted from the bank's capital and treating them more favourably as loan collateral could be the subject of further empirical research to obtain IPR risk data. The Basel Accord IV capital regulation (which has yet to be finalized) could amend section 67 Goodwill and Intangibles to better distinguish the collateral potential between the different types of intangibles. The wider class of intangible assets could be separated into new categories of loan collateral with more appropriate risk weighting for capital regulation purposes. In the author's view this would better reflect commercial reality and the corporate wealth and of its clients. The potential new and additional categories of IP monopoly rights under

---

[83]   E. Kübler-Ross, *On Death and Dying* (1969) Scribner Book Company Reprint Edition (12 August 2014). The Kübler-Ross model describes five stages of emotional and psychological response to grief, tragedy and catastrophic loss, and in behavioural economics, or in the case of the Covid-19 pandemic, it is used in a change management context.

section 67 are set out below, in order of most legally certain IPR to least legally certain IPR:

*   Registered granted IP monopoly rights (patents, trade marks, designs)
*   Registered IP monopoly right applications
*   Unregistered IP monopoly rights (copyright, database rights, confidential information, unregistered brands/trade marks).

3.3.2   The advantages of registered granted IPRs

Why is the distinction between registered and unregistered IPRs important in terms of loan security potential and valuation? Like a land title register or a share registry, the advantages of a system of national patent, trade mark and design registers are numerous but in the main relate to transparency of the monopoly granted and ownership. Registered IPRs have to be applied for and fulfil specific legal criteria under relevant national IPR legislation.[84] A central pillar of the modern system is that certain IPRs only come into existence if they are lawfully registered with the national IP office, granted to the 'first to file' registration of title to the IPR. The 'first to file' registration system incentivizes IPR owners to file the patent, trade mark or design application with the relevant national IP office as soon as is practicable. Once the application and registration process has been completed, a registered owner has the exclusive monopoly right to use the IPR across the UK as IPRs are territorial rights. The sooner the IPR is registered, the sooner the owner can exercise their monopoly right over their territory to exclude others in the market from using the invention, trade mark or design, back-dated to the date of registration. Registration of the title to the IPR results in a register entry being generated and maintained by the respective national IP office, the organization that centrally holds the details of all IPR ownership in the UK. The information on the register is important as it stakes out the boundaries of the IPR, providing a high degree of legal certainty regarding the asset. The relevant IPR registers confirm the person, natural or legal, who owns the stated monopoly IP rights and provides detailed information concerning the scope and boundary of those intangible IPRs. Third-party interests in the IPR can be recorded in the register. Additionally, the online IPR register can be searched by owner, registration number or key word very easily.

---

[84]   Patents Act 1977 (UK), Trade Marks Act 1994 (UK) and Registered Designs Act 1949 (UK).

3.3.3 Pioneering advances in the use of online IPR registers and databases

In the UK and the EU, the patent, trade mark or design register is public information, and at this time in the history of modern IPRs, freely electronically accessible and searchable, providing a clearer picture of the legal state of the IPR and the scope of the monopoly afforded by the registered right. Indeed, the online electronic register is a key development that arguably makes registered IPRs more attractive as loan security than in the past. The impact of online patent information databases has been a milestone for the global patent system and for innovation.

If registered IPRs are to be viewed more favourably from a banking capital risk perspective the challenge of transparency of registered IPR ownership arises and raises the question of the role of IP institutions such as the World Intellectual Property Organization (WIPO), the European Patent Office (EPO) and national IP offices. For example, Gorbatyuk asserts that the level of transparency be increased by mandating changes in title of patent ownership throughout the lifetime of a patent be recorded at national patent offices. Further, she proposes strict measures for non-compliance. In addition, it is argued that it would be beneficial if the EPO would register patent transfers of title during the lifetime of patents issued through the European Patent Convention system, beyond the opposition period.[85] Thus introducing a mandatory requirement to register sequential patent ownership (chain of title) would increase the level of transparency and legal certainty for third parties such as banks and more closely align with the system of registration of immoveable and moveable tangibles such land title, car registration and the like.

In the next section we analyse how the IPR legal framework has evolved to create a higher level of legal certainty as to the scope of the monopoly, using patents as our example as most relevant to UN 2030 SDG 9. We consider patent revocation proceedings, the timeframe between patent application and grant of the monopoly right, the UK's Green Channel to expedite inventions that involve the environment and how these modern developments enhance the loan security potential of registered IPRs.

The EU Intellectual Property Office's (EUIPO) pioneering Esp@cenet database integrates online patent information on a common platform on the Internet and is now over 20 years old, having launched on 19 October 1998. The Esp@cenet database substantially enhances the patent examination process in the UK and EU member states by ensuring only high quality

---

[85]   A. Gorbatyuk, 'Rethinking Registration of Intellectual Property: The Issue of (the Lack of) Transparency of Intellectual Property Ownership', in *Rethinking IT and IP Law. Celebrating 30 Years CiTiP* (2019) Intersentia, 235–242.

inventions, absolutely novel anywhere in the world, are granted monopoly rights in this jurisdiction.[86] Further, many national patent offices around the world work together to improve the overall quality of granted patents, through various mechanisms related to prior art search and examination work. The EPO defines prior art as *any* evidence that an invention is already known. Prior art does not need to exist physically or be commercially available. If anyone has previously described, shown or made something involving a use of very similar technology, this is sufficient to destroy novelty and thus the opportunity to patent. The most important place for further prior art searching is the world-wide patent system. Some patent databases (including the European Patent Office's free database Esp@cenet) contain 90 million documents, collected and indexed over many years by patent offices in many countries.[87] Examiners from different patent offices with complementary skills work together on the corresponding patent applications filed with those patent offices, resulting in higher quality examination.[88] The existence of comprehensive, freely available online patent searching is a relatively new modernizing factor that accentuates the attributes of registered IPRs as better suited for use as loan security than before. As noted above, the legal chain of title and transparency risks involved in searching for competing interests in registered IPRs are rooted in registers of title and secured transaction law, which can be improved and are not an inherent function of the usefulness, monopoly advantage or economic value of the inventions protected by the patents. In contrast, various unregistered IPRs also exist; the most well known is copyright, which comes into existence on creation, on fulfilling specific legal criteria under relevant national copyright legislation.[89] Registered and unregistered trade mark and design rights provide overlapping legal protection.

---

[86] 'Esp@cenet: 20 Years of Free Access to Patent Information in Europe' (19 October 2018) *The Patent Lawyer Magazine*, at https://patentlawyermagazine.com/espacenet-20-years-of-free-access-to-patent-information-in-europe/ accessed on 8 June 2020. Esp@cenet contains 100 million documents from over 100 countries, the single largest sources of technical information available.

[87] 'International Worksharing and Collaborative Activities for Search and Examination of Patent Applications' WIPO, available at https://www.wipo.int/patents/en/topics/worksharing/ accessed on 11 June 2020. See EPO, 'What is Prior Art', at https://www.epo.org/learning/materials/inventors-handbook/novelty/prior-art.html accessed on 13 March 2021.

[88] 'International Worksharing and Collaborative Activities', fn. 87, *supra*.

[89] Copyright Designs and Patents Act 1988 (UK).

3.3.4   Granted IPRs and the presumption of validity: a relatively low risk of patent revocation

The advantage of registered IP rights as loan security is that they are presumed to be legally valid unless revoked.[90] For example, in the UK granted patents are presumed valid, although this presumption is rebuttable with clear and convincing evidence. Section 72(1) of the Patents Act 1997 (UK) provides the Court or Comptroller with the authority to revoke patents only on very specific grounds, namely:

(a)   the invention is not a patentable invention;
(b)   the patent was granted to a person who was not entitled to be granted that patent;
(c)   the specification of the patent does not disclose the invention clearly enough and completely enough for it to be performed by a person skilled in the art;
(d)   the matter disclosed in the specification of the patent extends beyond that disclosed in the application for the patent, as filed, or, if the patent was granted on a new application filed under section 8(3), 12 or 37(4) above or as mentioned in section 15(9) above, in the earlier application, as filed;
(e)   the protection conferred by the patent has been extended by an amendment which should not have been allowed.

According to the UKIPO *Manual of Patent Practice*, revocation has effect *ex tunc* and the patent is therefore deemed never to have been granted.[91] The effect of patent revocation is to deprive the patent owner of their monopoly right of exclusivity. While this might sound catastrophic in terms of loan security, the CJEU has ruled in Genentech Inc v Hoechst GmbH, Sanofi-Aventis Deutschland GmbH (Case C-567/14) that EU competition law does not preclude patent licence agreements from including terms requiring the licensee to continue to pay royalties even after those patents have been revoked, so long as those agreements permit the licenses 'freely to terminate that agreement by giving reasonable notice'.[92] Further the CJEU held that in this case, the

---

[90]   C. Heer and K. Wei, 'The Differences between Unregistered and Registered Trademarks in Canada' (6 October 2019), at https://www.heerlaw.com/differences-unregistered-registered-trademarks accessed on 14 April 2020.

[91]   *Manual of Patent Practice* (last updated: April 2018) UK Intellectual Property Office (IPO), Sections 72.01–72.45, available at https://www.gov.uk/guidance/manual-of-patent-practice-mopp/section-72-power-to-revoke-patents-on-application, accessed on 8 June 2020.

[92]   'Royalties for Revoked Patents Do Not Necessarily Breach EU Competition Rules' (9 September 2016) Pennington Manches Cooper LLP, available at https://

royalty, even after patent expiry, could be considered to reflect a commercial assessment of the value attributed to the exploitation possibilities granted by the licence. The CJEU relied on its earlier decision in *Ottung* (Case 320/87)[93] whereby it held that requiring a licensee to pay a royalty, even if the term of the patent had expired, may reflect a commercial assessment of the value of exploitation resulting from the licence.[94, 95] Thus, from a cash flow and therefore a lender's banking risk point of view, in the EU royalties could continue to be payable under a licence even after the licensed patent has been revoked, provided that the licensee is free to terminate the licence on reasonable notice. The reasonable notice period could trigger risk mitigation action on the part of the borrower and lender. For example, each month the UK *Patent Journal*[96] reports all UK and European patents that have become void (s77(7) Patents Act 1977), revoked (under Article 102 of the European Patent Convention), ceased (through non-payment of renewal fees), or expired (after the termination of 20 years).[97]

As part of the literature search for this exploratory study, the author searched for empirical data regarding the rate or percentage of revoked patents per annum in the UK and EU to inform the analysis; however, she was unable to locate such information. This suggests the number of patents revoked every year is quite low as it has not warranted significant interest to date. Of interest, however, is a study of UK patent litigation commissioned by the UKIPO that identified 541 patent cases in the period between 2007 and 2013 or an average

---

www.penningtonslaw.com/news-publications/latest-news/2016/royalties-for-revoked -patents-do-not-necessarily-breach-eu-competition-rules, accessed on 8 June 2020.

[93]   Judgment of the Court (Sixth Chamber) of 12 May 1989 in Case 320/87 *Kai Ottung v Klee & Weilbach A/S and Thomas Schmidt A/S*. – Reference for a preliminary ruling: *Sø- og Handelsretten*, Denmark. Licensing agreement – Patent – Royalty and termination clause – Article 85 of the EEC Treaty [1989] ECR 01177, ECLI identifier: ECLI:EU:C:1989:195.

[94]   *Ibid.*

[95]   In contrast, note the US Supreme Court's decision in *Kimble et al. v Marvel Entertainment, LLC, Successor to Marvel Enterprises, Inc.*, Certiorari to the United States Court of Appeals for the Ninth Circuit, No. 13–720. Argued 31 March 2015, Decided 22 June 2015, at https://www.supremecourt.gov/opinions/14pdf/13-720_jiel .pdf accessed on 13 March 2021, which determined that the contractual obligation to pay royalties beyond the term of a patent was not enforceable, a decision that contrasts with the *Ottung* case.

[96]   See   https://www.ipo.gov.uk/pro-types/pro-patent/pro-p-os/pro-p-journal/p-pj -download.htm accessed on 8 June 2020. The National Archive holds the *Patent Journals* from 12 August 1988 to 26 March 2008. The UKIPO also publishes the *Trade Marks Journal* and the *Design Journal* with respect to those registered IPRs.

[97]   See the UK IPO instructions for patent searches, at https://www.ipo.gov.uk/ patent/p-journal/p-pj/p-pj-epuk/p-pj-epj-epuk-help.htm accessed on 8 June 2020.

of around 77 cases per year.[98] This study gives a snapshot of the volume of UK patent litigation that could result in a granted patent being revoked. When compared to the number of patents granted each year, the commercial risk in terms of deterioration or extinction of loan security is normally quite low. It is submitted that the volume of patent revocations per annum is smaller than the number of patents subject to litigation. However, such patent litigation may implicate commercially valuable patents. Patent litigation in the UK's High Court is dominated by large firms involved in the pharmaceutical, high tech and telecoms fields.[99] Arguably, large well-established firms are more likely to be able to provide alternative security in the event of patent revocation. There is scope for further research on this point to provide empirical evidence of the relative legal certainty afforded granted patents in a loan security and prudential banking regulation context. Similar arguments also apply to other registered IPRs.

3.3.5   Subsistence: unregistered IPRs offer less legal certainty

There are no unregistered patent rights. Unregistered trade mark, design rights, copyright and trade secrets must be proven in a court of law, which is costly and time-consuming. For example, the owner of an unregistered trade mark must provide that there is goodwill or reputation attached to the unregistered mark. A person must be able to prove at common law that they were the first creator and owner of an unregistered design right, as there is no confirming registration to presume ownership of the design right. The above provides a clear rationale for the superior loan security potential of registered IPRs (in contrast to goodwill, other intangibles and unregistered IPRs) in a similar vein to systems for registered land, vehicle and shares, for example.

As we are interested in suggesting rational reforms for prudential banking regulation, the first step in unbundling the wider asset class of intangibles is to create a subset of registered IPRs that could be treated more favourably for CAR purposes. Although patent, trade mark and design applications also have value, it is submitted that the value of IP applications is significantly less legally certain than granted monopoly rights until challenged, and thus less attractive for security and banking capital regulation purposes. Yet even so, IP-backed finance has made loans against unregistered rights with proven

---

[98]   C. Helmers et al., 'Examining Patent Cases at the Patents Court and the Intellectual Property Enterprise Court 2007–2013' (2015) UK Intellectual Property Office.

[99]   'How Much Patent Litigation is there in Europe? The United Kingdom' (11 April 2018) Simmons & Simmons, available at https://www.simmons-simmons.com/en/publications/ck0d8d8qwmlgz0b593vor6rjp/080218-how-much-patent-litigation-is-there-in-europe-uk accessed on 8 June 2020.

income streams that generate cash flow to service loan repayments and should not be excluded from the solutions proposed as many jurisdictions have active copyright registers.

3.3.6 The shorter time frame between application and grant of the IP monopoly

Another factor is the time frame between the date of the patent application through to grant of patent monopoly rights. This process usually takes no more than four years, but may be much less if the patent application comprises a 'green' invention eligible for expedited examination on the UKIPO's Green Channel for patents with environmental benefits.[100] If a green invention is being applied for, the time to grant could be reduced to as little as 18 months, especially if the invention is not complex. Further, the 'Patent Prosecution Highway' initiative significantly accelerates the patent application process if the patent has already been examined at another intellectual property office.[101] UK trade mark applications take even less time to be processed and typically take only approximately 4–6 months if the application is unopposed by any other registered trade mark owner with an additional 6 months if opposition proceedings are involved. A similar time frame applies to the design registration process.

In terms of volume, the EUIPO states that it registers almost 85,000 designs per year.[102] Given the fact that the time frame to register IP rights has improved over the last decade due to online processing, searching and examination discussed above, in the author's opinion there is less urgency for treating unregistered IP rights differently to intangibles generally for CAR and prudential regulation. As the level of legal certainty is likely higher for registered granted IPRs we must balance this with the goal of prudential regulation in providing a capital buffer for banks. In other words, from a prudential banking standpoint, the additional legal certainty provided by registration and grant of a 20-year monopoly option, in my view, are the rationale for carving out this type of IPR intangible from the wider class of intangibles on the basis of the differentiating characteristics that give rise to higher quality as security (collateral) than earlier, now-expired patents, granted pre-1998. Forward-looking studies, scenario analyses and stress tests could be performed as part of a UK Bank of England/ECB pilot initiative. In the next section, we turn to the views

---

[100] The UKIPO introduced the fee-free Green Channel for patent applications on 12 May 2009. This service allows patent applicants to request accelerated processing of their application if the invention has an environmental benefit, see https://www.gov.uk/guidance/patents-accelerated-processing accessed on 8 June 2020.
[101] *Ibid.*
[102] See https://euipo.europa.eu/ohimportal/en/designs accessed on 8 June 2020.

of a member of the Bank of England Monetary Policy Committee on the implications of increased investment in the intangible economy.

3.4 Professor Jonathan Haskel, External Member of the Bank of England Monetary Policy Committee (2020)

Professor Jonathan Haskel,[103] External Member of the Bank of England Monetary Policy Committee, gave a speech at the University of Nottingham on 11 February 2020 entitled, 'Monetary Policy in the Intangible Economy'[104] published by the Bank of England. Haskel focused on the implications of the movement to an economy with more intangible investment, for both the short-run transmission mechanisms and the long-run natural rate.[105] He referred to the Bean et al. (2002) study, which describes the 'bank lending' channel and the 'broad credit' channel.[106] The essential feature of the former bank lending channel is that monetary policy affects bank balance sheets, which in turn affects their appetite for lending.[107] The broad credit channel focuses on information frictions between borrowers and lenders, and how the mechanisms created to overcome these frictions can lead to amplification of financial shocks.[108]

In his speech, Haskel considers how these additional channels affect a more intangible-based economy. Haskel also confirms that intangible capital is less easy to pledge as collateral with creditors and young intangible firms may be more likely to have little or no earnings, which may result in an intangible economy that becomes disconnected from debt markets and (traditional) banks.[109] Haskel states that 'the move to an intangible economy, without financial innovation, may raise borrowing costs and give rise to less borrowing

---

[103] Jonathan Haskel CBE and Professor of Economics, London Imperial College London and author of J. Haskel and S. Westlake, *Capitalism without Capital: The Rise of the Intangible Economy* (2017) Princeton University Press. Haskel became a member of the Bank of England's Monetary Policy Committee (MPC) in May 2018.

[104] Speech published by the Bank of England, at https://www.bankofengland.co .uk/-/media/boe/files/speech/2020/monetary-policy-in-the-intangible-economy.pdf?la =en&hash=355DD0667ABC60E2BDEE465E05448E863D57CE54 accessed on 14 February 2020.

[105] *Ibid*, 3.

[106] C. Bean, J. Larsen and K. Nikolov, 'Financial Frictions and the Monetary Transmission Mechanism: Theory, Evidence and Policy Implications' In: I. Angeloni, A.K. Kashyap and B. Mojon (eds), *Monetary Policy Transmission in the Euro Area* (2003) Cambridge University Press, 107–130.

[107] See fn. 104, *supra*, 4.

[108] See fn. 104, *supra*, 4.

[109] See fn. 104, *supra*, 4.

and more internal funding' for IPR-rich borrowers with little tangible collateral such as land, buildings, equipment or vehicles.[110] Haskel advised there is evidence that intangibles may indeed interact with collateral constraints, so that with more intangibles in the economy there is heightened sensitivity of firms to monetary policy.[111] Delving deeper into this barrier to sustainable innovation finance, Haskel opines that the shift to intangibles might affect the monetary transmission mechanisms if intangibles are harder to borrow against and so firms seeking external finance find it harder to do so. He concludes that the conventional financial system finds it hard to value and so lend against intangible assets, then over the long-run risk spreads will rise as the economy becomes more intangible-based.[112] Haskel highlights that innovation and IP-rich borrowers may be credit constrained or even excluded from credit markets. This situation creates inequalities between borrowers and lenders (and among borrowers) with the starting point that if green innovation firms are credit-excluded, they cannot borrow. Hence, if they receive no income at all their innovations will never benefit the public or solve the climate change or Covid-19 problems facing the planet. The existing credit market, guided by compliance with Basel-driven monetary policy and CAR treatment of the class of intangibles, perpetuates inequalities and the outdated perception of the security value of registered IPRs.

The above extracts from high-level speeches by professionals involved in monetary policy in central banks demonstrate a growing awareness by central banks that they have a role to play in shaping access to sustainable finance, innovation and economic productivity. Since Basel III, the BCBS has been reviewing risk-measurement approaches internationally and among banks.[113] In an interview with the *Financial Times*, Valdis Dombrovskis referred to a proposal that would encourage banks to finance green investments including energy-efficient homes and zero-emissions transport by lowering capital requirements.[114] It is positive that two important central banks are actively and expressly supporting engagement with innovation, intangibles and IPRs (namely patents that provide monopoly protection for qualifying new innovations) as potential solutions to economic global productivity problems. Since 2019, under Basel III a bank's Tier 1 and Tier 2 capital must be a minimum of 8% of its risk-weighted holdings. The higher ratio provides a stronger buffer

---

[110] See fn. 104, *supra*, 8.
[111] See fn. 104, *supra*, 10.
[112] See fn. 104, *supra*, 10.
[113] S. Koch, 'Banking Regulation' (22 November 2017) *The Economic Times.*
[114] 'Brussels Eyes Easing Bank Rules to Spur Green Lending' (2019) *The Financial Times*, at https://www.ft.com/content/bddc3850-1054-11ea-a7e6-62bf4f9e548a accessed on 15 April 2020.

than the 2% ratio in place over a decade ago in 2008 and has greatly improved global banking financial stability.[115] The Group of Central Bank Governors and Heads of Supervision (GHOS) has indicated that it does not intend to increase the total regulatory capital requirements in the industry as a whole. Indeed, prior to the Covid-19 pandemic there was some discussion about potentially relaxing the CARs.

4. STATE OF FLUX DUE TO CLIMATE CHANGE AND DEVELOPMENTS TO SUPPORT GREEN FINANCE

On 12 November 2019, the keynote speech of Vice President Valdis Dombrovskis referenced the challenges and impacts of implementing Basel III.[116] As European Commissioner for Financial Stability, Financial Services and the Capital Markets, Dombrovskis has initiated discussions regarding potentially easing bank capital rules to facilitate green finance.[117] Dombrovskis stated that the proposal would encourage banks to finance green investments by lowering capital requirements, the CAR that measures a bank's ability to absorb losses.[118]

However, details are still lacking as to what the Group of Central Bank GHOS might do to improve the IPRs as loan security situation.

The case for carving out registered IPRs such as granted patents, trade marks and designs from the intangibles asset class (nonphysical assets with potential benefit in the long term) has been outlined in this chapter. Further, the international IPR system is sanctioned by the World Trade Organization (WTO)[119] and administered by WIPO.[120] The WTO's Agreement on Trade-Related Aspects of Intellectual Property Rights (TRIPS)[121] was negotiated over two

---

[115] S. Nikolas, 'What is the Minimum Banking Capital Adequacy Ratio under Basel III?' (21 July 2019), available at https://www.investopedia.com/ask/answers/062515/what-minimum-capital-adequacy-ratio-must-be-attained-under-basel-iii.asp accessed on 13 April 2020.

[116] See https://ec.europa.eu/commission/presscorner/detail/en/SPEECH_19_6269 accessed on 12 November 2019.

[117] B. Caplan, 'The Risks of Getting Green Finance Wrong' (3 December 2019) *The Banker*, The Financial Times Ltd.

[118] Corporate Finance Institute, at https://corporatefinanceinstitute.com/resources/knowledge/finance/capital-adequacy-ratio-car/ accessed on 7 January 2020.

[119] See https://www.wto.org and the WTO Text, at https://www.wto.org/english/docs_e/legal_e/legal_e.htm#TRIPs accessed on 7 January 2020.

[120] See https://www.wipo.org accessed on 7 January 2020.

[121] See https://www.wto.org/english/thewto_e/whatis_e/tif_e/agrm7_e.htm accessed on 7 January 2020.

decades ago during the 1986–94 Uruguay Rounds, introducing IPR rules into the multilateral trading system. TRIPS is legal recognition of the significance of links between intellectual property and trade. The WTO states that the new internationally agreed trade rules for IPRs were seen as a way to introduce more order and predictability.[122] Functional IPR legal frameworks are mandated for all WTO member states. The lack of GHOS attention to the global IPR system suggests a level of dissonance and lack of coherence as between the finance and IPR law disciplines that needs to be rectified. Central banks should be encouraged to re-evaluate the security potential of modern registered IPRs such as granted patents and consider the interaction between the hitherto independent legal ecosystems.

My hypothesis suggests that the potential of registered IPRs as loan security is underestimated when compared to the wider class of intangibles generally (a class that includes substantially more nebulous intangibles such as goodwill, know-how and unregistered IP rights e.g. copyright, confidential information and trade secrets). Further, in the financial sector specialist IP finance lenders already exist and are successful. In the UK these are authorized by the Financial Conduct Authority. There is potential for the central banks to study these specialist lenders' experience vis-à-vis prudential regulation requirements. The first cross-country study on how financial crises affect patenting shows the lack of access to bank credit that will result in firms dropping both ongoing (sunk costs) and new R&D projects. Hardy and Sever find that:

> [T]hese industries decrease their patenting more following a financial crisis than other industries. The effect is persistent, lasting upwards of 10 years, and is specific to banking crises. This indicates that when firms lose access to bank credit, they may be forced to drop new and ongoing R&D projects. This results in fewer patents over the following years. These results provide a link between financial crises and the sustained decline in output and productivity observed after a recession.[123]

Losing R&D projects that may lead to innovation to support global sustainability in the public interest makes it less likely that UN 2030 SDG 9 will be achieved. Banking CARs is one aspect of the 'financial channel to innovation' that this chapter has addressed; advocating a more contemporary approach to the categorization of intangibles would support UN 2030 SDG 9. Next, we consider how climate change is adversely affecting value certainty in the

---

[122] 'Intellectual Property: Protection and Enforcement', at https://www.wto.org/english/thewto_e/whatis_e/tif_e/agrm7_e.htm accessed on 7 January 2020.
[123] B. Hardy and C. Sever, *Financial Crises and Innovation* (4 March 2020) BIS Working Paper No.846 https://www.bis.org/publ/work846.htm accessed on 14 April 2020.

housing market and may provide further incentive for central banks to consider levelling the playing field for IPRs as loan security.

4.1   Tangible Assets: Value Uncertainty Challenges Due to Climate Change

We have seen that the main actors in the financial system are commercial banks (banks), the central bank and other financial institutions. Patents and other forms of IPRs are personal property rights that can be traded independently of the protected technology. For example, non-practising entities (NPEs) who acquire patents also use their patent portfolio as loan security. Asset markets are the money market, the stock market, the housing market and the other financial markets. There is currently no functioning IPR or patent market, although as mentioned earlier there are many purchasers and today patent intermediaries exist and patent auctions increasingly take place.[124] The housing market, however, plays an important role in the economy and houses are the main form of wealth of households (except for the very rich). Company directors of IPR-rich firms often have to rely more on personal tangible assets (as opposed to company assets) to overcome lending frictions by giving lenders a security interest (a director's guarantee) in their homes. Houses and the land they sit on are traditional loan security, but this type of fixed tangible security is facing new challenges. Dr Rhian-Marie Thomas, OBE and Chief Executive of the UK's Green Finance Institute, argues that within the context of 20- or 30-year mortgages (secured by buildings and homes), these times-cales are beyond the planning horizons of banks and building societies due to a variety of risks including climate change and flooding.[125] In a speech dated 8 November 2019 she stated:

> About 12% of land in England is adjacent to a river or a stream and these low-lying areas are more vulnerable to floods … As these flood risks become more prevalent due to climate change … these physical risks in the real economy clearly also pose a considerable risk to the financial sector. That is why 50 of the world's central banks, including the Bank of England, have formed the rapidly growing Network

---

[124] L. Tonnison, R. Millien and L. Maicher, 'Shortcoming on the Market for Intellectual Property: Qualitative Study among Intellectual Property Service Providers on Various Problems Related to Intellectual Property Markets' (March 2016) Fraunhofer Center for International Management and Knowledge Economy, available at https://www.imw.fraunhofer.de/content/dam/moez/de/documents/Working_Paper/Working-Paper_Shortcomings%20on%20the%20market%20for%20intellectual%20property.pdf accessed on 14 April 2020.

[125] *R.-M. Thomas: The Impact of Climate Change on the Mortgage Market* (November 2019) UK Annual Mortgage Conference.

for Greening the Financial System. They recognize that climate change represents the single greatest systemic risk to the stability of financial services and they are working together to explore and share best practice to mitigate the risk using all the supervisory and regulatory levers at their disposal to drive change – governance, capital adequacy and weighting, stress testing, disclosures, data provisions and so on.[126]

Essentially, banks lack the ability to measure exposure to climate risk (echoing their claim of inability to value patents). Professor Nigel Wright,[127] a flood risk expert, in online exchanges in September–November 2020 with the author, agrees that there may be an adverse impact on land and property values due to climate change in the future. Wright's research spans the use of computers to predict the movement of fluids in the natural and built environment expanding into cross-disciplinary aspects of flood risk management and climate change adaptation. Further, Wright suggests that climate change will create risks other than flooding that may also impact on asset value in the housing market. He counsels that there is insufficient data available to assess the likely impact on lender's security value at present. Wright advises that lenders could insist on additional measures to make properties more resilient to flooding to mitigate risk. Wright concurs with Dr Thomas that additional research on the subject of lenders' exposure to flood risk is vital, as some research suggests that existing desirable and expensive property, e.g. on the Thames to the West of London for example, would not be adversely affected.[128]

Brassell and King's research has confirmed that 'recent banking initiatives targeting growth businesses are finding that traditional fixed assets simply no longer exist'.[129] If the level of credit risk related to traditional tangible bank assets such as residential mortgages and real property is increasing, necessitating a reassessment of the CAR weighting, what does the future hold for loan security and capital regulation? Will the reduction in stock and quality of traditional residential loan security lead lenders to adopt a more risk-tolerant

---

[126] *Ibid.*

[127] Professor Nigel Wright is Deputy Vice-Chancellor for Research and Innovation at Nottingham Trent University, a Chartered Engineer and Fellow of the Institution of Civil Engineers. See N. Wright, 'Advances in Flood Modelling Helping to Reduce Flood Risk' (2014) 167(2) *Proceedings of the Institution of Civil Engineers-Civil Engineering*, 52; and N. Wright et al., 'Delivering and Evaluating the Multiple Flood Risk Benefits in Blue-Green Cities: An Interdisciplinary Approach' In: D. Proverbs and C.A. Brebbia (eds), *Flood Recovery, Innovation and Response IV* (2014) WIT Press, 131–124.

[128] J. Lamond, D. Proverbs and F. Hammond, 'The Impact of Flooding on the Price of Residential Property: A Transactional Analysis of the UK Market' (2010) 25(3) *Housing Studies*, 335–356.

[129] Brassell and King, fn. 74, *supra*, 13.

approach to monopolistic registered IPRs? In this chapter, I have laid out several arguments as to why registered granted IPRs could play a more important role in the credit market and sustainable innovation finance. Given the likely increase in value uncertainty facing the mortgage market due to climate change, treating registered IPRs more favourably in terms of banking CARs and risk weighting could potentially strengthen a country's ability to unlock and commercialize new inventions to tackle global challenges. Statutory granted IP monopoly rights such as patents, trade marks and designs provide unique commercial advantages as loan security that may not currently be recognized by the central bank regulators.

4.2 Elaborating the Case to Treat Registered IPR More Favourably for CAR Purposes

UN Sustainable Develop Goal 9 concerns innovation and technological progress. Inventions are state-sanctioned time-limited monopolies that provide the patent owner the important negative right to stop others using the invention without permission for up to 20 years as long as renewal fees are paid.[130] The links between innovation and sustainability are proven. Research confirms that IP-rich businesses are more sustainable in the long term and that there is a positive association between patenting and firm outcomes, in that they benefit from the time-limited monopoly advantage of patents.[131] Further, patenting is positively associated with future business growth and survival in the long term, and if the firm is unsuccessful, patents provide salvage value[132] for lenders. An important component of sustainability is sustainable finance, which refers to finance that takes into account environmental, social and governance considerations leading to increased investment in longer-term and sustainable activities.[133] Thus, a discussion of the role of IPRs to support green finance (climate change mitigation and adaptation and related risks) and blue finance (to support ocean resilience) is highly relevant to both SDG 9 and sustainable finance initiatives.

This section sets out arguments for potential reform to the categorization of Basel III Tier 1 capital to stimulate lending and cash flow to IP-rich busi-

---

[130] Patents Act 1977 (UK).

[131] B. Hall, 'Is there a Role for Patents in the Financing of New Innovative Firms?' (May 2018) Max Planck Institution for Innovation and Competition Research Paper No 18-06.

[132] *Ibid.*

[133] The European Commission Report, *Sustainable Finance*, see https://ec.europa .eu/info/business-economy-euro/banking-and-finance/sustainable-finance_en accessed on 18 June 2020.

nesses. Prioritizing lending to firms with registered granted IPR assets could be an important component of sustainable blue and green finance. Like the labour market, the credit market is essential to the functioning of a capitalist economy.[134] Money is at the centre of the loan transactions and, in simple terms, money is a 'store of value' as, for example, a firm's patented inventions are part of its net worth or corporate wealth. With loan funds, an innovating firm can invest the borrowed money and turn its innovations and inventions into goods and services that support sustainability in the public interest. Thus, borrowing and lending are about shifting capital as the technological innovations mature, are commercialized and produce income streams (the security/collateral), so long as the market desires the products and services. The venture capital and equity market has evinced a clear interest in funding the R&D and patent applications that may lead to registered patented inventions to combat climate change. Within the debt finance market, borrowing funds at commercially attractive rates enables a firm to further develop its R&D, innovations and inventions in-house and greatly reduces the risk of novelty-destroying disclosures that would prevent the grant of a patent monopoly[135] (plus future royalty income streams available as security).

Nonetheless, lenders – the debt financiers – are right to be wary. To date, lending funds to an IP-rich firm with a high ratio of intangible assets has mostly been viewed as a higher risk loan (with an interest rate calculated accordingly) than lending against traditional collateral such as real property, especially buildings and land. Experts – such as Brian Caplen, editor of *The Banker* – hold the view that relaxing CARs for green loans that are subsequently rolled up into securitizations and given AAA ratings would eventually crash resulting in a regulatory response to clamp down hard on green lending.[136] In response to this hypothetical argument, the purpose of capital regulation is to result in both higher and better quality capital. This chapter has put forward that registered granted patents and other registered IPR are better quality capital than traditionally perceived for the reasons elaborated above.

---

[134] *Economy, Society and Public Policy* (2019) CORE Economics Education, Oxford University Press, 388.

[135] See A. Falato, D. Kadyrzhanova and J.W. Sim, 'Rising Intangible Capital, Shrinking Debt Capacity, and the US Corporate Savings Glut' (November 2012) Finance and Economics Discussion Series, Divisions of Research & Statistics and Monetary Affairs, Federal Reserve Board, Washington, DC, at https://www.federalreserve.gov/pubs/feds/2013/201367/201367pap.pdf accessed on 11 January 2020.

[136] B. Caplen, 'The Risk of Getting Green Finance Wrong' (3 December 2019) *The Banker* https://www.thebanker.com/Editor-s-Blog/The-risks-of-getting-green-finance-wrong accessed on 3 December 2019.

4.2.1   One class for intangible assets may no longer suit all IPRs

Arguably as at 2020, certain tangible property such as house and land as loan security is a riskier proposition than in the past, while registered granted IPRs are less so given the modern IPR legal framework. It is true IPRs can be high risk and not all IPRs are valuable in a monetary sense. IPRs may have no financial or monetary value to a lender unless they assist to create, maintain or increase cash flow to service a loan, and they are less liquid. However, the class of intangibles is very broad, as is the class of IPRs, both registered and unregistered, yet they are all treated the same by CAR regulation with respect to Basel II Section 67 Goodwill and Other Intangibles discussed in section 2.2 above. Is this bank asset classification current and appropriate for the 21st century given the institutional support for IPRs from global institutions such as the WTO and WIPO? IPRs, as assets, may alter in value for many reasons, but that is also the case for other traditional loan security assets as seen in section 2.3 above with respect to bank assets and elastic risk weightings. While a patented invention for a new drug, for example, may begin its life as a unique solution to a problem, in time other pharmaceutical companies may find alternative solutions that reduce the patent's royalty income. On the other hand, successful promotion of the patented drug can ensure the patent remains valuable until it expires at the end of a 20-year term and much longer. Most registered trade marks gain value as they become better known and the licensing of the marks for use by third parties generate revenue to service a loan.[137] There is often positive valuation elasticity as the patented invention is commercialized, which reduces lender risk.

4.2.2   Advances in IPR valuation methodologies

It is only in the last few decades that the concept of 'patent value' has emerged. Now several well-established valuation methodologies for IPRs exist. The cost method and the market value method are based on past performance. In contrast, the income or economic benefit method and the relief from royalty method are based on the lender's assessment of likely future events. Each has its limitations and no one method is appropriate for every type of IPR. With respect to patents, the stage of technological development (or technology readiness level (TRL)), the availability of patent and strategic business information and purpose of the valuation will affect the final monetary value assigned. The UKIPO has published a transaction IPR valuation checklist scored on a scale of 0–5 (0 = no value, 2–3 = weak, 4 = strong and 5 = very strong). When patents are valid, even if the borrower defaults, the granted patent portfolio will likely

[137] 'Guidance: Valuing your IP' (12 February 2016) UK Government, see https://www.gov.uk/guidance/valuing-your-intellectual-property accessed on 13 April 2020.

provide lenders with salvage value. A bespoke standardized valuation system could be developed for prudential banking risk and loan security purposes.[138] If the IPRs are rated as strong or very strong, they could be treated more favourably as a form of loan security, without the requirement to be deducted in the calculation of Common Equity Tier 1 capital, for example. The BCBS might consider developing its own bespoke bank asset credit risk valuation methodology/analytics for IPRs as part of any revised capital regulation rules.

4.2.3   Aligning the IP-rich borrower and lender's interests

However, apart from valuing IPR, lenders face two further problems. These are not CAR problems. Rather the material below provides additional background to the IP finance lending landscape and wider concerns vis-à-vis IP-backed lending. First, banks suggest that when loans are taken out for investment in commercializing innovations and inventions, they cannot be sure that a borrower will exert enough effort to make the project succeed. A secured loan reduces the bank's risk; as long as the security (e.g. the house, painting, jewellery, land, patents, trade marks and designs) can readily be sold for more than the amount of money owed, the lender is secure. The borrower, by providing security, reduces the conflict of interest between the borrower and the lender because the borrower will tend towards prudent business decisions to ensure commercialization of the invention is a success. In addition to the arguments in section 3.3 above, the author argues that investment in filing and registering patents – via a lengthy 1–4 year high-level patent examination procedure – means the borrower is investing funds and resources into the venture, therefore their interest aligns with that of the lender. Registered IPRs, such as granted patents (in addition to having a higher level of legal certainty than patent applications or unregistered rights) are a good signal to the lender that the borrower believes that the invention is of adequate quality to succeed in the market or have a role within the company's IP portfolio.[139]

As we know, financing early-stage innovation (e.g. R&D, confidential information, trade secrets, pre-patent application) is usually regarded by the market as a high risk investment so that equity finance is common. Once an exclusive patent monopoly has been granted, the lender's risk is reduced to the commercialization of the invention. Although this stage of commercialization and technology readiness level is not without risk (typically TRL 4–9), it is arguably a significantly lesser risk than the risk level assigned to early stage, pre-patent application, intangible confidential information and know-how (TRL 1–3). The use of TRLs enables consistent, uniform discussions of techni-

---

[138]   *Ibid.*
[139]   *Ibid.*

cal maturity across different types of technology and could feature in banking prudential regulation credit risk weightings.[140] The TRL system is already widely used in the public finance domain.

Second, the borrower (the innovation firm) has more inside information than the lender about the quality of the inventions and the likelihood of successful commercialization. These problems arise from a difference (or conflict) of interest between the borrower and the lender, and from the difference between the information the borrower and the lender have about the borrower's project and actions. The problems impose costs of monitoring and loan enforcement that will increase the interest rate on the IPR-secured loan. If the borrower fails to repay the loan, with IPR as security the lender has to assume ownership of the patents, maintain them and find a buyer. It is easier to sell registered granted patents than unregistered IP rights. Although an important issue for Tier 1 banking capital classification is that there is no organized market for patents, as exists for other types of intangibles such as shares in companies (e.g. the London Stock Exchange, the NASDAQ etc.),[141] this clearly does not mean there are no buyers for the patents. Management buyouts, competitors and patent aggregating firms are all potential patent portfolio acquirers in the modern marketplace, and there are also private patent auctions as with antiques and other moveable valuables. Private banks could even set up their own IPR market to liquidate granted patents.

4.2.4 A long history of IPR-backed debt finance

It is important to bear in mind that IPRs have a long history of being used as security for debt. IPRs are currently increasingly being used to secure loans in many developed countries.[142] The proposal to revise the CAR for registered IPRs aims to enhance access to IP debt finance by innovation firms and make this category of intangible asset more attractive to lenders as security. Interesting research published in 2012 by Maria Loumioti, at the University of Dallas, made the following findings regarding the US credit market:

> Using a sample of secured syndicated loans, I explore the use of intangible assets as loan collateral and whether this credit practice was an innovation or a negative mutation in the corporate loan market. While intangible assets were not traditionally considered as eligible collateral, I find that twenty-one percent of U.S.-originated secured syndicated loans during 1996–2005 have been collateralised by intangi-

---

[140] See fn. 15, *supra*, 43.
[141] Tonnison, Millien and Maicher, fn. 124, *supra*.
[142] The UK, USA, Canada, Japan, Singapore and many others.

bles, with intangible asset collateralisation significantly increasing over this time period.[143]

Loumioti's invaluable contribution to this debate provides preliminary evidence that intangible re-deployability and borrower reputation are positively related to the probability of using intangibles as loan collateral and that collateralizing loans by intangibles significantly increases loan pricing and credit supply to firms. However, her key finding of interest for the purpose of capital regulation and CARs is that loans secured by intangibles perform no worse than other secured loans.[144] Loumioti's findings have important implications for the credit market, the largest capital provider of innovation finance, and capital regulation. Creditors have found ways of leveraging, financing and valuing intangible and IPR assets, benefiting both borrowers and lenders. Loumioti's research suggests that using intangibles as loan security did not significantly deteriorate lenders' credit profile. American commercial banks have also been seeking US Federal Reserve regulatory approval for counting intangible assets towards loan security for regulatory capital assets, from which they have been previously restricted.[145] Accordingly, there is some evidence for arguing that commercial banks could reduce their estimates of expected losses upon borrowers' default and their capital requirements.

4.2.5 Designing an IPR security friendly sustainable innovation finance system

We understand that a role of prudential capital regulation is to address bank asset valuation, legal risks and liquidity. Since 2014, central banks' awareness of IPRs and their role in innovation has increased as set out in section 2 above. Nevertheless, many IP-rich borrowers are excluded from the credit market and are unable to obtain a loan of any kind, necessitating reliance on savings, crowdfunding, business angels and venture capital, which is far more costly and less sustainable. Lenders often require company directors to give loan guarantees by taking out residential mortgages secured against their homes, which unacceptably shifts commercial risks to these directors and their families. Further, in June 2020, Nationwide, the UK's leading building society, announced that it would now only lend to borrowers with at least a 15%

---

[143] M. Loumioti, 'The Use of Intangible Assets as Loan Collateral' (1 November 2012), available at SSRN: https://papers.ssrn.com/sol3/papers.cfm?abstract_id= 1748675 accessed on 15 April 2020.

[144] *Ibid.*

[145] J.H. Eisbruck, 'Credit Analysis of Intellectual Property Securitization: A Rating Agency Perspective' In: Bruce Berman (ed.), *From Ideas to Assets: Investing wisely in Intellectual Property* (2002) John Wiley & Sons, Inc.

deposit, amid concerns about falling house prices and negative equity, where a borrower owes more than the home is worth.[146] The typical deposit used to be only 5%, so this is a dramatic increase in the amount home buyers will need to save. Nationwide confirms the 15% minimum deposit will apply to all new house purchase, remortgage and first-time buyer applicants.[147] If other lenders in the mortgage market follow suit, the opportunities for home ownership in the UK will be limited. Adverse developments in the mortgage market lend further weight to the argument that it is timely for central banks and lenders to re-visit the issue of intangibles and IPRs as risk-weighted bank assets for credit purposes. Perhaps designing a sustainable innovation finance system with a more expert classification of the intangibles asset class is the next logical and evolutionary step for the development of global prudential regulation.

4.2.6 A new role for IPR intelligence and analytics in calculating CARs and lending risk

Designing prudential regulation to adapt to the intangible economy could draw on innovations in the fields of artificial intelligence and fintech to analyse IPR portfolios for bank asset risk-weighting purposes. It could be feasible for central banks and lenders to devise algorithms and create IP portfolio intelligence software to calculate registered and unregistered IPR-related CAR risk weightings. As the borrower's IPR matures, active loan monitoring and lending risks could be updated and adjusted, positively or negatively, as part of the prudential regulation toolkit. If central banks and lenders are armed with knowledge about the IP landscape for CAR purposes, downstream lenders will be able to better understand and evaluate the credit risk of borrowers' IPR portfolios, empowering credit risk lending decisions. Loan agreements can be adapted to include relevant contractual terms to support such IPR evaluation and lender/borrower relationships.

Thus, in order to support SDG 9 and enhance sustainable innovation finance, the author recommends that the Basel Committee on Banking Supervision establish an international experts advisory group to explore the proposals put forward in this chapter, with a view to issuing IP finance guidance to members and potential reform of the Basel Accords bank asset risk weightings, Basel III section 67 Goodwill and Intangibles as applied to intangible, registered granted IPRs as loan security.

---

[146] P. Collinson, 'Nationwide Triples Minimum Deposit for UK First-Time Buyers' (17 June 2020) *The Guardian*, available at https://www.theguardian.com/business/2020/jun/17/nationwide-triples-minimum-deposit-for-uk-first-time-buyers accessed on 17 June 2020.

[147] *Ibid.*

5.   CONCLUSIONS AND RECOMMENDATIONS

Our national and global economies are part of our society, which lives in the Earth's biosphere and physical environment. Advances in technology may assist in producing innovation to tackle climate change and ensure our energy is supplied from less-polluting sources, with a greater reliance on wind, solar and other renewable sources. In the finance domain, intangible yet legally created and state expert-examined registered IP monopoly rights are part of our collective wealth. Granted patents arguably capture the world's best innovations, known as 'inventions', so-called as they are the state of the art in the field. Registered patented inventions represent the pinnacle of innovation and have an intrinsic store of value that, in theory, could be recognized separately from the wide category of intangibles, which is based on accounting terminology and not specifically bank credit risk. Certainly, many industry sectors presently comprise firms with a high ratio of intangible assets to tangible assets. For example, the technology sector relies on computer hardware patents, software copyright and its trade mark brands as key intangible assets. The green engineering and technology sectors rely heavily on design rights, patents and copyright protection. The medical sector relies on patented medicines and brands. The entertainment and media sector relies on copyright and related rights. All industry sectors rely to some degree on confidential information and Internet domain names, also classed as intangible assets.

However, registered IPRs are presumed to be legally valid and provide their owners with a potential commercial monopoly and thus 'insurance' against competition and reduce a lender's risk that the borrower's business will fail. Therefore, generally speaking, over time intangible assets enhance perception of a firm's value and, ultimately, the firm's intangible assets may become even more valuable than its tangible assets such as land, plant and equipment, thus bank credit risk is reduced. A firm that invests in long-term assets such as intangible IPRs (especially registered rights such as patents, trade marks, copyright etc.) is laying the foundation for long-term value creation, earnings and sustainable financial performance. However, a firm's long-term investment in IPRs is not only about the time frame, it also concerns alignment with long-term outcomes and structural trends such as digitalization, addressing climate change and the environment.

In this chapter I critically examined the activity of the Basel Committee on Banking Supervision and the Basel Accords[148] as they apply to intangible assets and IPRs as loan security and thus bank assets, with a view to

---

[148]   The second, third and fourth of the Basel Accords issued by the Basel Committee on Banking Supervision.

enhancing sustainable finance and, ultimately, supporting SDG 9. SDG 9 seeks to promote inclusive and sustainable industrialization while fostering innovation.[149] Presently, intangible assets (which includes registered granted IPRs such as patents, designs and trade marks) are not used in banks' CAR risk weightings as they are treated as very low quality capital, largely due to legal certainty and liquidity concerns. The interdisciplinary traditional law and qualitative analysis presented has enabled us to build an exploratory case to support a new approach to prudential regulation and its interrelation with IPRs. The original analysis evaluated why CAR risk weighting, as applied across the whole intangible asset class, could be reviewed and potentially reformed, as a possible solution to improve how funds are actively channelled to finance urgent innovation to support SDG 9, climate change and flood risk. My exploratory proposal involves treating registered IPR assets as a separate or distinct category within the general 'intangibles' category. Given the unique commercial monopoly advantages for product and service commercialization, low risk of revocation, proven use as loan security,[150] IPRs could now be viewed more favourably from a bank asset credit risk standpoint.

Further, IPRs increasingly have residual salvage value on insolvency of the borrower (liquidity), reducing lending risk. As long as a bank is able to meet the minimum liquidity ratio (LCR) to provide sufficient cash to cover funding needs for a 30-day period of stress; and the longer-term ratio net stable funding ratio (NSFR) intended to address maturity mismatches over the entire balance sheet, I theorized that prudential banking regulations should aim to adjust and fine-tune the bank asset risk weighting applicable to registered granted IPRs. Holding a small percentage of high quality granted IPRs as bank assets would arguably enhance the bank's credit risk, yet have the added benefit of potentially stimulating IPR-backed lending. According to Bhattacharya:

> [The] imposition of prudential norms like capital adequacy and stricter provisioning requirements as market-safeguards, demands a carefully drawn up policy framework for the lending activities of banks and financial institutions.[151]

As part of CAR policy, this research makes an original contribution to interdisciplinary IPR and banking law literature with new insights to nurture and advance sustainable IP debt finance transactions. Basel I was issued in 1988 and focused on credit risk and capital adequacy of financial institutions introducing the bank asset risk classifications. The Basel Accords have always

---

[149] See fn. 5, *supra.*

[150] See section 3, *supra.*

[151] H. Bhattacharya, *Banking Strategy, Credit Appraisal and Lending Decisions: A Risk-Return Framework* (2010) Oxford University Press, 386–388.

been intended to evolve over time. Two decades later, in 2020, the world's central banks could pay more attention to the treatment of WTO-sanctioned and state-registered monopoly IPRs with long useful lives as a form of loan security that offers more sanctuary from risk than in the past. The novelty, legal certainty and validity of registered granted patents is arguably higher than in the pre-computer technology and Internet age, circa mid-1980s. Yet, the CAR applicable to the intangibles asset class as a whole has not changed significantly, treating all intangibles uniformly as low quality capital. As standard maker, the BCBS has the power and legitimacy to make a real direct impact on banking CARs with respect to registered IPRs, which are, frankly, a commercial necessity in the market.

The evolving sustainable finance market is currently responding to the global targets set in the UNEP Principles of Responsible Banking (PRB) launched on 23 September 2019.[152] The PRB are accelerating the banking industry's contribution to achieving society's goals as expressed in the Sustainable Development Goals and the Paris Climate Agreement but do not address capital regulation.[153] While there are capital risks in getting IPR as loan security and green finance wrong, a top-down review of CARs with respect to intangibles and IPRs should be based on a thorough understanding of how CARs affect each type of intangible asset within the wider class. Potential reform to unbundle the goodwill and intangibles asset class, which is currently tied to the definition of intangibles as set out in IAS Intangibles 38, may improve the impact of regulatory constraints on innovation and economic productivity. Central banks could take a more holistic approach to CARs and more accurately classify intangible registered granted IPR assets against banking credit risk, thereby optimizing bank capital. Such an approach might assist the BCBS, BIS and GHOS to adapt prudential regulation to the shift in business models in the fourth and fifth industrial revolutions by modernizing capital-management plans and regulation. Designing a contemporary IPR-friendly regulatory banking environment, well-positioned to prudently lend to IPR-rich borrowers, may be an important component for sustainable finance. Appropriate IPR analytics software, now available, could be developed by the central banking community in conjunction with banks to assign more accurate lending risk to IPRs as capital with a view to adjusting banking capital adequacy weightings for registered granted IPRs.

---

[152] The PRB have been developed by the banking industry itself, together with the United Nations Environment Programme Finance Initiative (UNEP FI) – a UN–private sector collaboration that includes membership of more than 240 finance institutions around the globe, see https://www.unepfi.org/banking/bankingprinciples/ accessed on 14 April 2020.

[153] *Ibid.*

In conclusion, in this chapter I have evaluated the impact and potential reform to banking capital adequacy requirements and CAR for intangibles and IPRs as part of the wider green and blue finance initiatives to improve the flow of capital to innovation needed to solve planetary issues and support sustainability. This topic, to my knowledge, has not been addressed in the interdisciplinary academic sustainable finance or IPR literature in depth before. An exploratory case has provided qualitative and traditional legal analysis to inform an argument that the BCBS and central banks are aware and potentially more amenable to adopting a more risk-tolerant approach to IPRs, especially registered IPRs, in light of the deterioration of other bank assets such as residential mortgages. The shaky bridge that links IPR-rich borrowers with bank finance could be re-designed to provide better access for innovation firms and made stronger so that the central banks and financial sector can embrace financial technology, e.g. IPR portfolio analytics, to support bank asset credit risk assessments. Howard Crosse, former Vice President of the Federal Reserve Bank of New York, states that 'the very act of formulating a policy and expressing it in words that all agree will sharpen the issues and make the end product more effective'.[154] Of course, it is essential to balance prudential banking regulation with the interests of other stakeholders in the lending environment to achieve the best possible outcome and maintain trust in banks. A challenge for the Basel Committee will be to reflect on how bank asset capital risk weightings for the intangibles asset class could be activated across multiple jurisdictions, especially those without online IPR registers. Further debate is necessary in the finance world. In addition, empirical research and risk modelling on the impact of CARs on registered granted IPRs as bank capital assets, as a specific monetary policy factor in the overall mix of bank assets, is necessary. That said, it is timely for prudential regulation to evolve alongside business and the economies the banking community serves. This chapter has hopefully enriched the sustainable finance literature and provided original thinking that may act as a catalyst to improve access to sustainable innovation finance for IP-rich business borrowers, small or large, while achieving society's goals as expressed in the UN 2030 sustainability agenda SDG 9.

---

[154] H.D. Crosse, *Management Policies for Commercial Banks* (1962) Prentice-Hall, Inc.

8. Intellectual property rights, technology development and market dynamics in the renewable energy sector

Inger B. Ørstavik

1. INTRODUCTION

> I'd put my money on the sun and solar energy. What a source of power! I hope we don't have to wait till oil and coal run out before we tackle that.[1]

Almost 90 years after Thomas Alva Edison supposedly said this to his friends and giants of the automotive industry Henry Ford and Harvey Firestone, his vision is becoming a reality. However, immense resources have been invested in developing the capacity to utilize solar photovoltaic (PV) energy, from its first application as an energy source in space, to solar PV plants delivering power into the electric grid at prices competitive to electricity from fossil utilities. The patent system has supported this development, as the primary legal tool of policymakers to incentivize innovation.

Today, the patent system is challenged as sustainability targets and climate change spur policymakers to foster transformative innovations while at the same time supplanting unsustainable practices and technologies.[2] The Brundtland report from 1987 defined 'Sustainability' as the ability to meet the needs of the present without compromising the ability of future generations to meet their needs. In the context of energy, the term points to environmental

---

[1]   James D. Newton, 'Uncommon Friends: Life with Thomas Edison, Henry Ford, Harvey Firestone, Alexis Carrel, & Charles Lindbergh', Harcourt Brace Jovanovich, San Diego, California, USA, 31, describing a conversation between Thomas Edison, Henry Ford and Harvey Firestone taking place in March 1931. Here, the quote is cited for its anecdotal value, rather than for its accuracy.

[2]   See UNCTAD Technology and Innovation Report 2018, available at https://unctad.org/en/PublicationsLibrary/tir2018_en.pdf, accessed 13 October 2020.

sustainability, meaning not harmful to the environment and without depletion of natural resources to support long-term ecological balance. The transition to renewable energy from fossil energy sources is set out in UN Sustainable Development Goal (SDG) number 7, 'affordable and clean energy'. Mass adoption of renewable energy sources, in this chapter the focus is on solar PV, is dependent on a continued innovative process of technology development and deployment, for solar plants to become better, more efficient and cheaper, as well as responding to overreaching calls for sustainability in production of equipment and installations. This chapter looks at the role of the patent system as an incentive mechanism for innovation to support this transition.

A success criterion for the patent system's survival since the early 1800s has been its neutrality to industries and technology applications: it is not designed to drive innovation in some technologies over other technologies, but rather to award innovation regardless of use and application. Thus, the integration of the patent system in climate change mitigation policies is contentious. On the other hand, research shows that environmental policies also encourage innovation.[3] This chapter looks at the role of patent rights in the transition from fossil to renewable energy. In line with the project of this book, the chapter takes a contextual approach to patent rights, focusing on how patent law interacts with and is based upon economic theories on market dynamics. The chapter argues that policies may be structured to strengthen the functions of the patent system for renewable energy technologies over fossil fuel technologies, without requiring material changes to patent law. An integral part of the normative rationale of the patent system is that the exploitation of patent rights will take place within functioning markets. Thus, by aligning energy policies with the normative rationale behind patent rights, the market itself will award sustainable innovation, in the context of this chapter renewable energy technology over fossil energy technology, thereby contributing to sustainable energy markets.

---

[3] Cf. UNEP/EPO, 'Climate Change Mitigation Technologies in Europe – Evidence from Patent and Economic Data', http://documents.epo.org/projects/babylon/eponet .nsf/0/6A51029C350D3C8EC1257F110056B93F/$File/climate_change_mitigation _technologies_europe_en.pdf, accessed 13 October 2020, p. 65 with further references, and Adam B. Jaffe et al., 'A Tale of Two Market Failures: Technology and Environmental Policy', *Ecological Economics*, 54 (2005) 164–176, DOI:10.1016/j .ecolecon.2004.12.027.

2.   THE GAP BETWEEN ENVIRONMENTAL POLICY AND INNOVATION POLICY

In international policy instruments dealing with sustainable development and climate change mitigation, the importance of innovation and technology is highlighted, but there is a screaming silence regarding the main legal instruments for inciting innovation: intellectual property rights (IPRs).[4] Under the UN SDGs, the overall objective of sustainability dictates that renewable energy should replace fossil energy. Clean energy is also a sustainability goal in itself, as per goal number seven. To reach this goal, the UN recommends to increase public and private investments in energy, to focus on the relevant regulatory frameworks and on innovative business models.[5] The link to SDG 9 – industry and innovation – is also apparent.[6] Furthermore, to reach SDG 11, 'sustainable cities and communities', access to renewable energy sources and deployment of renewable energy systems will be required. As IPRs, and patent rights in particular, are the basic tools for policymakers to incentivize investments in R&D, thereby promoting innovation, IPRs will play a role in reaching the UN SDGs, regardless of their mention in the official texts.[7]

The Paris Agreement from 2016, the main international instrument for mitigating climate change on an international level, emphasizes the importance of access to technology, and prescribes a 'Technology Mechanism for Technology Transfer' in Article 10, but without mention of IPRs. Later rounds of negotiations have not yielded results on IPR policy, rather they have reiterated the need for cooperation in R&D and access to technology.[8]

---

[4]   Cf. Matthew Rimmer, 'Beyond the Paris Agreement: Intellectual Property, Innovation Policy, and Climate Justice', *Laws*, 8(1) (2019) 7, 8, DOI:10.3390/laws8010007, on p. 2 with further references, and Chen Zhou, 'Can Intellectual Property Rights within Climate Technology Transfer Work for the UNFCCC and the Paris Agreement?', *Int. Environ. Agreements*, 19 (2019) 107–122.

[5]   Cf. the UN General Assembly resolution 70/1 from 25.09.2015, the 2030 Agenda for Sustainable Development, available at https://sustainabledevelopment.un .org/post2015/transformingourworld, accessed 13 October 2020.

[6]   As highlighted by the Director General of WIPO, Francis Gurry, 'WIPO and the Sustainable Development Goals (SDGs)', 2017, https://www.wipo.int/export/sites/www/about-wipo/en/dgo/speeches/pdf/wipo_sdgs_022017.pdf, accessed 13 October 2020.

[7]   Cf. Hans Morten Haugen, *Chapter 2 of this volume, supra.*

[8]   Hence, the Agenda 21 and the Rio Declaration are still fundamental in facilitating technology transfer to mitigate climate change, cf. Abbe E. L. Brown, 'Intellectual Property and Climate Change', in Rochelle Dreyfuss and Justine Pila (eds), *The Oxford Handbook on Intellectual Property Law*, 2018, DOI:10.1093/oxfordhb/9780198758457 .013.34, available at https://www.oxfordhandbooks.com/view/10.1093/oxfordhb/

Among scholars and policymakers, there is an open discussion on whether and how IPRs can and should play a role in the transition from fossil to renewable energy.[9] One side of the international policy debate concerns access to sustainable technologies for developing countries.[10] The debate is concerned with both whether lower threshold protection should be available to protect local innovation, such as utility patents or design patents, and whether the TRIPS Article 66.2 flexibility should be used more to ensure technology transfer from industrialized to developing countries.[11] Another side of the debate concerns the consequences of the harmonization of important aspects of IP law through the TRIPS Agreement under the WTO framework. The TRIPS/WTO framework rests on the premise that strong intellectual property protection benefits international trade. However, these instruments in themselves may become obstacles for substantial reforms. While their widespread adoption contributes to international markets for innovation and patent rights, they are consensus-based, and radical changes to the treaties require international consensus.[12] Other policy recommendations encourage firms to engage in innovation by protecting their knowledge or to ensure open access to technologies contributing to sustainable development.[13] However, and of importance to the discussion in this chapter, my review of the literature does not suggest a consensus regarding what kind of changes, if any, to the patent system would

---

9780198758457.001.0001/oxfordhb-9780198758457-e-34, accessed 13 October 2020. See Rimmer, fn. 4.

[9] See Matthew Rimmer, 'Chapter 2: The Paris Agreement: Intellectual Property, Technology Transfer, and Climate Change', in Matthew Rimmer (ed.), *Intellectual Property and Clean Energy*, Singapore 2018, 33, DOI:10.1007/978-981-13-2155 -9_2, and Estelle Derclaye, 'Patent Law's Role in the Protection of the Environment – ReAssessing Patent Law and Its Justifications in the 21st Century', *IIC*, 40 (2009) 249.

[10] Only 1% of renewable energy patents are from the southern hemisphere cf. UNCTAD Technology and Innovation Report 2018, fn. 2. Further discussion by Joshua D. Sarnoff, 'Intellectual Property and Climate Change, with an Emphasis on Patents and Technology Transfer', in Cinnamon P. Carlarne et al. (eds), *The Oxford Handbook of International Climate Change Law*, 2016, Chapter 18.

[11] Cf. discussion by Peter Yu, *Chapter 3 of this volume, supra*, and Daniel Gervais, 'Of Clusters and Assumptions: Innovation as Part of a Full TRIPS Implementation', *Fordham L Rev*, 77 (2009) 2353, 2357–2361. See also Ahmed Abdel-Latif, 'Intellectual Property Rights and the Transfer of Climate Change Technologies: Issues, Challenges and Way Forward', *Climate Policy*, 1 (2015) 103–126, DOI:10.1080/14693062.2014 .951919.

[12] See Josef Drexl, 'The Concept of Trade-Relatedness of Intellectual Property Rights in Times of Post-TRIPS Bilateralism', in Hanns Ullrich et al. (eds), *TRIPS plus 20. MPI Studies on Intellectual Property and Competition Law*, 25 (2016) 2.4, DOI:10 .1007/978-3-662-48107-3_2.

[13] UNCTAD Technology and Innovation Report 2018, fn. 2. Cf. also discussion by Catherine Banet, *Chapter 10 of this volume, infra*.

help to promote climate-change-mitigating innovations while supplanting unsustainable innovations.[14]

This chapter suggests how policies aimed at promoting the transition to renewable energy can be more effective if aligned with the normative rationale of the patent system. Such measures are possible without international consensus on radical changes to intellectual property law. In section 3, I discuss how an overreaching coherent approach to innovation and environmental policy is necessary to ensure sustainable markets. The following sections discuss the concrete functions of the patent system in relation to energy policies. Section 4 explores how energy policies may enhance the incentive function of patent law. Section 5 critically discusses variables for policy settings in different markets. Finally, section 6 discusses commercialization of technology with conclusions and policy recommendations in section 7.

3.   THE ROLE OF PATENT MONOPOLY RIGHTS IN SUPPORTING SUSTAINABLE RENEWABLE ENERGY MARKETS

3.1   Externalities of the Patent System

This section looks at the patent system in a wider perspective: how can environmental policy supplement patent law to ensure that both innovation activities and results are sustainable in terms of energy consumption and carbon emissions (3.2)? The discussion concerns the interplay and consistency between industry and innovation policy (patent law) and energy policy.[15] The discussion takes a global perspective, as the renewable energy industry relies on global markets. This must be taken into account in policy settings within national or regional IP and energy law.

---

[14]   See for instance Zhou, fn. 4, 107–122. Brown, fn. 8 *supra*, points out that to overly limit the power of IP protection may reduce the positive effect of IP in inciting innovation and investment in innovation.

[15]   See Sufang Zhang et al., 'Interactions between Renewable Energy Policy and Renewable Energy Industrial Policy: A Critical Analysis of China's Policy Approach to Renewable Energies', *Energy Policy*, 62 (2013) 342–353. They discuss the difference between 'renewable energy policy as policy aimed at promoting the development and deployment of renewable energy, which provides a sustainable and stable domestic renewable energy market', and 'renewable energy industrial policy [which] is defined as policy aimed at enhancing the competitiveness and capability of renewable manufacturing industry' (p. 343). These authors argue that environmental policies should complement aggressive industrial policies in China to drive a change in overall energy consumption towards renewable energy.

A core feature of patent law is that it is technology neutral. The criteria for patentability are not tied to certain technologies or dependent on the application of the invention or its effect on carbon emissions.[16] TRIPS Article 27.1 requires that the invention is novel and represents an inventive step compared to prior technology, but leaves it to the market to sort those inventions that are useful to society from those that do not have a practically useful application.[17] True, reducing energy consumption in a process may suffice to prove an inventive step, but it is not relevant in patent law whether a process patent used in purification of silicon or in wafer production operates with energy from coal or from renewable energy sources. Similarly, issues concerning waste, use of chemicals, materials and recycling of waste and parts fall outside the scope of patent law.[18]

The research question examined in this chapter is whether an overreaching goal of sustainability can or should be part of the patent system. An *ex post* normative rationale for the patent system is that by making information about the invention public, duplication of innovative efforts is avoided, saving costs for society.[19] Thus, innovation in renewable energy technologies is likely to serve as basis for further innovation in renewable energy technologies. To include sustainability, innovative efforts should not only be steered towards 'white spaces' of technology and enhanced towards renewable energy technologies in general. Stronger deterring policies and more nuanced policies might be necessary to ensure sustainability. On the one hand, more or less radical changes to the patent system can be envisaged, such as exceptions from patentability for fossil fuel technology, or diversification of the inventive step

---

[16]   Derclaye, fn. 9, argues that the morality exception as in EPC Article 53(a) incorporates environmental concerns, and could potentially be applied to deny patentability for high-emissions inventions.

[17]   There is a long-standing and still on-going discussion whether patentability should be dependent upon actual social utility of the invention, and not just any utility as in current patent law, cf. Derclaye, fn. 9, with further references, see in particular Friedrich-Karl Beier, 'Future Problems of Patent Law', *IIC*, 3 (1972) 423.

[18]   I revert to some of these concerns when discussing 'green channel' initiatives in section 6.

[19]   Cf. Jay P. Kesan, 'Economic Rationales for the Patent System in Current Context', *Geo.Mason L. Rev.*, 22 (2015) 897, 899–900, 907, Mark A. Lemley, 'The Economics of Improvement in Intellectual Property Law', *Texas Law Review*, 75 (1997) 989, 996, and Stephen P. Maurer, 'Intellectual Property Incentives: Economics and Policy Implications', in Rochelle Dreyfuss and Justine Pila (eds), *The Oxford Handbook of Intellectual Property Law*, 2018, DOI:10.1093/oxfordhb/9780198758457 .013.30, 154–155, citing Edmund Kitch, 'The Nature and Function of the Patent System', *The Journal of Law & Economics*, 20 (1977) 265–290, 278–279.

requirement.[20] However, as many innovations are applicable across different industries, it is very challenging to direct such targeted changes to patent law at technology application. There are initiatives to facilitate patenting of green technology by making the administrative procedures less burdensome for green inventions, so-called 'green channels'. I revert to these initiatives in section 6. On the other hand, energy and environmental policies could serve to increase the expected market value of green energy innovation, as internal production costs come down (for instance by avoiding carbon taxes) and as licensing becomes more attractive. Thus, policies that bring sustainability into the market dynamics will bring sustainability into the incentive function of patent law. The following section discusses how these policies can contribute to markets that support sustainable innovation. The discussion here in section 3 is on a general level, as the following sections provide more detailed analysis of the arguments put forward here.

3.2   Sustainable Markets Depend on Coherence between Environmental Policy and Patent Law

Increased installations of solar PV capacity contribute towards fulfilling SDG 7, affordable and clean energy. However, there is a lack of mechanisms to guarantee that the upstream solar PV industry is low carbon and sustainable. I put forward two arguments: one, that market dynamics are an integrated part of patent law, and two, that policies aimed at affecting the market dynamics so that low carbon emissions is a requirement in downstream as well as upstream markets are likely to provide incitements to innovate within green technologies over high-emissions technologies. As patent law provides incentives to innovate, the market dynamics can enhance the incentives for green technologies and suppress the incentives for high-emissions technologies. A market that demands low emissions technologies both long term and short term, through the industry value chain, may be characterized as a sustainable market.

The solar PV industry provides useful illustration.[21] Solar PV (photovoltaics) generates electricity by converting sunlight into flowing electrons in a semiconductor material, usually high-purity silicon. The production process starts with a chemical process purifying metallurgical grade silicon to high-purity polysilicon. The polysilicon is grown to ingots and sliced into thin wafers, often using diamond saws. From the wafers, solar cells are produced

---

[20]   See Estelle Derclaye, 'Should Patent Law Help Cool the Planet?', *EIPR*, 31 (2009) 168–184 and 227–235.

[21]   The author of this chapter has from 2013 to 2021 been on the board of directors of REC Silicon ASA, a Norwegian-owned company producing high-purity polysilicon for the solar industry from its factory in the USA.

and assembled with inverters to solar modules, which again are installed in industrial energy parks or in domestic systems. Within the solar PV industry, production equipment is standardized, and access to state-of-the-art production equipment enables market entry at all levels of the value chain. The upstream market for high-purity polysilicon consists of a few large producers. There are some barriers to entry, not as a result of patents, as the chemical methods for silicon purification are well known, but because investment lead time is at least three years, sunk costs are high and the process is technology-intensive with a fairly long learning curve.[22] In downstream markets, cell production and module assembly, production is labour-intensive, but sunk costs are lower and the learning time is shorter. Patents do not form barriers to entry, confirmed also by the fact that there is very limited licensing of technology in the PV industry.[23]

Solar PV technologies were first developed in the US for the space industry from the 1950s, and the US was leading in technology development and in installed capacity until the mid-1990s. From 1995, Japan introduced radical subsidies to stimulate technology development and capacity installation, taking a leading role in installation. Following Germany's introduction of feed-in-tariffs in 2000, installations in Germany soared over the following decade. Since 2015, the People's Republic of China (PRC) has taken over as the world's largest producer of solar PV systems, with an international market share of more than 80% in all parts of the manufacturing value chain, slightly lower in the market for high-purity silicon.[24] The growth in China's market share across the solar PV industry corresponds with a sharp increase in renewable energy patenting activities.[25] A closer look at the growth of the PV industry in the PRC shows the lack of overreaching sustainability in an industry that, with its end product, is instrumental in reaching SDG 7, namely

---

[22]   Cf. Arnaud de la Tour et al., 'Innovation and International Technology Transfer: The Case of the Chinese Photovoltaic Industry', *Energy Policy*, 39 (2011) 761–770. The key to purifying silicon at a reasonable cost is the efficiency of the process, by precisely controlling the parameters of the chemical reactions.

[23]   de la Tour et al., *ibid*, 765.

[24]   de la Tour et al., *ibid*, 767. Zhang et al., fn. 15, points out that the underlying policies supporting this development have been industrial policies, and not environmental policies. Condensed information about the solar PV industry in the PRC on https://en.wikipedia.org/wiki/Solar_power_in_China, accessed 21 October 2020.

[25]   Cf. Shweta Khurana and Tapas K. Bandyopadhyay, 'Patenting in Renewable Energy Sector – An Analysis', *Journal of Intellectual Property Rights*, 23 (2018) 44–50, 45 and 48, and Sarah Helm et al., 'Renewable Energy Technology: Evolution and Policy Implications – Evidence from Patent Literature', *WIPO Global Challenges Report*, 2014, https://www.wipo.int/publications/en/details.jsp?id=3891&plang=EN, accessed 21 October 2020.

affordable and clean energy. The PRC still produces most of its energy through coal-fired power plants.[26] Based on the location of the energy-intensive parts of the solar industry, namely in northwestern parts of the PRC, it can be assumed that the solar industry is also fuelled by coal-fired power plants. Although the market has brought about solar panels producing electricity at a cost competitive to fossil fuels, the sustainability of the solar PV industry as such is questionable. The cost-competitiveness of the solar panels drives demand for renewable energy with end-consumers, but the production of panels and upstream products drives demand for fossil energy and increases coal-fuelled carbon emissions.[27] The problem is not unique to the Chinese industry, but is in various forms relevant for all industrial activities within the renewable energy sector. The significance of this point was recognized by policymakers in the PRC in the recently announced pledge that the PRC shall become carbon neutral by 2060.[28]

To tackle this challenge, the immediate or static effects of environmental policies must be balanced against their long-term or dynamic effects. For instance: very high carbon taxes internalize the costs of pollution with the fossil utilities, but is likely to lead to higher costs of electricity, thereby hampering the development of the solar PV industry and the deployment of solar PV power.

The premise for the discussions in this chapter is that innovation and technology development is necessary for a transition from fossil energy to renewable energy. In patent law, the dynamic efficiency of innovation policy is balanced against its static efficiency: to promote innovation, patent law awards an exclusive monopoly right, broadly defined to cover all technologies, for a period of up to 20 years. Exclusivity is balanced by the obligation to publish the knowledge inherent in the invention, and by allowing experimental use of

---

[26] Coal accounts for 2/3 of China's consumed energy (2013), cf. Zhang et al., fn. 15.

[27] In a study from 2012, domestic patenting activities in renewable energy were found to play an important role in CO2 emissions reduction in eastern PRC, but not in central and western parts of the PRC, where large parts of the solar PV industry is located. See Zhaohua Wang et al., 'Energy Technology Patents – CO2 Emissions Nexus: An Empirical Analysis from China', *Energy Policy*, 42 (2012) 248–260. See section 5 for a closer discussion of the role of patents in the various levels of the value chain in the solar PV industry.

[28] China's president Xi Jingping made the announcement during the annual meeting of the United Nations General Assembly, on 22 September 2020, and it was broadly covered in the media. See for instance Steven Lee Myers, 'China's Pledge to Be Carbon Neutral by 2060: What It Means', https://www.nytimes.com/2020/09/23/world/asia/china-climate-change.html, accessed 14 October 2020. It is unclear how China is planning to reach this target.

the invention.[29] Energy policies that only promote renewable energy industry, without addressing the pollution externalities of industry building, risk failing their objectives in the short term.[30] The literature is just beginning to look at how coherence between environmental policies and industry and innovation policies may be key to ensure sustainable markets.[31]

The question is how to correlate environmental policies with innovation policies. Research shows a positive relationship between environmental policies and innovation: firms innovate in order to comply with and compete in a market where environmental policies lead to an internalization of costs related to pollution.[32] Environmental policies lead to more innovation if they are stringent and not differentiated.[33] Innovation policy can lead to a more efficient innovation process, and the incentives to innovate in patent law can be enhanced for 'green' technologies over high emission technologies. This is discussed in more detail in the following sections.

Next, I put forward a few ideas for how some policies might promote a sustainable renewable energy industry. Environmental and trade policies may aim to stimulate demand towards producers who can demonstrate sustainability, for instance by documenting a low carbon footprint. Feed-in-tariffs (FITs) are long-term contracts providing guaranteed grid access and cost-based purchase prices for electricity to promote the dissemination of renewable energy. FITs could be differentiated with a higher tariff for projects demonstrating a low carbon footprint or with a minimum portion of consumed energy from renewable sources. Different quotas could also be structured to prioritize projects or producers who can document a low portion of fossil energy consumption or a low carbon footprint. Energy efficiency and carbon footprint measurements

---

[29]   See for instance The European Patent Convention Article 93 (publication), ref. Article 83 (disclosure of the invention) and Article 127 (European patent register). Examples of exemptions for research or experimental use of the patent in the German Patent Act § 11 No. 2, and the Norwegian Patent Act § 3(3) No. 3, allowed under TRIPS Article 30 and Article 31.

[30]   Critical analysis of Chinese renewable energy policy in Zhang et al., fn. 15.

[31]   Zhang et al., fn. 15.

[32]   Stefan Ambec et al., 'The Porter Hypothesis at 20: Can Environmental Regulation Enhance Innovation and Competitiveness?', *Review of Environmental Economics and Policy*, 2(7) (2013) 2–22, DOI:10.1093/reep/res016, on pages 13–14. See also the UNEP/EPO study, fn. 3.

[33]   Cf. Nick Johnstone et al., 'Environmental Policy Design Characteristics and Technological Innovation: Evidence from Patent Data', *OECD Environment Working Papers No. 16*, 2010, DOI:10.1787/5kmjstwtqwhd-en, accessed 13 October 2020. The study shows a positive effect of stringent, i.e. ambitious or strict, environmental policies on production efficiency and fuel use over time. It also shows that integrated innovation approaches are more efficient than end-of-pipe innovation to decrease the cost of emissions abatement, see pp. 6–7 and 28. See also Jaffe et al., fn. 3.

should be structured to include both energy usage in operation and energy usage in manufacture of products and equipment. In section 4, I will revert to a closer examination of the interrelation between different policy measures and the incentive function in patent law. Section 5 provides an analysis of the impact of policy measures depending on market dynamics and technology maturity. Certification procedures and marks may make such documentation cheaper and more reliable for investors and consumers, discussed more closely in section 6. Generally, the topic needs further research.

When setting targets for renewable energy deployment, these should rather refer to total energy consumption than total installed capacity of solar or wind power.[34] Installation targets may incentivize industry expansion as seen in the Chinese solar PV industry, but, without corresponding targets and initiatives concerning total energy mix that apply specifically to the PV industry, industry expansion is also likely to lead to inefficiencies, most prominently increased demand for fossil energy. In other words, an increase of renewable energy in the downstream energy mix in the Beijing area could thus be partly offset by an increase in consumption of fossil energy in rural areas where the upstream industry is located. In order to balance incentives for industry expansion and innovation with the higher costs of a higher portion of renewable energy in manufacturing, subsidies such as tax incentives and FITs could favour manufacturers who can demonstrate a low carbon footprint or who uses a high portion of renewable energy in production. Whereas a tax incentive can be applied with precision at a desired level of the industry value chain, a carbon footprint measurement will apply cumulatively to the value chain as a whole. FITs will apply to the downstream levels of the industry, i.e. solar PV systems and installation. Renewable energy policies would complement patent policy with the possible effect that innovation efforts are concentrated on lowering energy consumption in manufacturing of parts and inputs to solar panels, or for wind energy, windmills or turbines. Those advances of the production technologies that contribute to a sustainable industry are thereby likely to be preferred over less sustainable solutions already at the R&D stage.

Furthermore, the purchasing power of governments is so large that it can influence market dynamics. Thus, applying performance standards or requiring documentation of a product's environmental properties, for instance its carbon footprint, may contribute to sustainable technology and industry development.[35] Similarly, recycling and lifecycle cost analysis may be required in public bidding, see further discussion in section 6.

---

[34] Chinese environmental policies are moving in this direction cf. Zhang et al., fn. 15.
[35] Cf. Jaffe et al., fn. 3, p. 171.

As discussed, a long-term and dynamic perspective in energy policy would affect the long-term and dynamic functions of patent law. The value of a patent lies in the exclusive right, and thus the incentives to innovate (and patent) are highly dependent on the market for the innovation. Energy policies can impact market dynamics to the effect that the market creates stronger incentives to innovate in sustainable technology, incentives that are included in patent law and policy. Creating a sustainable market would also include sustainability in patent law. In the next section, I will explore in more detail the interrelation between energy and environmental policies and the incentive function in patent law.

4.   THE INCENTIVE TO INNOVATE AND THE DEMAND FOR RENEWABLE ENERGY

4.1   Incentive Theory

Under the public goods theory, IPRs provide incentives for private investment in innovation and creation.[36] The legal right creates an exclusive position not otherwise inherent in knowledge, and provides incentives to invest in innovation at a time when the result of the innovative effort is still uncertain. Under utilitarian law and economics incentive theory, the promise of an exclusive right to exploit significant innovations incentivizes the inventor to invent, and it provides incentives to bring the innovation to market.[37] National and international patent law systems temporarily restrict access to the invention, allowing the innovator to charge a higher price for its use.[38] However, the right holder must make knowledge about the invention available to society through publication of the patent application, allowing competitors to invent around the invention, and allowing further innovation based on the disclosed invention.[39] The overall objective of the patent system is to incentivize technological inno-

---

[36]   See, for example, Maurer, fn. 19, for a broader discussion.

[37]   This is a very brief synopsis of a modern utilitarian law and economics approach, building on the theories of Jeremy Bentham, but incorporating both the public goods theory and economic efficiency theories, see William M. Landes and Richard A. Posner, *The Economic Structure of Intellectual Property Law*, 2003, 295 and 14. See discussion in Ole-Andreas Rognstad, *Property Aspects of Intellectual Property*, 2018, 15–20.

[38]   Cf. Landes and Posner, fn. 37, 20.

[39]   In this regard, the patent right forms a contract between the inventor and society: in exchange for the exclusive patent right, the inventor has to provide information on their invention to society as published in the patent register. This reasoning is supported by property right theories, tracing back to John Locke, cf. Donald S. Chisum et al., *Principles of Patent law: Cases and Materials*, 1998, 35–37.

vation and development. To achieve this, the system must offer both incentives
to invest in innovation, and incentives to disseminate and commercialize
R&D results. In the short term, the dissemination of new technology allows
improved efficiency in the use of existing resources, and in the long term, it
allows new innovation based on the technology. However, the patent system
does not distinguish between different technologies, and the research question
examined in this chapter is if and how an overreaching goal of sustainability
can or should be part of the patent system. This section explores integration of
sustainability in the incentive function in patent law.[40]

The patent system is technology neutral and provides little flexibility to
direct investments towards renewable energy technologies over other technologies. The wide scope of patentable subject matter supports the incentive
function. First, the patent right is available for the results of R&D even though
the inventor might not know what will come out of their efforts when starting
new R&D projects. Second, R&D projects may be broadly defined and still be
able to secure (usually public) funding, as even if the project fails its primary
objective, other results may be patentable and provide sources of licensing
income.

This section 4 discusses more concretely how environmental or energy
policies may affect and possibly diversify the incentives ascribed to patent law
in incentive theories. The question is, given the technology neutrality of patent
law, and the broad nature of the incentive function, could the incentive function also include sustainability? More specifically, how can energy or environmental policies play into the incentive function of patent law to enhance the
incentives to invest in innovation in renewable energy technology and deter the
incentives to invest in fossil energy technology? The idea is that if energy and
environmental policies are aligned with the market-based rationales of patent
law, they may be more effective and efficient.

Patent law is market-based, and the normative rationales of patent law
depend on and closely interrelate with economic theories on competition and
market dynamics.[41] Firstly, investments in R&D are likely to correspond with
expected market demand. Secondly, patent law trusts the market to select
technology winners. Simplified, the market will bring forward those innovations that are beneficial to society, and suppress innovations that do not bring
benefits, as there will be no demand for them. It is obvious that this is only
a theoretical starting point.[42] Here, it suffices to point out that the individual

---

[40]   See also discussion by Derclaye, fn. 9, who argues that the rationales behind
patent law support integration of environmental concerns in patent law.

[41]   See Maurer, fn. 19.

[42]   The neoliberal economic schools, foremost the Chicago school of economic
thought, has most strongly subscribed to theories on the self-regulating market. A dif-

market actors' interests do not align with those of society in general. However, it illustrates that policies aiming at directing innovation towards renewable energy technologies and away from high-emissions technologies should take into account that innovation always takes place within a market context. Policies directed at the market can affect innovation and technology development, primarily by directing demand towards renewable energy technology and away from fossil fuel technology. The following discussion starts with a look at policies directed at the demand side of the market, and their effect on innovation (section 4.2). This analysis gives a basis for discussing policies and measures, including possible modifications to the patent system, that are directed at the technology supply side of the market (section 4.3).

4.2 Policy Measures Creating a 'Demand-Pull' for Innovative Green Energy Technology

4.2.1 Market trends supporting demand for renewable energy

World energy demand is expected to grow over the next 20 years, and the demand for electricity will grow most. The International Energy Agency (IEA) projects that low-carbon sources, especially solar PV and wind, will provide more than half of total electricity generation by 2040.[43] Here, I discuss how market trends and policies can contribute to innovation in renewable energy technologies by creating a demand-pull for innovation.

The energy transition is supported by changes in market dynamics in downstream markets, driven by societal trends spurring consumer demand for renewable energy. Policy measures playing into these changes can be cheap and effective, as they play on societal trends already in progress. Consumers are increasingly demanding that new products are sustainable, utilizing renewable energy over fossil fuels. This trend translates into demand for electric cars and trucks, batteries with capacity for long-range transportation and a sustain-

---

ference in the economic approach to the market may partly explain why radical policy measures to promote a transition to renewable energy were first introduced in political systems more influenced by ordo-liberalist economic theory, advocating more government intervention in the market to ensure competition. The introduction of FITs in Germany, with the Renewable Energy Act in 2000, is explained in this setting by Mishka Lysack, 'Economic and Political Foundations of Effective Transition to Renewable Energy: Ordoliberalism, Polianyi, and Cities as Hubs for Climate Leadership and Innovation', *Renewable Energy*, 2019, 3–37, DOI:10.1007/978-3-030 -14207-0_1. For the discussion in this chapter, it suffices to establish the interlinkage between patent law and market theory. Closer analysis of the relative effects of such policies would benefit from a sounder theoretical basis in market economics.

[43] Cf. IEA World Energy Outlook 2019, https://www.iea.org/weo2019/, accessed 13 October 2020.

able energy profile in homes. Consumers are asking for these products before the technology to support them is developed, contributing to a demand-pull for innovation in green energy technologies. When market demand is proven at the time of investment in R&D, investments in groundbreaking innovation are more likely, as financial risk is lower. This trend is observable in the on-going race for battery technology development.[44] The shift in consumer demand also means that future demand for unsustainable products is uncertain, and to minimize risk, investors are increasingly requiring that the companies they invest in can demonstrate a controlled or decreasing carbon footprint or otherwise to adhere to climate change mitigation policies. Such trends contribute to push production companies to switch to renewable energy sources to support production, and can stimulate investments in more efficient production methods. Policymakers and stakeholders can facilitate such changes by awarding improvements in corporate disclosure and reporting of results.[45] However, as such trends and measures address companies with already high sunk costs, they might not in themselves spur investments in groundbreaking innovation.

Another important market trend is that consumers are actively participating in electricity markets, evolving into 'prosumers', delivering excess energy from their local solar panels into the electric grid. This trend, combined with the demand from authorities and consumers for a more efficient grid adapted to efficient use of renewable energy, spurs investments in the grid itself. The grid becomes smarter, and uses digitization and sensor technology to heighten energy efficiency. The smart grid can accommodate a higher ratio of wind and solar power: as these sources are susceptible to weather changes and daylight, energy in the grid must be balanced accurately to maximize renewable energy while maintaining an efficient supplement of energy from fossil utilities. Employing two- or multi-sided business models in energy distribution allows more flexibility and variation in energy sources – to the benefit of renewable energy. Thus, policies contributing to the 'smart' grid, will also improve market access for renewable energy. The 'smart grid' has high priority among policymakers, cf. EU renewable energy directive, (EU) 2018/2001.[46] It con-

---

[44] The EPO recently published a study of patenting activity within batteries and energy storage, see http://documents.epo.org/projects/babylon/eponet.nsf/0/969395F58EB07213C12585E7002C7046/$FILE/battery_study_en.pdf, accessed 20 October 2020. The study show an annual increase in patenting in energy storage of 14% since 2005.

[45] An example of private stakeholder influence is how the London Stock Exchange has set up a Green Bonds Market, where investors may invest through green bonds, financing companies that fulfil certain sustainability requirements, cf. https://www.lseg.com/green, accessed 13 October 2020.

[46] Directive (EU) 2018/2001 of the European Parliament and of the Council of 11 December 2018 on the promotion of the use of energy from renewable sources.

tains measures such as rights for 'prosumers' to deliver electricity into the grid, cf. Article 21.

4.2.2 Policy measures directed at the demand side of the market

When policies are aimed at the demand side of the market, they can stimulate investments in innovation as they mitigate the riskiness of investment and expand the market size for renewable energy.[47] It may be assumed that the possibility of patent protection for R&D results is more important the riskier the investment. Investment risk depends, among other things, on the amount of capital required, the likelihood of success and the time from project initiation to market. While demand-side incentives generally can be assumed to stimulate innovation, they are likely to have a stronger effect for technology that is already in the market or close to market, thus first enhancing the incentive to commercialize. Economic research concerning the effect of FITs has called into question the efficiency of such measures when it comes to incentivizing groundbreaking innovation.[48] Spain and Germany have experienced a rapid increase in installed solar PV capacity as a result of FITs. FITs allow renewable energy to be distributed at the same price to consumers as energy from fossil utilities, while still covering the costs of the renewable power producers. By creating a powerful incentive to install solar PV to offer energy to the end-market, these price-based policy instruments have been shown to increase efficiency in production and learning-by-doing.[49] For renewable energy technologies that are close to competitive with utilities, broader market-based policy measures stimulating market activities may be effective to improve their competitiveness. The mentioned study also shows a massive increase in installed solar PV capacity over the same period. In general, creating a demand-pull may be effective to stimulate smaller scale innovation and increased efficiency, and as renewable energy technologies are becoming closer to competitive on price, less expensive policy measures may have a sufficient effect on demand to stimulate further follow-on innovation. For solar PV and offshore wind, FITs might soon no longer be necessary, and they could be substituted with cheaper measures, such as green certificates, guaranteed market access for small energy producers (and 'prosumers'), grid regulations, quotas, requirements in public bidding etc., and still stimulate innovation and increased competitiveness.

---

[47] See also Jaffe et al., fn. 3. A review of research examining the effects of environmental policy on innovation in UNEP/EPO report, fn.3.

[48] Christoph Böhringer et al., 'The Impact of the German Feed-in Tariff Scheme on Innovation: Evidence Based on Patent Filings in Renewable Energy Technologies', *Energy Economics*, 67 (2017) 545–553, with further references.

[49] Böhringer et al., *ibid.*, 546.

Demand-side policies, such as FITs, are attractive from a policymaker perspective, because they yield fast and solid results, i.e. a rapid increase in installed solar PV or wind capacity. When guaranteed a minimum price over a long time, the incentive to commercialize technology and enter the market is strong, as is the incentive for producers already in the market or close to market to invest in learning-by-doing and small scale innovation to bring down production costs thus increasing margins. To stimulate groundbreaking innovation, however, it appears to be necessary to create stronger incentives to innovate in the technology supply side of the market, i.e. to create a technology-pull. This may be better achieved by policies directed at R&D activities, or at least policies that are stable enough to provide the long-term certainty that is necessary to take on the risk inherent in investments in groundbreaking innovation.[50] FITs that need annual or regular confirmation under national law on taxation or public spending are therefore not likely to sufficiently incentivize long-term investments in bringing forward groundbreaking technology where the outcome of R&D is uncertain.[51]

4.3   Policy Measures Stimulating Innovation through the Supply Side

Production of renewable energy is based on a traditional value chain, using known methods, but there are still areas where the industry is searching for groundbreaking solutions to technology challenges. Within battery technology, a large number of initiatives are engaged in a wide search for more efficient energy storage, spanning various technologies. The risk with investing in groundbreaking R&D is higher than when investing in technology improvements closer to the final product for two main reasons: the outcome of R&D efforts is uncertain, and the lead time is long, even for successful initiatives.

---

[50]   Cf. Johnstone et al., fn. 33, and Antoine Dechezleprêtre et al., 'Climate Change Policy, Innovation and Growth', *Grantham Research Institute Policy Brief*, 2016, http://www.lse.ac.uk/GranthamInstitute/publication/climate-change-policy-innovation-and-growth/, accessed 21 October 2020.

[51]   See Kenneth Arrow, 'Economic Welfare and the Allocation of Resources for Invention', in *The Rate and Direction of Inventive Activity: Economic and Social Factors*, 1962, 610–614, 609. Arrow argued that risk aversion would result in under-investment in innovation, as there is an inherent risk with R&D that it is not successful. To incentivize investment, the risk must be mitigated sufficiently to reward the investment long enough to give a comparable return on the investment, and the policy must be in place at the time the invention is brought to market, not only at the time of investment. Thus, policies should take into account both the timing of investments and the timing of expected returns.

Policies that can contribute to mitigate these risks may provide incentives to invest in groundbreaking innovation.

As discussed above, demand-side incentives are likely not sufficient to create incentives for groundbreaking innovation. Measures directed at the supply side, i.e. the technology side, may directly contribute to making investments in certain R&D more attractive by ensuring that the returns on the investments are higher than what the financial market would offer. Such measures can be tax incentives, public research or access to public funding.[52] These measures lower the costs of investment, thus lowering risk. Within solar energy, there are differences between national policies. In the US, tax incentives are frequently used, whereas the PRC has rather used publicly funded research, evidenced by public research institutions being among the largest patent holders.[53]

Environmental policies have been shown to have a positive effect on innovation, as companies look for new technology in response to stringent environmental policies.[54] However, policies must be technology neutral and flexible so as not to create lock-in effects or inefficiencies such as duplicated efforts.[55] Technology neutrality is a core feature of the patent system. To incentivize innovation in renewable technologies over other technologies, policies should therefore be more effective if they maintain the neutrality of the patent system as to the technological solutions resulting from R&D, and avoid policies that lock in technology, such as technological standards.[56]

The following discussion looks at ideas for aligning environmental policy with patent law incentive policy. Patent law awards new and inventive solutions to technical problems. Interacting with environmental policies, the award for the innovative effort is already a function of patent law, but environmental policies may induce innovators to prioritize problems within renewable energy technology rather than in fossil technology, and to solve them by sustainable means. Such policies could be either incentive drivers or deterrents.

Drivers can be funding for R&D in renewable energy technologies in particular, co-funding, public research, tax incentives etc.[57] Tax incentives and

---

[52]   Sarnoff, fn. 10, highlights the need for publicly funded research within the market-driven approach to technology in the UN legal framework.

[53]   See Helm et al., fn. 25, 26.

[54]   Ambec et al., fn. 32, on pp. 13–14, Johnstone et al., fn. 33, 6–7, and Dechezleprêtre et al., fn. 50, 2.

[55]   Johnstone et al., fn. 33, 7.

[56]   Cf. also Böhringer et al., fn. 48, arguing that broad stimuli that are not technology-specific will provide better incentives to invest in more groundbreaking innovation.

[57]   Jaffe et al., fn. 3, 170.

R&D funding can be narrowly designed to benefit specific research projects.[58] It is possible to specifically target problems relevant to renewable energy technology and require that solutions are sustainable without being overly specific with regards to R&D outcome.

Measures can also be designed to deter innovation in fossil energy technologies. Such deterrents can be further exceptions from patentability, like the existing exceptions for medical therapeutic methods or for human embryos.[59] The literature has proposed a number of changes to the patent system, such as applying a lower threshold for the inventive step for green technologies or exceptions from the exclusive right for green applications of patented technology.[60] However, all such changes require that the balance between the patent holder's exclusive right and the benefits of patent protection to society, herein the incentive function of patent rights, is struck anew. It is difficult to strike a balance that restricts the incentive function of the exclusive right but does not lead to wide dissemination and use of unsustainable technologies due to the cost–benefit with free access to non-patentable innovation.[61] To supplant innovation in high-emissions technologies, policies that deter investments in unsustainable technologies, and can be designed independently of this internal balance in patent law, may be better. Such measures can be environmental policies that restrict the use of carbon fuel, tax incentives such as emissions taxes, or emission caps, certificates and certificate trading, which will increase the costs related to new technology in fossil energy manufacturing compared to renewable energy technologies.[62] In the next section, I will look at how policies may be adapted to the varying market dynamics in different markets within the solar PV value chain.

---

[58]   Jaffe et al., fn. 3, 170.
[59]   Cf. The European Patent Convention, Directive 98/44/EC, Article 53 on the legal protection of biotechnological inventions, Article 6 and ECJ ruling in case C-34/10, *Brüstle*. The TRIPS Agreement Article 27 allows member states to deny patents to inventions whose commercial exploitation would be contrary to *ordre public* and to morality. Scholars have advocated that these exceptions could be developed to avoid patent protection as an incentive for innovation in oil and gas, and to ensure that patents are granted to sustainable technologies only if they meet current environmental standards, ref. Derclaye, fn. 20, and Brown, fn. 8, section 5.2.3 with further references.
[60]   Brown, fn. 8, section 5.2.3 with further references.
[61]   Cf. Derclaye, fn. 20, 231.
[62]   Ref. also Dechezleprêtre et al., fn. 50.

5.　THE COMPETITIVE IMPACT OF PATENT RIGHTS IN DIFFERENT MARKETS

5.1　Incentive Theory and Market Structure

Investing in R&D is risky, as there is risk relating to the market penetration and success of the new technology, risk of competing innovation and risk concerning the profitability of the innovation. Companies perceive the risk as high since new and innovative technology might become obsolete before the costs with developing it have been recovered, following Schumpeter's theory of 'creative destruction'.[63] As the exclusivity of patent protection enables a higher price than in a perfectly competitive market, it mitigates the risk of innovation, thereby contributing to incentivize innovation.[64] Schumpeter's theory is that a monopoly or a highly concentrated market presents the best conditions for promoting innovation.[65] The incentive to innovate follows from the anticipation of a period of increased market power, achieved through either patent exclusivity, barriers to entry or vertical integration.

Depending on the market, the incentives work differently. In markets where innovation takes large leaps, market challengers are likely to have the best incentives to innovate, as they will take over the leading position in the market with a successful innovation. In less innovative markets, competition on innovation will be similar to price competition, and the market leader or monopolist will have the best incentives to innovate, as they will maintain a leading position, whereas smaller agents will only achieve a small increase in profitability. Markets for mature technology can develop into a segmented market, where a few large companies form a top end of high quality producers, who invest more in R&D to develop significant, if not groundbreaking, technology. In solar PV, the top four producers of solar panels are all Chinese companies.[66] The smaller market actors would spend less money on R&D, innovating to reduce production costs, thereby increasing profits. Thus, the low end of the market would consist of a large number of low-cost, but low(er)

---

[63]　Joseph Schumpeter, *Capitalism, Socialism and Democracy*, 3, London reprint 1994, Impression, 81.

[64]　Cf. Kesan, fn. 19. The patent does not grant market power in itself, but its attributes are such that it can give basis for market power if the technology is successful in the market, cf. Lemley, fn. 19, 989, 996.

[65]　Significant literature challenges Schumpeter's theory regarding the concentrated market, arguing that more competition will lead to more innovation, referred in Kesan, fn. 19, 900.

[66]　Jinko Solar, JA Solar, Trina Solar and LONGi Solar (2019) cf. https://en.wikipedia.org/wiki/List_of_photovoltaics_companies, accessed 27 October 2020.

quality producers. The PRC dominates the downstream solar PV industry, and the low-end producers are serving mostly the Chinese domestic market.

In section 5.2, I discuss the different market dynamics in upstream and downstream markets, using solar PV as an example. In section 5.3, I explore the interrelation between technology maturity, cost development and patent activity. The overreaching question is how policies may be aligned with the incentive function of patent rights to promote the transition to renewable energy, as per SDG 7.

5.2   Patent Rights in Upstream vs. Downstream Markets

Production of renewable energy, such as solar, wind and hydro, is based on a traditional value chain, where the equipment is produced through refinement of hardware (silicon, cells and panels for solar PV), but using known chemical and physical processes. Consequently, patent protection is only available for components or intermediate goods, and the final product is not subject to a single patent that grants market monopoly.[67] This is different from other markets. In pharmaceutical markets, patent protection is available to the active substance in itself, thus granting market exclusivity in the downstream market, enabling high prices and representing a high barrier to market entry for the term of the patent. In telecommunication markets, on the other hand, patents are available for small components, and in combination with the network effects of technology standardization (such as the 3G or 4G standards), the upstream patents enable high licence fees putting upwards pressure on prices in downstream markets.

A common denominator in renewable energy technologies is that although patent rights confer competitive advantages and represent concretized value to investors, patent rights do not confer market dominance or exclusivity in any part of the value chain.[68] Competition on innovation is likely to focus on learning-by-doing and smaller innovative steps to reduce costs and improve production quality and efficiency. This sharply contrasts pharma markets where competition on innovation takes the form of a race for the active substance, and telecom markets where competition on innovation is concentrated on patenting very small inventive steps. Although there are differences between renewable energy technologies – in wind turbine technology, for example, there are very valuable patents – many new solutions in renewable

---

[67]   For the wind sector, cf. Jacob Funk Kirkegaard et al., 'It Should Be a Breeze: Harnessing the Potential of Open Trade and Investment Flows in the Wind Energy Industry', *Peterson Institute for International Economics Working Paper No. 09-14*, available at http://ssrn.com/abstract=1521651, accessed 21 October 2020, pp. 27–28.

[68]   See de la Tour et al., fn. 22, 763.

energy technologies are likely to be off-patent and rather kept secret. Patenting of small innovative steps is less attractive, as the publication of the patent can help competitors invent around the patent.

The question discussed here is whether and how policies to promote innovation within renewable energy technologies can be more effective if the dynamics of competition on innovation in the relevant market are taken into account.

The emergence of China as the dominating country in the solar PV industry over a very short period illustrates how public policy can spur industry development, especially if it is adapted to market dynamics.[69] The growth in China's market share across the solar PV industry corresponds with a sharp increase in renewable energy patenting activities.[70] Research suggests that this is not only a result of market induced private innovation, but that the underlying industry development is spurred by state policies supporting technology development and patenting.[71] In the downstream markets, policies have included aggressive installation targets and generous FITs for installed PV capacity. This has ensured Chinese producers' entry in and later dominance of the downstream market for cell production and module assembly. Although the first developed parts of the value chain were the downstream segments, a study from 2009 shows that innovation activity was higher in upstream markets (silicon and ingots/wafer manufacturing) than in the downstream markets for cell production and module assembly.[72] Innovation, especially in the downstream segments, was found to be carried out directly on the production lines and not in specialized R&D departments, and protected by secrecy rather than patenting.[73] This illustrates that market-based policies to increase demand, such as FITs and installation targets, may quickly contribute to market entry and smaller step innovations in the downstream markets, confirming the findings in section 4.2 above.

The PRC's entry in the upstream industry segments – silicone purification and cell/wafer production – has been slower, and only subsequent to the establishment of a broad downstream market, consisting of a large number of panel producers. Hence, the policies stimulating end-market demand, FITs and

---

[69] Overview of Chinese legal framework and policies in the energy sector in Lina Yan, 'China Energy Efficiency Report', *International Energy Charter*, 2019, 52–68, available at https://www.energycharter.org/fileadmin/DocumentsMedia/EERR/EER -China_ENG.pdf, accessed 21 October 2020.

[70] Cf. Khurana and Bandyopadhyay, fn. 25, 45 and 48, and Helm et al., fn. 25.

[71] See Khurana and Bandyopadhyay, fn. 25, 45, who point to four factors to explain the high patenting frequency in China in this sector: (1) China has a big market and low production costs; (2) China offers patent prosecution and grant; (3) there is a high probability of technology infringement in China; and (4) state policies support patenting.

[72] de la Tour et al., fn. 22, 766.

[73] de la Tour et al., fn. 22, 767.

installation targets, may likely have had an indirect positive effect on development in the upstream industry, as the establishment of a downstream industry promises an offtake for cells/wafers and polysilicon that induces long-term investments and innovation in these segments, as described in section 3.2.

The upstream market is much more concentrated, but more innovative than the downstream markets. The high patenting rate in silicon and cells/wafers up to 2009 shows massive investments in technology development. A significant portion of the patenting activity has been through public research organizations, confirming that this effort to gain market share in the upstream market is also a result of public policies supporting R&D and patenting.[74] This would align with the findings in section 4.3 above: as investments in polysilicon purification, cells and wafers have a long lead time, investments in these segments carry high risk. Policies that mitigate this risk, government funded R&D, long-term tax incentives or subsidized R&D, would be more likely to stimulate investments in these segments than demand-side stimuli.[75]

Finally, the example of the Chinese solar PV industry shows that policymakers should consider the market structure. In the downstream part of the industry, solar panels and installation, barriers to entry are low, there is a high number of market participants, and innovation takes small leaps. Policies to stimulate development in these segments can be directed at the demand-side of the market, such as FITs or quotas. They do not need to be very long term, as the objective is to incentivize investments in optimizing production methods and use of materials to reduce costs and in making solar power more competitive. A competitive market with many suppliers is likely to present the best landscape for gradual improvement of production processes to achieve better price competitiveness, ref. 5.1 above. As for the upstream part of the industry, silicon purification and cells/wafers, the investment lead time for production facilities form high barriers to market entry. In more capital-intensive segments, when investment risk is high due to the lead time, a concentrated market might present better conditions for investments in technology.

---

[74]   In 2011, the Chinese operators were just entering the top 20 technology holders in solar PV, measured in patenting activity. There are variations between renewable energy technologies. In wind technologies, universities and public sector research institutions are not among the top technology owners. Ref. Helm et al., fn. 25, and Zhang et al., fn. 15.

[75]   Cf. Jaffe et al., fn. 3, 170.

5.3   Technology Maturity and Energy Cost Development

Renewable energy technologies are maturing, and in some areas, patent land-scaping analyses show that they have reached a very high level of maturity.[76] As the technologies mature, both innovation and patenting activities as well as market dynamics change. Most notably, the price comes down, increasing market penetration and market share for renewable energy, and competition becomes cost-driven rather than technology-driven.[77] Patenting activity for both solar PV and wind peaked in 2011–2012, and as patenting activities have receded over the last decade, the comparative price for electricity for solar PV and wind has come down to a range that is competitive with fossil energy.[78]

For mature technologies, innovating activities are likely to be concentrated on follow-on innovations, i.e. innovations that improve on existing technology.[79] If the improvement makes use of the teachings of an existing patent, the consent of the original patent holder is necessary to use it. This has two implications: first, in-house improvements are less likely to be patented but rather kept secret as the exclusive right conferred by the original patent also controls the improvement, and by patenting the improvement, it is disclosed to the public.[80] Second, external improvers need a licence to the original patent to use the improved technology, and licence fees add costs to technology diffusion.[81] Follow-on innovation is thus likely to drive down costs, but less likely to drive technology dissemination.

To promote the competitiveness of mature renewable energy technologies to supplant fossil technologies, it follows from the discussion hereto that policies may be short term and directed at the demand side. FITs and quotas have been effective to overcome a price disadvantage, and can be substituted with less

---

[76]   Khurana et al., fn. 25, have found that patenting activity was most intense in 2009–2011, indicating maximum research activity during 2008–2013. Earlier land-scaping analysis saw exponential growth in patenting activities in 2006–2011 compared to the previous 30 years (24% average annual growth in CCMTs as opposed to a 6% global average for all technologies), ref. Helm et al., fn. 25.

[77]   Ref. Khurana et al., fn. 25, 46.

[78]   The price drop has been most dramatic for solar PV, with a drop of 50% in 2011 alone, ref. Helm et al., fn. 25.

[79]   Cf. Kilian Raiser et al., 'Corporization of the Climate? Innovation, Intellectual Property Rights, and Patents for Climate Change Mitigation', *Energy Research & Social Science*, 27 (2017) 1–8, 5, with further references.

[80]   It means also that high concentration of technology ownership is indicative of a mature technology, as only the large owners will have incentives to patent innovation. One example is wind technology cf. Helm et al., fn. 25.

[81]   Cf. Raiser et al., fn. 79, 4.

expensive measures such as 'prosumer' rights, public bidding requirements and quotas as price parity is achieved.

However, some parts of the renewable energy industry still face very high technology risk due to the immaturity of the technologies. One example is battery technology, where current solutions are insufficient for long-term high capacity storage, and there is a race for new and groundbreaking solutions. In the search for groundbreaking technology, the technology risk is very high.[82] Similarly, biofuel technology is lagging behind other climate change mitigation technologies (CCMTs), evidenced by the large number of public research institutions among the top technology owners.[83] Another example is developments of the 'smart' grid, as the network effects are very strong. As the technical qualities of the grid must be standardized, there is a high risk that new technology will not be adopted. When technology risk is high, incentives must be strong enough for the companies to carry the risk that a successful innovation still does not reach the market.

In these industries, IPRs may play a more important role. A patent right will confer an exclusive right, and for emerging technologies such as battery technology, it is more likely that the exclusive right will translate to an exclusive market position than in more mature industries.[84] To stimulate ground-breaking innovation, policies directed at the demand-side of the downstream market might not be sufficient, as discussed under 4.2 above. For instance, tax incentives to promote consumers purchasing electric trucks over combustion engine trucks can incentivize smaller investments to improve production and distribution of electric cars, but may have only a limited effect on the incentives to invest in groundbreaking battery technology. To spur investments in developing groundbreaking battery technology, policies should be long term and contribute to a technology-push, such as R&D subsidies, investment tax incentives, or publicly funded R&D.[85]

---

[82]   Following the theory of 'creative destruction' ref. Schumpeter, it is likely that the first groundbreaking technology developed that answers to demand (long-distance truck transportation or night-time electricity supply off-grid) will be the market winner. Whether there also will be network effects is unknown, as the winning technology has not been identified yet.

[83]   Cf. Helm et al., fn. 25.

[84]   See Kitch, fn. 19, 265–290, discussed below.

[85]   Cf. Dechezleprêtre et al., fn. 50.

6.   THE INCENTIVE TO COMMERCIALIZE AND 'SOFT' GREEN-TECH POLICY INITIATIVES

6.1   The *Ex Post* Rationales of Patent Law: Incentive to Commercialize

To facilitate a transition to renewable energy, renewable energy technology innovations must be distributed and applied. Connected to the normative rationales of patent law: the patent right should have such characteristics that it not only incentivizes innovation *ex ante*, but also incentivizes the commercialization of the innovation *ex post*.[86] To attract investors to bring the invention to market, the incentives are stronger if the patent right is a safe and easily transferable object of investment.[87] Thus, characteristics that bring down transaction costs contribute to the incentive to commercialize. A characteristic of the patent system is its transparency concerning who owns the patent, the scope of the invention and who invented it. When this information is public through registration of the patent, it helps establish a market for the invention and brings down transaction costs, as licensing or transferring the rights does not increase the risk of misappropriation, and as the rightful owner can be easily traced.[88] Patent documents are standardized, largely on an international level, and they are therefore known to investors.[89] The question discussed here is how so-called 'soft' green-tech policy measures can enhance the incentive to commercialize renewable energy technologies over fossil energy technologies.

6.2   The Impact of 'Soft' Green-Tech Policy Initiatives

Intellectual property institutions have initiated policies to CCMTs,[90] designed to work within the current regulatory regime of patent law. These initiatives seek to enhance the visibility of green technology patents and ease promotion of green technology. As such, they can be termed 'soft' initiatives. I discuss

---

[86]   See F. Scott Kieff, 'Property Rights and Property Rules for Commercializing Inventions', *Minn. L. Rev.*, 85 (2001) 697, 707–712; Landes and Posner, fn. 37, 295 and 14; Kitch, fn. 19, 265–290.

[87]   In bringing the invention to market, Jaffe et al., fn. 3, show that the involvement of industry in government funded research is more likely to lead to commercial success and bringing the innovation to market.

[88]   Cf. Landes and Posner, fn. 37, 328–330 and Kesan, fn. 19, 904–905, with further references.

[89]   Kesan, fn. 19, 909.

[90]   Climate change mitigation technologies include renewable energy technologies as well as carbon capture and storage.

only a selection of initiatives to illustrate how they relate to the normative rationale of patent law.

The European Patent Office (EPO) is tagging inventions within CCMTs with certain codes, Y02/Y04.[91] This highlighting of CCMTs enables better patent landscaping and technology analysis. The codes are searchable in the EPO database, thus enabling data mining and making statistical and mathematical data on patents and technologies readily available. WIPO's international patent classification system (IPC) also includes a green inventory that categorizes patents in a similar nomenclature for green technologies.[92]

'Soft' initiatives may play into the commercialization function of patent law. First, the tagging enhances the visibility of existing technology, ensuring against duplicated efforts and promotes dissemination of information about green technologies. Second, the tagging as green technology can help attract investors, as more investors are seeking sustainable investment opportunities and the EPO or WIPO codes are objective and standardized, adding credibility to the classification.[93] Especially for smaller businesses and start-ups, for whom patenting is important in securing funding, the coding may enhance the value of their patents.[94] Lastly, this increased visibility of the patent and innovation landscape gives a better basis for designing other policies.[95]

---

[91] See V. Veefkind et al., 'A New EPO Classification Scheme for Climate Change Mitigation Technologies', *World Patent Information*, 23 (2012) 106–111. Climate change mitigation technologies includes carbon-capture and -storage technologies, which are not discussed in detail here.

[92] Some national intellectual property authorities have put in place measures to fast-track patent applications within green technologies, see Antoine Dechezleprêtre, 'Fast-tracking Green Patent Applications: An Empirical Analysis', *CTSD Programme on Innovation, Technology and Intellectual Property*, Issue Paper No. 37, available at https://www.lse.ac.uk/GranthamInstitute/wp-content/uploads/2014/02/WP107-fast-tracking-green-patent-applications.pdf, accessed 21 October 2020. These measures may reduce patenting costs and contribute to technology dissemination, especially if combined with earlier publication.

[93] Cf. Morgan Stanley's survey from 2017, 'Sustainable Signals', available at https://www.morganstanley.com/pub/content/dam/msdotcom/ideas/sustainable-signals/pdf/Sustainable_Signals_Whitepaper.pdf, accessed 21 October 2020.

[94] A study from 2008 revealed that start-ups and entrepreneurs tend to see patent rights as a means to attract investors, and not as an incentive for innovating. Cf. Stuart J. H. Graham et al., 'High Technology Entrepreneurs and the Patent System: Results of the 2008 Berkeley Patent Survey', *Berkeley Technology Law Journal*, 24 (2009), 1255–1327.

[95] Cf. Helm et al., fn. 25. See also EPO and NIPO 'Green Technologies and Renewable Energies – Innovating and Patenting', Proceedings of the conference 20 November 2018, available at https://www.patentstyret.no/globalassets/om-oss/rapporter/green_technologies_renewable_energies_oslo_nov2018_conference_report.pdf, accessed 21 October 2020. Analysis of patent data in UNEP/EPO report, fn. 3.

Other initiatives from international organizations are not directly tied in with the patent system.[96] The WIPO GREEN initiative is a database and a network to enable connections between technology and service providers from both public and private sectors. Based on the United Nations Framework Convention on Climate Change (UNFCCC), the UNFCCC Climate Technology Centre and Network is a UN initiative to promote technology transfer as set out in the Paris Agreement.[97] These initiatives can facilitate technology licensing where the market fails to do so, and can promote technology dissemination from developed countries in the Northern hemisphere to developing countries in the south.[98]

In bringing the technology to the market, patent law borders on trademark law, and eco-labelling and certification schemes may communicate with consumers to ease commercialization from the demand side of the market. Especially certification marks may be suitable to highlight those properties of a product that are relevant to climate change mitigation, for instance the product's carbon footprint.[99]

7.   CONCLUSIONS

In this chapter, I have explored whether an overreaching goal of sustainability can or should be included in the patent system. In result, I have argued for better coherence between environmental policy and innovation policy as a path forward in fulfilling SDG 7 'affordable and clean energy', as per the call for action in the 2030 Agenda for Sustainable Development.[100] While patent law is the main instrument of policymakers to incentivize innovation, the patent system has shortcomings when it comes to prioritizing green technology over unsustainable technologies. As discussed above, research shows a positive

---

See also patent landscaping analysis done by the Canadian Intellectual Property Office in 2017, available at https://www.ic.gc.ca/eic/site/cipointernet-internetopic.nsf/eng/h _wr04289.html, accessed 21 October 2020.

[96]   Broad discussion by Abdel-Latif, fn. 11, 103–126, DOI:10.1080/14693062.2014 .951919.

[97]   Cf. Rimmer, fn. 4. Rimmer also discusses other technology networks and alliances.

[98]   Cf. discussion by Sarnoff, fn. 10.

[99]   Cf. EUD in C-317/2019 (Öko-test), showing that it was not a trademark infringement to use the trademark Öko-test with test result 'very good' for a product for which the trademark was not registered. The protection for a well-known trademark that is independent of product categories was still open, but it was clear that protection for a mark for an eco-test service would be much stronger if the service provider had chosen a certification mark.

[100]   Gurry, fn. 6.

relationship between environmental policies and innovation: firms innovate in order to comply with and compete in a market where environmental policies lead to an internalization of costs related to pollution.[101] The positive effect on innovation is stronger if environmental policies are stringent and not differentiated.[102] Environmental policies may be aligned with patent law and policy to more effectively promote development of renewable energy technologies. It is important to maintain the openness of the patent system towards R&D results, and its neutrality towards technologies – as also renewable energy technologies are dynamic. If policymakers supplement patent law with policies that align with the normative rationale of the patent system, they may strengthen the functions of the patent system to work better for renewable energy innovation than fossil fuel innovation. Carbon taxes or carbon footprint measures are likely to roll back in the industry, dissuading innovation in high-emissions technologies, and to promote innovation that contributes to a lower carbon footprint. A diversification of policies, aligning with the economic theory concerning competition and the market, might be necessary to incentivize both learning-by-doing and improved production efficiency as a response to environmental policies or demand-pull incentive policies such as feed-in-tariffs, but also groundbreaking innovation as a response to technology-push incentives, such as tax incentives or R&D funding. Whereas fundamental changes to patent law may be difficult because of the integration of patent law in the TRIPS Agreement under WTO, 'soft' initiatives, such as 'green channels' or WIPO green, may contribute to the role of 'green' patents in securing funding for green technology R&D, as they play into the *ex post* rationale of patent law.

As patent law is market-based, market dynamics and technology maturity have a significant impact on the incentives for innovation and the risks connected with innovation in different markets. Careful analysis of market dynamics, industry development and investment risks and lead time can be very important to balance effective policies within the different renewable energy industries. By looking closely at the solar PV industry, this chapter has shown that the normative rationales of patent law, together with market economics, might provide a basis for designing policies that play into the market dynamics, contributing to sustainable markets for renewable energy.

Finally, the chapter has pointed to the problem of externalities of the technology neutrality of patent law. Patent law does not discriminate between innovative activities in renewable energy technologies and fossil technologies. Patent law struggles to handle the externalities of bringing inventions to market, illustrated by the problem of the solar PV industry relying heavily

---

[101]   See section 3.2 and references in fns. 32 and 33.
[102]   *Ibid.*

on coal-fired utilities to supply electricity for production. These externalities occur as patent law interacts with market dynamics. Policies that affect market dynamics are therefore also likely to affect innovation. This chapter has aimed to rationalize and operationalize coherence between patent law and energy or environmental policies under the concept of sustainable markets. Sensible directions for policy orientation have been offered from an interdisciplinary perspective with the aim of contributing to and shaping the debate and signposting future topics for research.

9. Smart Grid standards development and patent protection in the United States: striking the balance between dramatic overhaul of the electric grid and encouragement of innovation

Joel B. Eisen and Kristen Jakobsen Osenga

1.   INTRODUCTION

Over the past decade, dramatic changes have been taking place in the United States in the resources used to generate electricity and the technologies available to use, store and transmit it. In response, the US has embarked on a comprehensive effort to overhaul its electric grid and make it into a modern, interactive network. The term 'Smart Grid' has been used to describe the wide variety of technical, legal and societal transformations necessary to foster interactivity and create a more capable grid.[1] This chapter will also use the term 'grid modernization', which has been more increasingly used in recent years to describe specific regulatory proceedings in which progress toward a smart electric grid is taking place.[2] Grid modernization has been encouraged by a panoply of state laws and programs, and by federal laws and regulations,

---

[1]   Joel B. Eisen, *Smart Regulation and Federalism For the Smart Grid*, 37 HARV. ENVTL. L. REV. 1 (2013) [hereinafter Eisen, *Smart Regulation and Federalism For the Smart Grid*]; 42 U.S.C. § 17381 (2012) (defining the Smart Grid in over ten separate objectives and related goals).

[2]   Shelley Welton, *Grid Modernization and Energy Poverty*, 18 N.C. J. OF L. & TECH. 565 (2017); NC Clean Energy Tech. Ctr., 50 STATES OF GRID MODERNIZATION: Q1 2018 QUARTERLY REPORT (2018), *available at* https://nccleantech.ncsu.edu/wp -content/uploads/Q12018_gridmod_exec_final.pdf (noting that over half of the states are engaged in these activities, and listing and describing grid modernization proceedings underway).

including the 2007 Energy Independence and Security Act (EISA)[3] and regulatory initiatives of the Federal Energy Regulatory Commission (FERC).

Some compare the evolution of the Smart Grid to the development of the Internet in scale and complexity.[4] The US Department of Energy's first Smart Grid report observed in 2009 that the Smart Grid 'may transform America as much as the Internet has done, redefining every aspect of electricity generation, distribution, and use'.[5] The focus of this chapter is on the development of the technical standards that serve as a foundation for interoperability on the Smart Grid led by the 'Smart Grid Interoperability Panel' (SGIP),[6] and in particular on the protection of intellectual property in the standard setting process. Specifically, we evaluate the balance struck in the standard setting process between encouraging innovation and potential for dominance of the standard setting process by individual firms to the exclusion of the public interest.

Accordingly, in the remainder of this chapter, we discuss the standard setting process for the Smart Grid and the procedures for protecting intellectual property. We conclude that in the Smart Grid, as in other industries, while the processes of patenting and standard setting may seem to be contradictory, they are in fact complementary. To protect companies other than the patent holders, standards developing organizations (SDOs), including those involved in the Smart Grid effort, require that a patentee (a) disclose any patents to the standard setting body that are necessary to practice the standard and (b) provide a licence under [fair], reasonable and nondiscriminatory ([F]RAND) terms.[7] This, we claim, has struck an appropriate balance between the need for rapid standards development and the goals of intellectual property protection.

2.   THE PROMISE OF GRID MODERNIZATION

Until recently, America's electric grid operated much as it had for the better part of the past century. Large, central power plants generated electricity from fossil fuels, and utilities and other suppliers delivered it to consumers.[8] The grid operated in a strictly one-way relationship, and there was no two-way flow

---

[3]   Eisen, *Smart Regulation and Federalism For the Smart Grid*, fn. 1, *supra*, at 4–5 discusses the relevant statutory provisions.

[4]   Eisen, *Smart Regulation and Federalism For the Smart Grid*, fn. 1, *supra*, at 6.

[5]   Eisen, *Smart Regulation and Federalism For the Smart Grid*, fn. 1, *supra*, at 6.

[6]   Natl. Inst. of Stds. & Tech., *Smart Grid Interoperability Panel*, *available at* https://www.nist.gov/programs-projects/smart-grid-national-coordination/smart-grid -interoperability-panel-sgip.

[7]   Fns. 65–70, *infra*, and accompanying text.

[8]   Emily Hammond & David B. Spence, *The Regulatory Contract in the Marketplace*, 69 VAND. L. REV. 141 (2016).

of power – or information – between generators and consumers.[9] Distribution utilities supplied power to consumers at the moment it was generated, with no ability to save it in real time.

Today, many assumptions that undergird this settled view of the grid are being discarded.[10] As recently as a decade ago, coal provided nearly half of the electricity generated in the US. Since then, the mix of resources used to generate electricity has changed dramatically and is increasingly clean. In 2018, hydropower and other renewables accounted for almost 20% of US electricity generation,[11] and that share is rising rapidly as costs of solar and wind technology fall.[12] Even the most conservative estimates of renewable energy growth envision substantially increased deployment of renewables over the next several decades.[13] By current US federal government projections, taking current policies into account, renewables will account for 64% of total electric generation growth in the US through 2050,[14] yielding significant benefits for mitigating the adverse impacts of climate change.

Increasingly, consumers are challenging the grid's one-way nature. Many are producing their own solar, wind or geothermal power, and much more often than before, they are delivering this power back to the grid under net metering or similar programs when they have more electricity than they need.[15] The proliferation of electric vehicles has added additional impetus for the development of a two-way electric grid, as some foresee the use of EV

---

[9] Eisen, *Smart Regulation and Federalism For the Smart Grid*, fn. 1, *supra*, at 7.

[10] *Ibid.*

[11] U.S. Energy Info. Admin., *What is U.S. electricity generation by energy source?*, https://www.eia.gov/tools/faqs/faq.php?id=427&t=3 (17.1% in 2017).

[12] James H. Williams *et al.*, Energy & Entvl. Econ., Inc., *Pathways To Deep Decarbonization in the United States* 1 (2015), *available at* http://deepdecarbonization.org/wp-content/uploads/2015/11/US_Deep_Decarbonization_Technical_Report.pdf.

[13] In 2018, the US Energy Information Administration predicted that renewable energy sources would see explosive growth in the US between then and 2050. U.S. Energy Info. Admin., Annual Energy Outlook 2018 with Projections to 2050 20 (2018), *available at* https://www.eia.gov/outlooks/aeo/pdf/AEO2018.pdf. The National Renewable Energy Laboratory's (NREL) Renewable Electricity Futures Study explains that renewables could meet 80% of the nation's electricity demand by 2050. Nat'l Renewable Energy Lab., *Renewable Electricity Futures Study* (2012), *available at* https://www.nrel.gov/analysis/re-futures.html.

[14] *See* U.S. Energy Info. Admin., Annual Energy Outlook 2018 with Projections to 2050, fn. 13, *supra*. In addition, natural gas surpassed coal as the main source of electricity in the United States for the second year in a row in 2017, further contributing to improved climate benefits.

[15] States' net metering policies are listed and discussed at Natl. Conf. of State Legislatures, *State Net Metering Policies*, *available at* http://www.ncsl.org/research/energy/net-metering-policy-overview-and-state-legislative-updates.aspx; *see* Database of State Incentives for Renewables & Effic'y, *available at* http://

batteries to provide power back to the grid.[16] Also, the advent of less expensive storage technologies has prompted many to contemplate a future where power generated from intermittent renewable technologies can be saved and provided back to the grid when needed, or consumed on a customer's premises.[17]

A smarter grid would support a wide variety of objectives, including two-way interactivity and more widespread integration of renewables, and as such would yield efficiency, environmental and social gains. It might create 'spectacular technological breakthroughs, the rise of entire new industries, and consumer uses far beyond anyone's wildest dreams'.[18] To begin with, it would have significant potential benefits for the grid itself. Although grid upgrades have already cost billions of dollars in front-loaded expenses, these investments will eventually yield considerable savings to electricity consumers. An updated grid operates 'more efficiently, would need less maintenance and large-scale infrastructural investment, and would fall victim to fewer "power disturbances" such as outages and overloads that impose significant costs on the U.S. economy'.[19] And, by matching supply more closely to demand and decreasing the need for peaking plants (plants that are expensive to run and operate only at times of highest electricity demand), it would 'avoid unnecessary expenses of building new generation, transmission, and distribution infrastructure'.[20]

In addition, a smarter grid will yield enormous benefits to consumers. It will enable delivery of power to end users as needed, depending on demand, but also foster networked interaction among customers, utilities and other participants in the grid. Consumers can save money on their electric bills, and become more active participants in the grid. Experimentation with creating marketplaces or other means for consumers to participate in the grid is beginning, and eventually consumers will be able to sell power to one another.[21]

---

programs.dsireusa.org, for a compendium of initiatives for self-generation for each state.

[16] *See, e.g.*, Jonathan Susser, *Not Just a Car: The Possibilities of Vehicle to Grid Technologies*, ADVANCED ENERGY, 4 Oct. 2017.

[17] FERC recently encouraged the growth of storage with its Order 841 that lowers barriers to its participation in wholesale electricity markets. Electric Storage Participation in Markets Operated by Regional Transmission Organizations and Independent System Operators, 83 Fed. Reg. 9580 (Mar. 6, 2018). States have also acted to promote storage. *See, e.g.*, State of Charge: Massachusetts Energy Storage Initiative, https://www.mass.gov/files/2017-07/state-of-charge-report.pdf.

[18] Eisen, *Smart Regulation and Federalism For the Smart Grid*, fn. 1, *supra*, at 3.

[19] Welton, fn. 2, *supra*, at 577.

[20] *Ibid.*

[21] Joel B. Eisen & Felix Mormann, *Free Trade in Electric Power*, 2018 UTAH L. REV. 49 (2018).

In the not too distant future, new companies will provide services such as advanced energy management to consumers, driving the growth of entire new industries and capabilities. Grid modernization is already creating new jobs in the energy sector: 'solar panel installer' was the fastest growing job category in the US in 2017.[22]

For these objectives to be fully achieved, '[c]onsumers must be given the tools and knowledge to become participants in the electric grid'.[23] Achieving grid modernization's touted benefits requires new infrastructure, new companies, new business models and new pricing structures that promote smarter use of electricity. Accordingly, upgrading the grid's physical infrastructure and developing new regulatory frameworks are the core goals of grid modernization efforts.

Reworking the grid's physical architecture focuses largely on upgrades to utility-owned 'transmission infrastructure, voltage support devices, and network monitoring systems'.[24] Fuller integration of renewables requires new technologies to handle renewable resources that generate electricity intermittently, when the sun shines or the wind blows. Involving consumers more fully in the grid requires substantial investments, reworking of regulatory structures and establishment of new frameworks to govern consumers' interactions with the grid, combined with comprehensive reevaluation of how consumers relate to the electric grid (and associated outreach and education efforts).

Until recently, a major obstacle to embarking on this transformation was the lack of smart metering infrastructure. Unlike the less capable electric meters of the not too distant past, smart meters record electricity consumption in granular detail, providing real-time information on electricity consumption and demand.[25] This allows utilities and other companies to obtain more comprehensive data on consumer electricity usage, enabling them to use that data to manage energy consumption and tailor other products and services to individual consumers.

---

[22]   Jordan Yadoo, *These Are the Fastest Growing Jobs in the U.S.*, BLOOMBERG BUSINESS, 24 Oct. 2017.

[23]   Welton, fn. 2, *supra*, at 574.

[24]   *Ibid.*

[25]   Eisen, *Smart Regulation and Federalism For the Smart Grid*, fn. 1, *supra*, at 16. The privacy concerns raised by the availability of this data are important and as yet not fully resolved. *Ibid.*; Welton, fn. 2, *supra*, at 584 (noting that, 'Nor is it clear whether and how consumers might access all the data that smart meters provide about their individualized use, as state laws regarding this data remain unsatisfactory or inconclusive on this point'). *See generally* Katrina Fischer Kuh, *Personal Environmental Information: The Promise and Perils of the Emerging Capacity to Identify Individual Environmental Harms*, 65 VAND. L. REV. 1565 (2012).

Given the necessity of smart meters as a precondition to grid interactivity, grid modernization efforts often fund their installations.[26] Billions of dollars in funding from the 2009 American Recovery and Reinvestment Act jumpstarted smart meter deployment by matching utilities' expenses with federal funds, enabling utilities to install smart meters for hundreds of thousands of consumers. With smart meters in place, the US may see more widespread development and deployment of 'smart appliances' and storage systems that interact with the grid (including the batteries from electric vehicles at times when they are not being used or charged), and a shift to 'time of use' and other 'dynamic' pricing techniques to prompt consumers to better manage their electricity demand.[27]

3. TOWARD A SMARTER GRID: THE ROLE OF FEDERAL AND STATE GOVERNMENTS IN SETTING AND USING INTEROPERABILITY STANDARDS

From the beginning, standards development – and particularly the development of interoperability standards to govern interactions on a modernized, digital grid – has been recognized as extremely important to the development of a Smart Grid. A standard is 'any set of technical specifications which either does or is intended to provide a common design for a product or process' and is 'related to characteristics such as quality, safety, or interoperability'.[28]

---

[26]   As of late 2016, utilities and other grid operators had installed 62 million smart meters in approximately 49% of US households (and an additional 8 million in businesses and industrial operations). U.S. ENERGY INFO. ADMIN., *How Many Smart Meters are Installed in the United States, and Who Has Them?*, https://www.eia.gov/tools/faqs/faq.php?id=108&t=3. States sometimes reject requests for utility smart meter installations if they believe the future benefits are too speculative in nature. *See, e.g.*, Jeff St. John, *Massachusetts Rejects Smart Meter Rollouts, as Competitive Energy Undermines the Business Case*, GREENTECHMEDIA, 17 May 2018 (discussing the rejection of 3 Massachusetts utilities' smart meter plans).

[27]   Eisen, *Smart Regulation and Federalism For the Smart Grid*, fn. 1, *supra*, at 11–13. For a discussion of demand reduction techniques (including 'demand response' and others) and their historical uses, *see* Joel B. Eisen, *Demand Response's Three Generations: Market Pathways and Challenges in the Modern Electric Grid*, 18 N.C. J. OF L. & TECH. 351 (2017).

[28]   Herbert Hovenkamp, IP & ANTITRUST: AN ANALYSIS OF ANTITRUST PRINCIPLES APPLIED TO INTELLECTUAL PROPERTY LAW n.73, 35.1a–35.3 (2002); Jorge L. Contreras, *Technical Standards and Ex Ante Disclosure: Results and Analysis of an Empirical Study*, 53 JURIMETRICS 163, 164 (2013) ('Technical standards are detailed sets of instructions, specifications, or protocols that are used to achieve a particular technical purpose').

Standards are generally created in one of three ways: government selection, de facto market selection, and standards development (or standards setting) organizations (SDOs or SSOs). SDOs are 'voluntary collectives in which representatives from multiple private companies, who are often competitors of each other, work together to establish technology standards'.[29]

Because grid modernization requires a combination of new technologies and transformative regulatory change heretofore unseen in the American electric grid, scholars and policymakers understood that development of effective interoperability standards would be a foundation for Smart Grid advances for decades to come. Before discussing the standards development process, however, it is necessary to note that jurisdiction over the electric grid is split between the states and the federal government in the United States. This jurisdictional split heavily influenced the process of developing Smart Grid interoperability standards. Under the Federal Power Act, the FERC oversees interstate transmission and wholesale sales of electricity; the states regulate retail sales of electricity. The regulatory structure of every US state establishes and gives authority to state regulatory bodies known as public utility commissions (PUCs) that oversee electric utilities and set electricity rates at 'just and reasonable' levels.[30]

PUCs are the principal forums in which grid modernization is taking place. At present, dozens of states are conducting grid modernization proceedings aimed at making the grid smarter, more efficient, and receptive to handling more renewable power.[31] In these proceedings, utilities have requested billions of dollars in reimbursement from their customers for the expenses they plan to incur – including upgrades to the transmission and distribution infrastructure. PUCs are currently deciding whether to allow utilities to recoup these costs from their customers, and are also figuring out how customers with distributed

---

[29] Jay P. Kesan & Carol M. Hayes, *FRANDs Forever: Standards, Patent Transfers, and Licensing Commitments*, 89 IND. L. REV. 1, 4 (2009). In addition to private companies, SSO participants may also include governmental delegates and academic researchers. Joseph Scott Miller, *Standard Setting Patents and Access Lock-in: RAND Licensing and the Theory of the Firm*, 40 IND. L. REV. 351, 364 (2007) (noting that SSO participants include 'volunteers from interested firms (and sometimes from government agencies and academic departments) who are technical, not legal or business, experts').

[30] Joel B. Eisen, Emily Hammond, et al., ENERGY, ECONOMICS, AND THE ENVIRONMENT 77–79 (describing the basic elements of public utility regulation), 455–460 (describing rate regulation by PUCs) (2015). *See also* William C. Boyd, *Public Utility and the Low Carbon Future*, 61 UCLA L. REV. 1614 (2014) (discussing the historical origins of public utility law).

[31] Herman K. Trabish, *Grid Mod Policy Actions Jump 75%, with Storage Playing a Central Role*, UTILITY DIVE, 5 June 2018 (discussing 50 STATES OF GRID MODERNIZATION: Q1 2018 QUARTERLY REPORT, fn. 2, *supra*).

energy resources such as solar arrays will interconnect to the grid and supply extra power to it.

It is difficult to generalize about these proceedings, as they often involve utilities' requests to undertake many different projects simultaneously.[32] Typically, though, grid modernization initiatives have several goals as described above: (1) overhauling the grid's antiquated architecture and replacing outmoded components with modern, digital technologies; (2) incorporating new resources (particularly distributed energy resources such as wind and solar power), reducing carbon emissions, and thereby mitigating the adverse impacts of climate change; and (3) providing consumers with new options for generating, using, conserving and transferring electricity, converting the current one-way grid to an interactive, participatory grid.

4.   THE INTEROPERABILITY STANDARDS DEVELOPMENT PROCESS

Without interoperability standards to govern interactions on the grid, the most well-intentioned grid modernization efforts could falter. Interoperability standards are different from standards of minimum quality for one product, as they establish the foundation for networking, defining how entities and devices on the Smart Grid interact.[33] For example, for an electric vehicle to provide power from its battery to the electric grid, there must be standards that define the physical connection and the governance of the power flow. A state could theoretically develop its own technical standards within the context of a modernization project. But from the outset, the development of interoperability standards was recognized as a federal function, not one to be undertaken by each of the 50 states operating independently.[34] Fostering interactivity on the grid requires uniform national standards that govern interactions across an interstate grid (although those standards are implemented by PUCs in grid modernization proceedings). Federal involvement was necessary to assure reliability of the grid and protection against cyberattacks. Moreover, PUCs

---

[32]   For example, the North Carolina PUC recently approved a multi-billion-dollar grid modernization effort by the utility Duke Energy that included investments in battery storage, data access and vehicle electrification components, voltage optimization upgrades. Robert Walton, *Duke Agrees to Cut North Carolina Grid Modernization Plan by $5.3B*, UTILITY DIVE, 4 June 2018.

[33]   Eisen, *Smart Regulation and Federalism For the Smart Grid*, fn. 1, *supra*, at 23–24.

[34]   Eisen, *Smart Regulation and Federalism For the Smart Grid*, fn. 1, *supra*, at 35 (noting that, 'Having 51 different points of approval may lead to balkanization, in which states choose different technologies and standards, and uniformity suffers').

had little expertise in developing technical standards, and it would have been a cumbersome and lengthy process for any PUC to create them.

Given the primary role of the states in grid modernization, some hybrid process was needed in which the federal government would lead the standards development process but leave it to the states to implement any standards resulting from that process. Moreover, in the normal process of technical standards development in the US, there is little if any role for governments to play. Instead, standards development is generally left to private industry under the aegis of SDOs or SSOs.[35] Thousands of SDOs, such as the Institute of Electrical and Electronics Engineers, develop and publish industry-specific standards.[36] SDOs have been responsible, at least in part, for the development of important interoperability standards, including standards that underlie the Internet and telecommunications.[37] Recognizing the strong tradition in favour of voluntary private sector standards development, and the familiarity that participants in the Smart Grid have with it, the Smart Grid standards process would have to be designed to take advantage of SDO expertise, not bypass it.

From the start, there was also a widespread recognition that the Smart Grid standards process would be fundamentally different from that of normal standards development. For one, hundreds of standards were required. The timeframe of an individual standard setting process, much less that of hundreds developed at the same time, was simply too slow to allow for the progress toward a smarter grid. A frequently cited example was that of the Internet networking technology Ethernet, which took ten years from conception to implementation, and even longer to broad acceptance.[38] In addition, the Smart Grid standards development process would require different SDOs to interact with one another. For example, the manner in which an electric vehicle might interact with the grid to provide power back to it from its battery would require collaboration between electrical and automotive SDOs. Although cooperation and interaction between different SDOs had been occurring in the telecommunications space, it was not routine for other technology sectors in the United States, and thus a process for fostering collaboration was required to encourage SDOs in a variety of industries to work together.

---

[35]   Peter L. Strauss, *Private Standards Organizations and Public Law*, 22 Wm. & Mary Bill Rts. J. 497, 499–501 (2013).

[36]   IEEE Standards, https://www.ieee.org/standards/index.html.

[37]   For example, the World Wide Web Consortium (W3C) 'develops open standards to ensure the long-term growth of the Web'. *See* www.w3.org. The 3rd Generation Partnership Project (3GPP) is a group of seven SDOs working to produce standards related to cellular telecommunications. *See* About 3GPP, http://www.3gpp.org/about-3gpp.

[38]   Eisen, *Smart Regulation and Federalism For the Smart Grid*, fn. 1, *supra*, at 33.

To act more quickly than the normal standards development process, the US Congress established, in the Energy Independence and Security Act of 2007, a form of fast-track process in which it tasked two federal agencies, the National Institute of Standards and Technology (NIST) and FERC, to (respectively) develop and approve standards, working in conjunction with private sector SDOs.[39] To begin with, the NIST was given 'primary responsibility to coordinate the development of a framework that includes protocols and model standards for information management to achieve interoperability of smart grid devices and systems'.[40] In keeping with this mandate, the NIST has issued several versions of a 'roadmap' for interoperability standards[41] that has yielded important benchmarks for technical advances in the Smart Grid, such as conceptual models for governing the numerous types of interaction on a modern electric grid.

NIST led an effort, originally known as the SGIP,[42] aimed at developing individual standards. The SGIP did not directly develop or write standards, but instead participated in and coordinated their development, ultimately approving any standards by action of its governing board. The standards roadmap consisted of 'priority action plans', identifying dozens of standards for information management and exchange, data management and other purposes as essential to the future of the Smart Grid and valuable for consumers, utilities and other Smart Grid participants.[43] Each priority action plan in turn chose an SDO to lead the effort and produce a standard in a working group. The resulting standard was then required to achieve a supermajority of 75% of the SGIP governing board.[44] While the SGIP process began with federal governmental oversight, it has now moved in its entirety to the private sector.[45]

The EISA empowered FERC to approve standards for use in the portion of the electric grid over which it has jurisdiction (defined in the statute as, 'interstate transmission of electric power, and regional and wholesale electricity markets') once the process of developing them, led by NIST, had achieved

---

[39] 42 U.S.C. § 17385 (2012).

[40] 42 U.S.C. § 17385(a) (2012).

[41] The third and final version of this framework and roadmap was Natl. Inst. of Stds. & Tech., NIST FRAMEWORK AND ROADMAP FOR SMART GRID INTEROPERABILITY STANDARDS, RELEASE 3.0 (2014) [hereinafter NIST FRAMEWORK RELEASE 3.0].

[42] Natl. Inst. of Stds. & Tech., *Smart Grid Interoperability Panel*, fn. 6, *supra.*

[43] NIST FRAMEWORK RELEASE 3.0, fn. 41, *supra*, at 4.

[44] The SGIP supermajority voting requirement reflected the principle that, 'substantial agreement' is 'general agreement, but not necessarily unanimity'. Eisen, *Smart Regulation and Federalism For the Smart Grid*, fn. 1, *supra*, at 39–40.

[45] In 2017, the SGIP merged with the Smart Electric Power Alliance (SEPA) under the SEPA brand and organizational structure. Jennifer Runyon, *SEPA and SGIP To Merge*, RENEWABLE ENERGY WORLD, 1 Feb. 2017.

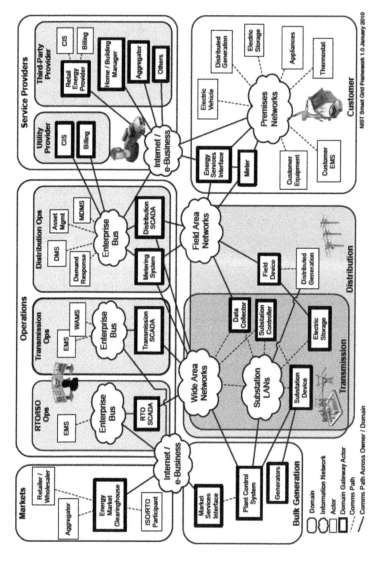

Figure 9.1   *NIST conceptual model for the Smart Grid (featuring the suite of interactions between customers and other entities through a 'Home Gateway')*

'sufficient consensus'.[46] As a practical matter, however, there is no physical separation between those parts of the grid over which the federal and state governments have authority. Thus, any standards approved in federal juris-dictional areas would effectively preclude any state from approving its own standards. Congress did not appear to recognize that FERC's approval of any Smart Grid standards might be seen as overreach into state jurisdiction.

Nonetheless, that issue is no longer salient, as FERC deftly sidestepped any potential problems when NIST submitted the first family of five standards to it for approval. The standards were not controversial, and FERC could have approved them. Instead, it neither approved nor rejected them; it found that the standards had not achieved sufficient consensus, but saluted NIST's work and encouraged it to continue.[47] Since then, FERC has not had any standards submitted to it for approval. Instead, almost one hundred standards developed through the SGIP process are incorporated in a 'Catalog of Standards' that serves as a valuable resource for utilities, regulators and other participants in the grid.[48] Although these standards are therefore not legally binding, they have found widespread acceptance as standards considered most relevant for the Smart Grid's development.

A noteworthy example of both the standards development process and adoption of the resulting standards by utilities working with PUCs is the 'Green Button Data'[49] initiative. This was announced by US Chief Technology Officer Aneesh Chopra in January 2012 as an effort to give consumers 'stand-ard, routine, easy-to-understand access to their own energy usage data'.[50] Today, utilities that use Green Button 'provide utility customers with easy and secure access to their energy usage information in a consumer-friendly and computer-friendly format'.[51] The ability for utilities and others to provide for standardized data presentation and exchange with third-party vendors who have developed applications to take advantage of the data derives from a stand-

---

[46]   The statutory text reads, 'At any time after the Institute's work has led to suffi-cient consensus in the Commission's judgment, the Commission shall institute a rule-making proceeding to adopt such standards and protocols as may be necessary to insure smart-grid functionality and interoperability in interstate transmission of electric power, and regional and wholesale electricity markets', 42 U.S.C. § 17385(d) (2012).

[47]   Eisen, *Smart Regulation and Federalism For the Smart Grid*, fn. 1, *supra*, at 44–46.

[48]   Catalog of Standards, *available at* https://sepapower.org/knowledge/catalog-of-standards/.

[49]   Green Button Data, http://www.greenbuttondata.org/.

[50]   *Ibid.*

[51]   *Ibid.*

ard – the North American Energy Standards Board's ESPI (Energy Services Provider Interface) that was developed in the SGIP process.[52]

Figure 9.2   *'Green Button' implementation, allowing for one-click downloading of electric usage data in standardized format*

5.   BALANCING STANDARDS AND PATENT PROTECTION

Although the advantages of standardization are clear, both for Smart Grid and more generally, what is less understood is how standards are developed. Participating in SDOs is often a costly proposition and yet, the success of any SDO is based on active participation by innovative firms. To encourage these firms to engage with the SDO process, there must be incentives. One of these incentives is allowing firms to recoup some of their costs by obtaining revenue from licensing patents that cover the technology a firm contributes to a standard. However, the relationship between standards and patents is a tense one. This section will discuss these issues in more detail.

Standard setting is a complex, time- and resource-intensive process that carries significant risks for participating firms.[53] In addition to membership dues and significant hours spent preparing for and attending SDO meetings, many firms also contribute technology to be considered for possible incorporation in the standard.[54] These contributions require substantial research and development costs with a very uncertain return on investment, as tens or

---

[52]   Natl. Inst. of Stds. & Tech., *Green Button Initiative*, https://www.nist.gov/engineering-laboratory/smart-grid/hot-topics/green-button-initiative.

[53]   Contreras, fn. 28, *supra*, at 171.

[54]   Andrew Updegrove, *The Essential Guide to Standards*, CONSORTIUMINFO.ORG §4.2.1, http://www.consortiuminfo.org/essentialguide/participating1.php.

even hundreds of technology contributions from many different firms may be considered for any given aspect of a standard, and perhaps only a handful are selected.[55] SDOs succeed where an individual firm may not, in part, by having the ability to select between numerous possible solutions to any technological issue. The success and robustness of a standard thus depends on encouraging multiple, technologically innovative firms to contribute their inventions and ideas to SDOs.

Beyond technology contributions, SDOs also benefit from their collaborative nature. As is typical in many SDOs, the firms that have collaborated to develop Smart Grid standards are, at the same time, firms that otherwise engage in competition with each other. This is not uncommon, especially for SDOs working on interoperability standards. After all, a primary goal in developing the standard is to ensure that products, services and networks from many different manufacturers and providers are able to interface and work together seamlessly. From the perspective of the SDO, there are great benefits in having companies that compete in the same or complementary industries come together to identify issues and select the best solutions to those issues because each of these competitors is likely to bring different strengths, resources and ideas to the SDO. Although the firms are invested in developing the interoperability standards, there still must be additional incentives to encourage these firms to also work to the benefit of their competitors.

To offset the direct costs (and risks) of participating in an SDO, as well as the indirect costs of collaborating with competitors, firms must receive some benefits from this participation. To be sure, active involvement in an SDO allows a firm to influence the direction and outcome of standard setting.[56] For some firms, this may be sufficient incentive, particularly if the firm is not itself contributing technology, but is simply participating in the collaborative discussions. On the other hand, if a firm is actively engaging in research and development efforts to submit technology to the SDO, a greater incentive may be necessary to offset the R&D costs. If a firm's technology contribution is selected to be incorporated into a standard, the firm may gain a potential income stream in the form of revenue from licensing patents covering that technology to any company that wants to design and manufacture products that implement the standard. These benefits, especially the possible income stream, provide sufficient incentive to encourage innovative firms to actively participate in the standard setting process.

---

[55]   *Ibid.* at §2; Justus Baron et al., *Unpacking 3GPP Standards*, §4.1 (Nw. L. & Econ., Research Paper No. 18-09, 2018), https://papers.ssrn.com/sol3/papers.cfm?abstract_id=3119112.

[56]   Updegrove, fn. 54, *supra*, at §2.1.

There is a natural tension between patents and standards. Patents are intellectual property rights (IPRs) that grant the patent holder a right to exclude others from making, using and selling the technology covered by a patent. Standards, on the other hand, are intended to be widely used. This is especially true for interoperability standards that benefit from network effects and are more valuable as more users adopt the standard.[57] The possibility to exclude others from freely using standardized technology, because various aspects of this technology is subject to patent protection, has been often cited as a potential hurdle to development of Smart Grid standards. Utilities and others call for open, freely available standards to catalyse further grid modernization efforts.[58]

While patents may seem to be an obstacle to standard setting, this observation is short-sighted and neglects the need to encourage innovative firms to participate in the SDO process. If incentives, such as potential revenue from licensing patented technology, are eliminated, these firms will be less likely to participate in the collaborative efforts or submit technology for consideration to the SDO.[59] Additionally, the objections to including patents in standards can be addressed through two lines of argument. First, these objections are based on erroneous understandings of the effects of patents and their exclusive nature and the reality is that patents are not the obstacle they are claimed to be. Second, to the extent any of the objections are actually problematic, many SDOs (including those involved in Smart Grid standards) have implemented policies that strike an appropriate balance between incentivizing participation in the SDOs and promoting a widely adopted standard.

There are two primary misunderstandings about patents and standards that are often raised as objections. First, patent holders are assumed to have undue influence over the standards setting process, resulting in their technology being selected over other options so that they can tap into the potential licensing stream. Second, patent holders who own standard essential patents are believed to engage in unfair, opportunistic behaviour that harms companies wishing to implement the standard. Neither of these beliefs is accurate.

---

[57]   James C. DeVellis, *Patenting Industry Standards: Balancing the Rights of Patent Holders with the Need for Industry-Wide Standards*, 31 AIPLA Q.J. 301, 305 (2003).

[58]   Rod Kuckro, *Tech CEOs Evangelize about Need for Open Standards*, ENERGYWIRE, 6 June 2018.

[59]   This is not an theoretical concern. Ron Katznelson has empirically studied firms' reactions to changes in SDO policy that decreased or eliminated these incentives and found a significant decline in participation. Ron D. Katznelson, *Presentation of IEEE's Controversial Policy on Standard Essential Patents at the Symposium on Antitrust, Standard Essential Patents, and the Fallacy of the Anticommons Tragedy*, Berkeley, CA (29 October 2016), http://bit.ly/IEEE-LOAs.

Patent holders do not unduly influence the standard setting process. It is true that technology underlying a firm's contributions is often protected by patents or patent applications pending while the standard is being developed.[60] However, the working groups that are considering the various contributions for inclusion in the technology standard are focused on selecting the best technological solution to achieve the desired outcome. Often the working groups do not know which contributions are covered by intellectual property, and some SSOs have specifically discouraged discussing patent rights until a standard is agreed upon.[61] Further, the collaboration and selection of technology for incorporation into a given standard is not being done by business or legal experts who would be in a position to leverage a firm's technology position; instead, the true work of SDOs is done by working groups composed of engineers, scientists and technical experts who focus on finding the best technological solution to the issue at hand.[62]

Firms that participate in and contribute patented technology to SDOs do not engage in the alleged opportunistic behaviours that are routinely raised in discussions about patents and standards, including patent hold-up and royalty stacking.[63] Patent hold-up theory hypothesizes that patent owners can use the possibility of an injunction to force implementers to pay what are alleged to be excessively high royalty rates to use the patented technology necessary to practise a standard.[64] Royalty stacking theory hypothesizes that since final products incorporating standardized technology, as sold to end users, incorporate a large number of patented inventions from a variety of firms, implementers are forced to pay an excessive 'stack' of royalties that far exceeds the value of the underlying patented innovation.[65]

---

[60]   Nat'l Acad. of Sci., PATENT CHALLENGES FOR STANDARD-SETTING IN THE GLOBAL ECONOMY (Keith Maskus & Stephen A. Merrill eds., 2013).

[61]   Mark A. Lemley, *Intellectual Property Rights and Standard-Setting Organizations*, 90 CAL. L. REV. 1889, 1956 (2002).

[62]   Daniel S. Sternberg, *A Brief History of RAND*, 20 B.U. J. SCI. 211, 213–214 (2013). This was certainly true in the case of the Smart Grid standard-setting process, where working groups convened under each of the SGIP's Priority Action Plans featured experts in technical disciplines. NIST FRAMEWORK RELEASE 3.0, fn. 41, *supra*, at 27 (noting that the SGIP brought together experts in 'power engineering, information communication technologies, architecture, systems engineering, and life-cycle management').

[63]   Mark A. Lemley & Carl Shapiro, *Patent Holdup & Royalty Stacking*, 85 TEX. L. REV. 1991, 2010–2017 (2007).

[64]   J. Gregory Sidak, *Holdup, Royalty Stacking, and the Presumption of Injunctive Relief for Patent Infringement: A Reply to Lemley & Shapiro*, 82 MINN. L. REV. 714, 714 (2008).

[65]   *Ibid.*

The reality, however, is that allegations of patent hold-up and royalty stacking are generally unfounded. First, both the existence and the extent of both of these behaviours is unclear. Although much ink has been spilt on the theories of patent hold-up and royalty stacking, more recent empirical work demonstrates a significant lack of support for either theory and, in fact, has examined evidence to the contrary.[66] There remains significant controversy over the existence of patent hold-up and royalty stacking and whether patent holders, particularly in the context of standardized technology, can behave anti-competitively. Recently, however, one of the primary competition enforcement agencies in the United States – the Antitrust Division of the US Department of Justice – issued a clear statement that enforcement of standard essential patents (SEPs) is not itself anticompetitive.[67] Additionally, the Department of Justice views the development of standards to be a form of competition.[68]

To the extent either of the above allegations – that patent holders unduly influence standard setting and engage in opportunistic behaviour regarding SEPs – are true, many SDOs have adopted various policies related to patent and other IPRs to help ameliorate these concerns. The two most salient policies are those related to disclosure and licensing of IPRs. Disclosure policies mandate whether and what disclosures are required by an SDO, as well as whether a firm must affirmatively search for IPRs to disclose or simply disclose known IPRs.[69] Licensing policies explain what licensing terms are permitted and what licensing terms are required for IPRs that are covered by the standard.[70] The most common provisions mandate that firms must license standard essential patents at either a reasonable royalty or no royalty (royalty-free). Additionally, SDOs generally require that standard essential patents be licensed fairly and on nondiscriminatory terms, giving rise to the

---

[66] Damien Geradin & Miguel Rato, *Can Standard-Setting Lead to Exploitative Abuse? A Dissonant View on Patent Hold-up, Royalty-Stacking, and the Meaning of FRAND*, 3 Euro. Competition J. 101, 101–102 (2007); Kirti Gupta, *The Patent Policy Debate in the High Tech World*, 9 J. Competition L. & Econ. 827 (2013); F. Scott Kieff & Anne Layne-Farrar, *Incentive Effects from Different Approaches to Holdup Mitigation Surrounding Patent Remedies and Standard-Setting Organizations*, 9 J. Competition L. & Econ 1091 (2013).

[67] Alexander Okuliar, *Ensuring the Proper Application of Antitrust Law to Standards Development*, at 5, 28 May 2020, *available at* https://www.justice.gov/opa/speech/file/1281926/download (noting that patent holders are not in violation of antitrust law for exercising the rights that patents confer).

[68] *Ibid.* at 6.

[69] *See* Lemley, fn. 61, *supra*, at 1943.

[70] *Ibid.* at 1973.

FRAND moniker (fair, reasonable and nondiscriminatory).[71] These disclosure and licensing policies are then enforceable as contract commitments against the firms participating in the SDO, even by parties that are not SDO members that are seeking to license the technology.[72] SDOs involved in setting Smart Grid standards have fairly standard disclosure and licensing policy provisions. Specifically, firms participating in the SDO must disclose any patent to the SDO that is necessary to practice the standard.[73] Additionally, firms must agree to provide a licence to Standards Essential Patents (standards where a patent controls any part of the technology used in a standard) under [fair], reasonable and nondiscriminatory ([F]RAND) terms.[74]

6.   CONCLUSION

It is understood that patents may increase innovation – and so does standardization, by marshalling greater resources and human knowledge than any individual firm can possess. While it is easy to believe that patents and standards are in tension, and there is extensive literature that supports this notion, there is more to the story. Patents and standards can, and do, work hand in hand to encourage innovative firms to participate in SDOs, allowing these SDOs access to the best technological options when setting the standards. This side of the story is often lost when commentators raise objections to the inclusion of patented technology in standards.

A better, and more accurate, story is that patented technology should be allowed for consideration into standards and may result in better, more robust and eventually more widely adopted standards. The idea that patents are obstacles in standardization is largely theoretical and is not borne out by empirical work. However, to the extent patents may yet be an obstacle, SDOs have specifically developed IPR policies to ameliorate any concerns. In the Smart Grid field, NIST and the SGIP have addressed these issues from the outset. Thus, we argue the appropriate balance has been struck.

---

[71]   *See* Kesan & Hayes, fn. 29, *supra*, at 244.

[72]   Joanna Tsai & Joshua D. Wright, *Standard Setting, Intellectual Property Rights, and the Role of Antitrust in Regulating Incomplete Contracts*, 80 ANTITRUST L.J. 157, 158 (2015).

[73]   NIST FRAMEWORK RELEASE 3.0, fn. 41, *supra*, at 54.

[74]   *Ibid.* (noting that 'This does not mean that all of the standards and specifications are available for free, or that access can be gained to them without joining an organization (including those organizations requiring a fee). It does mean that they will be made available under fair, reasonable, and nondiscriminatory terms and conditions which may include monetary compensation').

10. The treatment of intellectual property rights in open innovation models: new business models for the energy transition

Catherine Banet

1.   INTRODUCTION

The transition to cleaner sources of energy is not only a question of technology; behavioural change is equally important. Moreover, there will be no sustainable, low-carbon and fair energy transition without the development, transfer, diffusion and adoption of new low-carbon technologies adapted to new production and consumption patterns. New technology and knowledge will be fundamental to enable the energy transition. This is reflected by the steadily increasing number of patent filings in relation to low-carbon energy technologies,[1] as reported by the World Intellectual Property Organization (WIPO) and the International Renewable Energy Agency (IRENA).[2] The central role played by technology innovation in addressing climate change is also recognised in the Paris Agreement to the United Framework Convention on Climate Change (UNFCCC).[3]

---

[1]   Patent trends are good indicators of technology progress and can be used to forecast innovations. IRENA, 'Intellectual Property Rights – The Role of Patents in Renewable Energy Technology Innovation', June 2013, 5.

[2]   In its patent landscape analysis of clean energy technologies (covering solar, wind, bioenergy, hydropower, geothermal, wave and tidal, hydrogen, carbon capture and storage, waste-to-energy), WIPO depicts a significant increase since the 1990s: an increase by 10% in the early 1990s, and by 25% between 2001 and 2005. In the next decade (2002–2012), the number of patent applications for renewable energy technologies published under the Patent Cooperation Treaty (PCT) increased by 547%. Although this figure has declined in 2019, it was still 3.5 times higher than in 2002. WIPO Magazine, 'Patenting Trends in Renewable Energy', March 2020.

[3]   See Article 10 of the Paris Agreement, and particularly Article 10.5 that provides that: 'Accelerating, encouraging and enabling innovation is critical for an effective,

This chapter concentrates on how new knowledge is created in the specific collaborative ecosystem that is open innovation (OI). It considers the role of intellectual property (IP) law in supporting the OI process and its interplay with energy sector regulation. As inventions[4] once again become crucial to economic growth, embracing a new industrial revolution[5] and the twin green and digital transitions,[6] nations and companies tend to be protective of their technologies and innovations. This leads to techno-nationalist behaviour for states and fierce competition between companies.[7] However, there is also a growing awareness of the need to collaborate in the creation of innovative solutions. This was already true at the very beginning of the electricity industry and is still true today. The famous inventor Thomas Edison quickly understood that he would need external inputs to nourish his own inventions. It is only by combining his own improved version of the modern light bulb with the external knowledge of experts on grid infrastructures that he realised a breakthrough and developed the first direct-current circuit electrical system.[8]

IP tools, such as patents, trade secrets, trade marks, copyrights and industrial designs,[9] are the traditional ways by which to protect inventors from unlawful use of their knowledge and to secure a return on investments. In his lifetime, Thomas Edison held more than 1,000 patents. However, as expressed by Edison himself, 'the value of an idea lies in the using of it'. Access to this knowledge can be free of charge, but because of its commercial value, it is usually ensured through contractual agreements. The most common contract mechanism for knowledge transfer is licensing, but other mechanisms exist,

---

long-term global response to climate change and promoting economic growth and sustainable development.'

[4]   Meaning both technologies and intangibles.

[5]   For a general reflection on the ongoing new industrial revolution, see K. Schwab, *The Fourth Industrial Revolution* (Currency, 2017).

[6]   Since the adoption of its Communication on the European Green Deal in December 2019, the European Commission has consistently referred to the 'twin green and digital transitions' including as part of the post-COVID-19 recovery plan. See the communications from the Commission: 'The European Green Deal', COM (2019) 640 final, 11 December 2019; and 'Europe's Moment: Repair and Prepare for the Next Generation', COM (2020) 456 final, 27 May 2020.

[7]   C. Banet, 'Techno-Nationalism in the Context of Energy Transition – Regulating Technology Innovation Transfer in Offshore Wind Technologies', in D. Zillman et al. (eds), *Innovation in Energy Law and Technology* (OUP, 2018) Chap. 5, 74–99.

[8]   I. Wills, *Thomas Edison: Success and Innovation through Failure* (Springer, 2019) Chap. 9.

[9]   Trademarks and copyrights, which are other traditional forms of IPR, are less relevant for the purpose of low-carbon energy technologies and will therefore not be covered.

such as assignment agreements or spin-offs.[10] Intellectual property rights (IPR) are effective incentives for innovators and investors. As stressed by IRENA, IPR protection plays an important role throughout the entire 'technology life cycle' for renewable energy technologies, from R&D to commercialisation and diffusion.[11] IPR form a central part of a framework in which contributing parties can engage in an innovation process ideally based on fair terms. But innovations can also be difficult to access and can be an obstacle to the development of new technologies. This is the main criticism raised by anti-patent movements that argue that patents inhibit technology transfer and diffusion.[12] This is a shortcoming that several international agreements under the World Trade Organization (WTO) and the UNFCCC regimes aim to address by promoting technology transfer.[13]

In the emerging global 'knowledge economy' associated with the fourth industrial revolution,[14] knowledge itself has become the key resource, and access to knowledge drives innovation. In other words, innovation builds on innovation. By blocking access to knowledge, innovation progresses at a slower pace. In the context of the energy transition, a slow development and diffusion of new low-carbon technologies may prevent us from attaining the set emissions reduction targets and may come at a higher cost for energy consumers.

In the pure context of technology innovation, collaboration based on knowledge sharing across fields and market players may be a prerequisite for creating new technologies, following an 'open innovation' approach. It is now becoming common practice within an energy sector that is subject to the driving forces of decarbonisation, decentralisation, digitalisation and democratisation (the 4 Ds), as well as the upcoming challenges of sector coupling and sector integration. Companies like Equinor, Engie or Elia have launched innovation platforms where they publish calls to capture innovative ideas. This

---

[10]   For a short introduction, see: The European IPR Helpdesk, 'Commercialising Intellectual Property: Knowledge Transfer Tools', July 2015.

[11]   IRENA, 'Intellectual Property Rights – The Role of Patents in Renewable Energy Technology Innovation', June 2013, 9–14.

[12]   Anti-patent activists see the patent system as inhibiting implementation of technology, rather than fostering its development. They take the view that green technology should be available for all to use. A manifestation of this concern is the global movement for compulsory licensing in third world countries, with respect to green technology. See Hillson and Daulton, 'Patenting Green: Issues Relating to the Emergence of Patents Concerning Green Technologies', The 2009 Midwest Intellectual Property Institute (2009): 5.

[13]   See C. Banet, fn. 7, *supra.*

[14]   See K. Schwab, fn. 5, *supra.*

contrasts with former, closed innovation (CI) models mostly based on internal R&D or bilateral collaboration with selected external partners.

The purpose of this contribution is to explore the concept of OI in the context of the energy transition and to question how IPR should be treated – by law or contracts – to create attractive and successful OI models in this sector. Because an innovation ecosystem is dependent on the regulation of its sector, the chapter also evaluates the interaction between IP law and energy law, and the phenomenon of 'inter-regulation'.

The chapter starts by briefly defining the concept of OI (Section 2), before analysing how the development of low-carbon technologies is increasingly relying on OI models (Section 3). This includes a categorisation of some existing OI models and an analysis of the legal framework applied to them. The chapter continues by discussing the implications of OI models on IP law and energy market regulation (Section 4) and then provides concluding remarks (Section 5).

The chapter aims to fill a gap in the legal literature and stimulate further research. Although there is a large body of literature on the treatment of IPR in OI models in the fields of business administration and organisational studies, no study has researched in detail its legal application to the energy sector. Similarly, few scholars have questioned the interaction between IP law and energy law or have attempted to ascertain how the regulation of OI models in the energy sector should evolve.

2.   THE CONCEPT OF 'OPEN INNOVATION'

2.1   Open Innovation as a Collaborative Process

The term 'open innovation' was first coined by Henry Chesbrough in 2003 in his book *Open Innovation: The New Imperative for Creating and Profiting from Technology*.[15] The phenomenon had already been observed in the 1960s and developed progressively since then, but Chesbrough contributed to its conceptualisation and promotion. Chesbrough defines OI as 'the use of purposive inflows and outflows of knowledge to accelerate internal innovation, and expand the markets for external use of innovation, respectively. OI assumes that firms can and should use external ideas as well as internal ideas, as well as internal and external paths to market, as they look to advance their technology.'[16]

---

[15] H. Chesbrough, *Open Innovation: The New Imperative for Creating and Profiting from Technology* (Harvard Business School Press, 2003).
[16] *Ibid.*

An organisation does not rely merely on its own internal knowledge, sources and resources for innovation, but also uses multiple external sources to drive innovation. External actors nourishing innovation would typically be start-ups, small and medium-sized enterprises (SMEs), research organisations or individuals and communities. Following a systematic approach, Von Hippel categorises the different actors contributing to an OI process, distinguishing between manufacturer-centric (top-down) and user-centric (bottom-up or democratic) innovation.[17] The fact is that no company can afford to continue innovating in a vacuum, in particular in highly competitive sectors that require putting new products on the market regularly while the Research, Development and Innovation (R&D&I) timeline is usually longer.[18] There is also a series of advantages in terms of shortening the time to innovate, sharing risks, reducing costs and getting preferential access to markets.[19] This is certainly true in a context of decentralised, digitalised and integrated energy systems, with an increased share of flexibility production from renewable energy sources and demand response from consumers.[20] Rapid and continuous innovation has also become necessary for success in the marketplace, in rapidly evolving technology environments. Therefore, OI can be described as an innovation model combining 'internal and external ideas into an architecture and systems whose requirements are defined by a business model'.[21]

Indeed, OI corresponds to new *business models* that encourage innovation with a variety of external actors. This change is based on a new model for economic development, but also other values such as social aspects, low carbon content or local benefits. However, open models for collaboration on innovation are not free, and an underlying legal question is how to value, incentivise and reward the external inputs through law. This has deep implications for the manner in which IP is used and managed.

OI models are in essence collaborative. They are not limited to *cooperation* (side-by-side, one after the other), but take advantage of *collaboration* to develop new ideas, products and services. They relate to new collaborative movements such as 'crowdsourcing', resulting in 'crowd-based innovation'.[22]

---

[17]   E. Von Hippel, *Democratizing Innovation* (MIT Press, 2005).
[18]   O. Gassmann, 'Opening up the Innovation Process: Towards an Agenda', R&D Manag (2006) 36(3): 223–228.
[19]   The European IPR Helpdesk, 'Intellectual Property Management in Open Innovation', Fact Sheet, October 2015, 2.
[20]   See a further discussion on the changes the energy sector is facing in Section 3 *infra*.
[21]   A. Markman (ed.), *Open Innovation: Academic and Practical Perspectives on the Journey from Idea to Market* (OUP, 2016).
[22]   T. Pellerin-Carlin and P. Serkine, 'Crowd-based Innovation for a Competitive Energy Transition', Institut Jacques Delors, 2016.

There is a link to the 'sharing economy', a greater involvement of citizens and the 'Creative Commons movement'.[23]

Fifteen years after the publication of his book, Chesbrough observed that OI practices have spread from academic research to industrial practice and into the public policy domain. He also noted the increasing awareness of the need to consider both commercial and non-profit purposes and a diversity of stakeholders to obtain a more complete picture of how innovation can work efficiently and effectively.[24]

The degree of control over the collaborative process and its end-result (protected by IPR) will vary according to the choice of OI model. This is the topic of the next two sections.

2.2 Open Innovation as a Formalised and Structured Process

Collaboration between entities – public or private – to generate innovation may be structured in different ways, supported by different forms of contractual agreements or laws. The literature distinguishes three basic models associated with OI models: 'inside-out', 'outside-in' and 'coupled OI processes'.[25]

- In the first case of inside-out OI (or 'outbound open innovation'), organisations share their innovative solutions with external partners on commercial or non-commercial terms. A series of well-known legal instruments can be used to ensure lawful access to the knowledge and the attached IPR. In the case of a commercial transaction, the original IP owner will be selling its IP or out-licensing it.
- In the second case of outside-in OI (or 'inbound open innovation'), which is the counterpart situation, companies acquire external knowledge instead of developing it internally. The external knowledge can be acquired through e.g. in-licensing agreements, merging and acquisition operations, or corporate venture capital (joint venture).
- The third alternative is a combination of the first two and consists of 'real' collaborative work in a coupled OI process. Pre-existing knowledge is

---

[23] In his book *The Zero Marginal Cost Society*, Jeremy Rifkin argues that monopoly capitalism will be displayed by a collaborative commons (Griffin, 2014) 226–231.

[24] M. Bogers, H. Chesbrough and C. Moedas, 'Open Innovation: Research, Practices, and Policies', California Management Review (2018) 60(2): 5–16.

[25] On the distinction between the three models, see: A. Gorbatyuk, G. Van Overwalle and E. van Zimmeren, 'Intellectual Property Ownership in Coupled open Innovation Processes', IIC – International Review of Intellectual Property and Competition Law (2016) 47: 262–302; E. Enkel, O. Gassmann and H. Chesbrough, 'Open R&D and Open Innovation: Exploring the Phenomenon', R&D Manag (2009) 39(4): 311–316.

pooled to create new knowledge, including collaboration with new potential third partners. This combination of pre-existing and newly co-created
knowledge has been tagged as 'background IP' and 'foreground IP'
respectively.[26] The IP legal framework for coupled OI processes will be
more complex to elaborate and track, with additional challenges related
to inventorship, ownership of the new knowledge co-created and rights to
future exploitation of this knowledge.[27]

Energy companies have used both models, the outside-in process and the
coupled OI process, supported by different legal forms of collaboration.
However, the coupled OI process is deemed to be the most integrated process
of co-creation in an OI environment.

OI is a strategic model of innovation for companies, but different OI models
exist. According to the OI model chosen, the extent to which companies keep
control over the collaborative process and the co-created knowledge will vary.
This will directly affect the level of trust in the OI process and the willingness
to contribute. Empirical research has demonstrated that commercial OI always
tends to be managed or controlled, in either a formal or informal way.[28] This
calls for a form of governance structure, notably over how the claims of the
different claim holders are prioritised. The regime for IPR treatment within the
OI model will be a key criterion for all partners to the co-creation. This chapter
argues that structured and formalised OI models, such as platforms and certain
patent pools, are more attractive because they increase the level of control over
the co-created knowledge, and therefore the level of trust between participants.

2.3   Less Formalised and Structured Forms of Open Innovation: Open Licensing and Open Source Development

In some circumstances, companies have chosen to soften the level of protection over their IPR as part of their OI strategy and to engage in open licensing,
open source development or even IP donation.[29] The value of applying open
source licensing within low-carbon energy technologies has been praised for

---

[26]   For a detailed definition of those two concepts, see A. Gorbatyuk, fn. 25, *supra*,
283–285.

[27]   *Ibid*, 264.

[28]   N. Lee, S. Nystén-Haarala and L. Huhtilainen, 'Interfacing Intellectual Property
Rights and Open Innovation', Lappeenranta University of Technology, Department of
Industrial Management Research Report No. 225, SSRN (2010).

[29]   For an analysis of the phenomenon, see N. Ziegler, O. Gassmann and S. Friesike,
'Why do Firms Give Away their Patents for Free?', World Patent Information (2013)
37: 1–7.

several years, with the objective of ensuring innovation diffusion.[30] Licensing is a common process for obtaining the right to use IPR. Open licensing is a way for the copyright holder – creator or other right holder – to grant the general public the legal permission to use its work. The applied open licence is usually indicated directly on the work or product. Open licensing for solutions result-ing from the implementation of these projects in the regulated distribution area could significantly reduce the risk of investing in new technologies and could accelerate innovation processes, which is especially important for countries that are filling the technological gap, such as developing countries. Another motivation for open sourcing is to further incentivise innovation in a sector. The clear backdrop of this approach is that companies lose control over the OI process and the results. Open licensing could be considered as one option or one step in OI models, but it can neither foresee nor structure how innovation will be created or IPR valorised.

3. ENERGY TRANSITION AND THE RELIANCE ON OPEN INNOVATION MODELS

3.1 Driving Forces in the Energy Transition Benefiting from Open Innovation Models

The energy transition is moved by some driving forces, commonly depicted as the 4 Ds of decarbonisation, decentralisation, digitalisation and democra-tisation. The 2015 Paris Agreement aims to strengthen the global efforts in response to climate change and limit the increase in global average tempera-ture to 'well below 2°C' above pre-industrial levels.[31] Because it is still mainly based on fossil fuels at the global scale, energy production and use are among the main contributors to GHG emissions, among them carbon dioxide (CO_2). The reduction of CO_2 emissions from this sector is key to reach the reduction targets (*decarbonisation*), based notably on an increased reliance on renewable energy sources and energy efficiency and energy savings. With a higher share of renewable energy sources, the forms of energy production, consumption and storage are evolving, becoming more distributed across territories and bringing new benefits in terms of flexibility and reliability (*decentralisation*). A more decentralised and integrated energy system brings new challenges in terms of grid management and market operations, but also opportunities, all

---

[30] In Europe, the organisation 'EDSO for smart grids' (https://www .edsoforsmartgrids.eu/) has argued in favour of open licensing for solutions resulting from the implementation of its projects.
[31] Paris Agreement, Art. 2.1(a).

supported by digital solutions (*digitalisation*). Similarly, energy consumers are facing challenges and being offered new opportunities. The United Nations have defined 'access to affordable, reliable, sustainable and modern energy' as the 7th of its 17 Sustainable Development Goals (SDGs), which form part of the 2030 Agenda for Sustainable Development.[32] In addition to access to energy, a more decentralised and digitalised energy system also empowers energy consumers who can produce, consume and trade their own energy as well as provide flexibility services to the grid (*democratisation*).

Another strong driver for exploring the benefits of OI models in the energy sector is the need to look at interfaces between technologies and sectors as part of 'sector coupling' (connecting gas, electricity and heating & cooling sectors) and 'sector integration' (with a tighter integration of the different sectors, e.g. transport, heating and industry). In that sense, smart sector coupling should rely on smart innovation policies across sectors, including through OI. The energy system strategy from the European Commission (EC) identifies innovation as 'a key enabler to create and exploit new synergies in the energy system', without going further into details.[33]

The ongoing transformation of the energy system results in the diversification and multiplication of actors as well as grid and market operations. It impacts the tasks performed by grid operators at both transmission and distribution levels and renders the tasks of supervisory authorities more complex. While closed innovation corresponds to the classic model of vertically integrated companies, OI models are becoming increasingly attractive to energy companies in terms of keeping track and staying ahead of market, technology and social evolutions, while complying with market design requirements.[34] This becomes even more necessary when different sectors interact.

3.2   Endorsement of OI by Energy Companies and Public Authorities

Because IP is crucial for their business development, companies involved in clean energy technologies are very conscious about protecting their IP rights from unauthorised use or infringement by third parties. Tesla Motors states repeatedly in its annual reports that: 'Our success depends, at least in part, on our ability to protect our core technology and IP. To accomplish this, we rely on a combination of patents, patent applications, trade secrets, including

---

[32]   UN SDG 7 homepage: https://www.un.org/sustainabledevelopment/energy/.

[33]   Communication from the European Commission: 'Powering a climate-neutral economy: An EU Strategy for Energy System Integration', COM (2020) 299 final, 8 July 2020.

[34]   See Section 5, *infra*.

know-how, employee and third-party nondisclosure agreements, copyrights laws, trade marks, IP licenses and other contractual rights to establish and protect our proprietary rights in our technology.'[35] As of 2020, Tesla Motors has been granted approximately 290 patents and has around 280 patent applications pending.[36] Tesla is licensing patents and other IP from third parties for the use of external technologies in their processes. Tesla Motors also stresses the increased risk of breach of their IPR and the need to engage patent or trade mark infringement claims, for companies engaged in international operations.[37]

Nevertheless, this does not cause Tesla to refrain from engaging in OI innovation. With the now famous phrase 'All our patents belong to you', Tesla's CEO announced in 2014 that their patents had been 'removed, in the spirit of the "open source movement", for the advancement of electric vehicle technology'.[38] Tesla will not initiate patent lawsuits against anyone who, 'in good faith', wants to use their technology. In his statement, Elon Musk made two strong arguments related to the development of low-carbon technologies and competitiveness. First, he recalled that the original purpose of Tesla Motors at its creation was to accelerate the advent of sustainable transport, and that if they were to 'clear a path to the creation of compelling electric vehicles, but then lay intellectual property landmines behind [them] to inhibit others, [they] are acting in a manner contrary to that goal'. Second, he stressed that there is a business model behind the 'removal' of the patents: 'that applying the open source philosophy to our patents will strengthen rather than diminish Tesla's position in this regard'.[39] To support this strategy, Tesla has developed a dedicated webpage concerning the use of its patents.[40]

However, it is not clear if Tesla is in fact ceding all its rights. It appears instead to be simply promising not to proactively sue those who enter the electric car market and use a similar technology. Furthermore, the move is not unprecedented, and the US Patent Office has a mechanism to allow companies to cede their patent rights. This move also corresponds to an increasing trend by patent holders in a range of fields to make pledges to limit the enforcement

---

[35] Tesla Motors, *Annual Report for the Fiscal Period ended December 31, 2012*, 23.

[36] United States Patent & Trademark Office.

[37] Tesla Motors, fn. 35, *supra*, 45.

[38] Tesla Motors, press release, 12 June 2014: https://www.tesla.com/blog/all-our -patent-are-belong-you. For an analysis of Tesla's strategy, see M. Rimmer, 'Elon Musk's Open Innovation: Tesla, Intellectual Property, and Climate Change', in Matthew Rimmer (ed.) *Intellectual Property and Clean Energy: The Paris Agreement and Climate Justice* (Springer, 2018) 515–551.

[39] Tesla Motors, press release, fn. 38, *supra*.

[40] https://www.tesla.com/about/legal#patent-pledge.

of patents. Patent pledges have been in part a response to concerns about patent over-enforcement.[41]

At the institutional level in Europe, the need to promote OI has also been recognised by the EC, which has previously stated: 'Fostering low-carbon innovations, energy efficiency projects and renewables requires a system of OI. Companies and industries increasingly understand that the complexity of today's world means that no single entity can come up with a complete solution. Furthermore, the most interesting market-creating innovations are happening at the intersection of different sectors, disciplines and approaches.'[42] The EC emphasises the role of energy consumers in this new OI system, as mirrored in its 2016 Communication on *Accelerating Clean Energy Innovation*.[43] OI is one of three policy goals of EU research and innovation policy,[44] and one of the pillars of the 'Horizon Europe' research programme.

3.3   Existing OI Models in the Energy Sector and Corresponding IPR Treatment Options

The energy sector has a long tradition of collaboration in R&D development with external partners. Traditionally, energy companies have done so using a wide range of agreements, from memorandum of understanding (MoU) to licensing agreements, to joint venture or consortium agreements to co-create. Those forms of collaboration are still widely used today and can also lead to co-owned IP. For example, two of the four pillars in Shell's current OI strategy, called 'Idea Factory', relate to collaborative agreements with universities (often licensing agreements) and the 'Shell Technology Ventures', which deals with venture capital. However, if the agreement is limited to a number of preselected partners, the collaboration is more a 'closed collaboration', in contrast to an 'open collaboration', when the number and types of partners is undetermined.[45]

---

[41]   J. Contreras and M. Jacob (eds), *Patent Pledges: Global Perspectives on Patent Law's Private Ordering Frontier* (Edward Elgar, 2017).

[42]   Communication by the Commission: 'Accelerating Clean Energy innovation', COM (2016) 763 final, 30 November 2016, 14.

[43]   *Ibid*, 4.

[44]   See RISE report: 'Europe's Future – Open Innovation, Open Science, Open to the World: Reflections of the Research Innovation and Science Policy Experts (RISE) High Level Groups' (2018). See Commission website 'Open Innovation Resources': https://ec.europa.eu/info/research-and-innovation/strategy/goals-research -and-innovation-policy/open-innovation-resources_en.

[45]   G.P. Pisano and R. Verganti, 'Which Kind of Collaboration is Right for You?', Harvard Business Review (2008) 86(12): 79–86.

Nevertheless, certain valuable lessons for IPR treatment can be drawn from those traditional forms of collaboration. Before starting the collaboration, the parties should sign a detailed agreement covering central IPR issues.[46] To start, confidentiality should be preserved, and contractual provisions should cover the risk of information disclosure. The issue is even more important in the case of a joint venture, when subsidiaries may have access to patents or trade secrets. Parties should clearly identify, up front, the background IP and secret information they are bringing into the collaboration. Companies often sign a joint venture non-disclosure agreement and ensure its implementation by internal routines consisting in marking documents and identifying trade secrets and confidential information. In case of co-creation of knowledge, the agreement should notably define who is responsible for filing the patent application, how IPR should be allocated, how royalties should be shared, what the conditions are for using the co-created knowledge (e.g. through a system of royalty fee licence), and how to deal with inventorship disputes. The agreement should also foresee how IPR are acquired or transferred in the event of a change of JV partner, following e.g. an M&A operation.[47]

Those closed models of innovation still consider IPR as defensive tools and do not promote collaboration with a broad audience of actors. To foster OI in the energy sector, international organisations within the IP and energy sectors have established a series of initiatives mostly focusing on promoting the patenting of 'green' technologies. Most of those initiatives take the form of patent platforms and IP clearing houses with the objective of putting patent holders and technology seekers into contact. For example, the WIPO GREEN database is an online marketplace operated by WIPO for connecting environmental technology[48] and service providers with those seeking innovative solutions. The referenced technologies are available for licence, collaboration, joint ventures and/or sale. The International Standards and Patents in Renewable Energy (INSPIRE) Platform[49] managed by IRENA offers information to users on the characteristics and use of patents and standards for the deployment of renewable energy technologies, facilitating dialogue between different stakeholders. The platform guides users in searching for renewable energy technologies and shows them how to use the information.

---

[46] See Section 4.1, *infra*.

[47] J. Roscetti and C. Collins-Chase, 'How to Protect IP in Energy Industry Joint Ventures', Law360, 24 August 2015.

[48] At present, the database includes seven technology categories: building and construction; energy; farming and forestry; pollution and waste; transportation; water; products, materials and processes.

[49] INSPIRE Platform website: https://www.irena.org/inspire.

The move observed today in the energy sector consists in the development of more structured and formalised OI models, where foreseeable and balanced IPR treatment is a key factor in attracting diverse inventors, accelerating innovation and securing benefits for all partners and for society. In addition, developing an innovative clean energy technology today often requires accessing a large number of patents (forming 'IP bundles'),[50] and the overlapping of IPR make it very challenging if the company does not have a structured approach to the innovation development process, both internally and externally.

The following paragraphs identify some OI models used by the energy sector and characterise how they are structured, focusing on IPR treatment:

- *Incubators* – Certain energy companies have established incubators, hosting start-ups with a view to generating patents. Elia, Engie, Shell and Equinor all offer such programmes. The Belgian TSO Elia runs an 'Open Innovation Challenge', based on a call for ideas giving the winner the opportunity to develop a proof of concept with them.[51] Under the Shell 'Game Changer' programme,[52] the company will receive idea submissions, sometimes based on a call for ideas, where the successful projects can be turned into an R&D programme, a commercial licence or a new venture. A similar approach is followed by Equinor's 'Techstars Energy Accelerator' programme, which is a 13-week intensive start-up accelerator programme for preselected companies or individuals working on disruptive solutions within oil and gas, renewables, new business models and digitalisation.[53]

- *IP clustering, including patent pools* – A patent pool is a common form of IP clustering, which may in turn follow different models and be more or less open. It can consist of an agreement between two or more patent owners to license one or more of the patents to one another or third parties.[54] It can also consist in the aggregation of IPR that can be cross-licensed, either transferred directly to the licensee(s) or through the setup of a joint venture.[55] In terms of governance structure, patent pools often rely on

[50]	IP bundles are formed through the combination of complementary technologies to increase the value of the individual parts. See A. Watson and A. Livingstone, 'Intellectual Property Clustering', *Technology Transfer Practice Manual*, AUTM 3rd edn, vol.4, (2010) 7.

[51]	https://innovation.eliagroup.eu/.

[52]	https://www.shell.com/energy-and-innovation/innovating-together/shell-gamechanger.html.

[53]	https://www.techstars.equinor.com/en/about.html.

[54]	C. Ayerbe and J. Eddine Azzam, 'Competitive Practices in Open Innovation: Lessons from Patent Pools', International Management (2015) 19(2): 96–114.

[55]	A. Watson and A. Livingstone, fn. 50, 2.

a central entity, which will exploit the collective rights of the multiple patent holders by licensing, manufacturing or both.[56] A joint venture can also be established to administer the patent pool. The Eco-Patent Commons initiative, supported by companies and the World Business Council for Sustainable Development (WBCSD), is an IP clearing house intended to facilitate sharing and accessing of IP rights, mostly patents, relevant for environmental technologies. The commons is open to any company that contributes at least one patent related to technologies having environmental benefits. One challenge with patent pools is that the technology is only open to members of the pools, and this may limit the extent of innovation and technology diffusion.

- *Standard Setting Organisations* (SSOs) – SSOs resemble patent pools but serve the purpose of developing a catalogue of technical standards to which member companies commit to comply. The SSO will govern the collaboration between member companies and coordinate the ownership of patents applicable to the standards that the SSO members adopt. They will notably require the owner of a patent deemed to be essential to a standard to make it available on fair, reasonable and non-discriminatory terms (FRAND). Renewable energy technologies and smart grids account for a large number of SSOs, as they need common standards to operate.[57]
- *Competitive clusters including OI* – Other companies have decided to join forces with business associations – and sometimes also with authorities, non-governmental organisations (NGOs) and civil society – for the creation of *clusters*. The EC (DG GROW)[58] has promoted the idea that a cluster approach to energy transition could enable the creation of ecosystems of collaboration involving OI, based on concrete needs and solutions. Clusters could be administered by a cluster intermediary and benefit from common solutions, including the terms of contractual arrangements pertaining to IPR to facilitate and ensure fairness in the collaboration.
- *OI platforms* – OI platforms are becoming increasingly popular. They can be used as an interface for launching calls for ideas, recruiting candidates to

---

[56] R. Merges, 'Contracting into Liability Rules: Intellectual Property Rights and Collective Rights Organizations', California Law Review (1996) 84(5): 1293–1393.

[57] On SSOs, see: N. Gandal and P. Régibeau, 'Standard-Setting Organisations: Current Policy Issues and Empirical Evidence', in P. Delimatsis (ed.), *The Law, Economics and Politics of Standardization* (Cambridge University Press, 2015); JRC Science for Policy Report, 'Making the Rules. The Governance of Standard Development Organizations and their Policies on Intellectual Property Rights', European Commission, 2019.

[58] European Commission, Industrial cluster policy website: https://ec.europa.eu/growth/industry/policy/cluster_en.

incubators or as intermediaries for OI partnerships. The operators of the OI platform can be a single company, a cluster, a public organisation or a third party. If a third independent party, not involved in the knowledge creation process, runs the OI platform as this is the practice in other sectors such as crowdfunding, the platform could put inventors into a relationship with one another, sometimes unanimously at the start, before they enter into a collaborative agreement.[59] Several energy companies have established their own platforms, often for the purpose of launching calls and connecting with start-ups. The most advanced OI platforms in the industry at the moment are the ones combining the publication of the company energy production and operation data,[60] even patents, with a model for cooperation for the development of new common knowledge. In those platforms, the manner in which submitted knowledge is dealt with will be a key factor. The Terms and Conditions for the Shell portal of the Game Changer programme require that the submission on the platform be non-confidential.[61] This is a common practice in the industry, often accompanied by statements suggesting that those who submit must rely on their prior-obtained patent rights. A drawback in considering every new idea as non-confidential is that it may inhibit openness and communication.[62] Another approach is the one proposed by the Finnish energy technology company Wärtsilä that has developed an 'Open Innovation Playbook'. The Playbook is a guide and a toolbox to run OI projects inside and together with Wärtsilä. The Playbook was conceived as a guide, and not a process that needs to be followed closely. The Playbook is being brought to fruition at the Smart Partner Campus, a virtual and physical OI facility within Wärtsilä's Smart Technology Hub.[63]

4.   THE IMPLICATIONS OF OI MODELS ON THE TREATMENT OF IPR

This section discusses the issue of legal novelty arising from OI models, taking the standpoint that the most successful models follow a formalised and structured approach to the treatment of IPR (4.1). An adequate level for addressing

---

[59]   E.g. ideXlab: https://www.idexlab.com.
[60]   See e.g. Elia's Transparency on Grid Data portal: https://www.elia.be/en/grid -data.
[61]   Shell asserts that it has no duty to treat ideas or other material as confidential and may pass on any ideas or other material submitted to its VC and other partners.
[62]   J. Harris, 'Patent Issues in Open Innovation', Landslide, American Bar Association (2014) 6(6).
[63]   https://www.wartsila.com/about/co-creation-playbook.

IPR treatment issues in OI models, harmonisation by law (4.2) or harmonisation by contracts (4.3), is discussed below.

4.1   Traditional and New IP Law Issues Raised by OI Models and Legal Response

Open Innovation does not mean that knowledge is shared for free or that there are no IP rights. Successful OI models aim to strike the right balance of interests between, on the one hand, protection of IPR between co-creators and, on the other hand, a sufficient level of openness to secure exploitation rights for third parties interested in using the co-created knowledge. A clear legal framework for OI to operate within will enable co-creators to work together with trust. This would also motivate further innovation for the benefit of society. In many ways, the legal framework for OI models is crucial to ensure their ability to deliver new knowledge and guarantee the many benefits of OI. Clear agreements and rules around ownership and property rights, IPR creation and exploitation, stimulate knowledge sharing and innovation.

OI models raise relatively traditional IPR treatment issues, but often exacerbate them, notably:

- Confidentiality issues: There is an underlying risk of disclosure during the collaboration process in relation to prior acquired knowledge that can be leaked by partners or the lack of rules for capturing the newly created knowledge. Trade secret laws may provide certain protection if the owner takes reasonable secrecy precautions.[64]
- Terms of use for the background IP: The identification of the terms of use of background IP brought into the OI process is a common issue not novel to OI models, although it can be extensive and demanding. Therefore, it will be important to valorise the IP, through for example an IP due diligence process for assessing the value of the IP and any risks attached to it. This mapping exercise is often part of an IP audit.[65]
- The tracking of inventorship: Since several actors are associated with the process of creation, it may be difficult to determine who 'originated' the idea. Inventorship laws do exist to address the situation of co-inventorship, based on criteria such as conception of the idea, material contribution to the development of the invention, implementation of the innovation. The

---

[64]   R.G. Bone, 'Trade Secrecy, Innovation, and the Requirement of Reasonable Secrecy Precautions', Boston University School of Law, 2014.

[65]   European IPR Helpdesk, 'IP Due Diligence: Assessing Value and Risks of Intangibles', Fact Sheet, 2015.

identification of the inventor is also important because this is the first person having the right to be granted a patent protection for the creation.[66]

- Allocation of IPR ownership of jointly created knowledge: Partners need to agree on which knowledge they have created together and how they share the IPR related to it. This can be done in an assignment agreement.
- Management of IPR: Not all partners may be able to afford the costs and time constraints related to this, in addition to the protection of co-created knowledge.
- Exploitation of IPR: Partners need to decide whether the jointly created knowledge will be exploited separately or jointly, whether there will be a system of compensation and benefits among them, and how the exploitation of the co-created knowledge by third parties will be organised (e.g. exclusive licence with one of the co-creators).
- Sharing benefits but also obligations/liability, including liability for final products.

All of the above issues are further complicated when the OI process involves different types of actors such as start-ups, consumers, suppliers or public entities that all contribute in some way to the process.

As an additional traditional challenge, the new IP created during the OI collaboration may not be exploited immediately. This is not seen as a cost, rather as an additional opportunity where the IP can be placed on a so-called 'intermediate market' or 'secondary IP market' for further exploitation.[67] Such a market would offer the opportunity to sell or license unexploited IP to specialised companies bringing the technology to maturity and/or making different use of it. The legal challenge, however, will be to ensure an efficient IP management regime for the commonly created IPR and their further exploitation.

This chapter argues that the main novelty arising from successful OI models lies in the form of the response to the IPR treatment issues. This involves offering a formalised and structured framework to collaborative innovation based on a strategic approach to IPR treatment on three levels: (i) the terms of use for the background IP brought into the OI process; (ii) the inventorship and ownership of the new knowledge co-created (co-ownership); (iii) the exploitation of co-owned IPR, particularly patents, through licensing.

---

[66] E.g., Convention on the Grant of European Patents (European Patent Convention), Art. 60, 81 and Implementing Regulations, Rule 19.

[67] H. Chesbrough and R. Ghafele, 'Open Innovation and Intellectual Property: A Two-Sided Market Perspective', in H. Chesbrough, W. Vanhaverbeke and J. West (eds), *New Frontiers in Open Innovation* (Oxford University Press, 2014) 191–207.

The question that arises next is the nature of the legal response. Two main approaches are classically identified, i.e.: harmonisation by law, with a legislation-based regime; and contractual arrangements, with a contract-based regime.

4.2 The Role of Legislative Harmonisation of IPR Treatment in OI Models

This section questions the role of harmonisation by legislation of (i) IPR treatment within OI models (the content) and (ii) OI platforms (the support) since those platforms are becoming increasingly important and relevant for OI in the energy sector.

4.2.1 Harmonisation of IP inventorship, co-ownership and IP exploitation rights in OI models

For the sake of clarification, the issue at hand is not harmonisation of IPR as such, but of IPR treatment in OI models.

The definition and the protection of IPR are already harmonised to a great extent as a result of international instruments such as the Agreement on Trade Related Aspects of Intellectual Property Rights (TRIPS Agreement) under the WTO, the Paris Convention for the Protection of Industrial Property and the Patent Cooperation Treaty (PCT).[68] Patent law is also largely harmonised, but primarily at national level, or regional level in the European Union. For the results of coupled OI activities, the patent law provisions of the majority of jurisdictions determine that jointly developed inventions are generally co-owned (Art. 59 of the Convention on the Grant of European Patents (European Patent Convention, EPC); Art. 116 of the US Code (U.S.C.), Title 35).[69] When OI collaboration involves partners from different countries, this could be a challenge.[70] The literature is also almost unanimous in criticising the still 'defensive, sales-oriented, proprietary model' of patent law that 'may be incongruous with open innovation'.[71] Others argued, in support of the con-

---

[68] J. Pila, *The Subject Matter of Intellectual Property* (Oxford, 2017) Chap. 2; H. Grosse Ruse-Khan, *The Protection of Intellectual Property in International Law* (Oxford, 2016).

[69] A. Gorbatyuk et al., fn. 25, *supra*, 267.

[70] E.M. Shinneman, 'Owning Global Knowledge: The Rise of Open Innovation and the Future of Patent Law', Brook. J. Int'l L. (2010) 35(3): 938.

[71] K.J. Strandburg, 'Accommodating User Innovation in the Intellectual Property Regime: A Global Administrative Law Approach', ACTA Juridica (2009) 284; K. Sawyer, 'The Collaborative Nature of Innovation', Wash. U.J.L. & Pol'Y (2009) 30: 293, 308.

tinued growth of OI, that international patent law harmonisation must evolve and the underlying goals of the patent regime must be re-evaluated: 'Rather than a defensive exclusion of others, IPRs should serve to further knowledge production, ease the sharing of ideas, and promote and police an ever growing international IP market.'[72]

The question, therefore, is not so much about further harmonising IPR, but about harmonising IPR treatment. Indeed, the international law instruments mentioned above do not regulate co-ownership or shared rights in IPR, i.e. IPR as property rights. At a national level, the question of IP inventorship and ownership allocation (co-ownership) is quite well harmonised,[73] but the default rule for co-ownership varies between jurisdictions.[74] The variations in national property law regulating use of IPR under shared ownership, or contract law regulating licences or transfers, are significant and present problems. The challenge is even higher in the case of cross-border collaboration. Then, the manner of how the claims of the different OI contributors (claim holders) can be prioritised is rarely a question addressed by the legislation. A minimum harmonisation of the prioritisation of the claims could reduce the risks of dispute.

Next, general rules in national patent legislation may also regulate the joint exploitation of co-owned patents – although this is not always the case. Those default rules may limit the freedom of the co-owners in deciding upon the exploitation of the IPR through, for example, licensing. They may need to acquire consent from each other, which can be quite burdensome, imposing 'a constant cooperation obligation' between them even after the completion of the OI project.[75]

Beyond that, it remains difficult to regulate all aspects of OI with IP law, due notably to the dynamic nature of the OI process and the multiple parameters and alternatives.[76] It might be difficult to foresee the type of new knowledge that will be created. It may be that a general rule will be sufficient, but not always, and this will rapidly call for supplementary contractual tools. As an example, many energy companies seek to collaborate with other sectors such as the aeronautic industry. The collaboration may result in two situations. The companies develop new knowledge together and may co-own the IPR. Alternatively, the energy companies identify a relevant patented technology developed by the other industry but will use it in a different manner than originally conceived. If

---

[72] E.M. Shinneman, fn. 70, *supra*.
[73] J. Harris, fn. 62, *supra*.
[74] See R.J. Paradiso and E. Pietrowski, 'Dilemmas of Joint Patent Ownership', NJ Law J (2009) 197: 912–913.
[75] A. Gorbatyuk et al., fn. 25, *supra*, 267.
[76] For a similar conclusion, see N. Lee et al., above fn. 28, *supra*.

this new use is not covered by the patent, it will normally lead to the filing of new patents, where the IP ownership will need to be agreed.[77]

4.2.2   Harmonisation of OI platforms regulation

As identified above, OI platforms are playing an increasingly important role in OI models in the energy sector. This trend corresponds to a 'platformisation' of the economy ('platform economy'), where digital platforms contribute to value creation and delivery.[78] It has become a business model, supported by digitalisation. OI platforms represent the meeting point of two trends, OI and platformisation.

The legal question is: (i) to what extent the OI platforms can and should be harmonised by law; and (ii) whether this can provide a more harmonised solution to IPR treatment.

The regulation of digital platforms is currently a priority area for regulators. Legislation at the national and European level already regulates activities on platforms, ensuring a minimum of harmonisation, often in relation to electric commerce and consumer and data protection. The EU adopted the Platform-to-Business (P2B) Regulation[79] as a first step to establish a fair and transparent business environment pertaining to online intermediation services. A new EU legislative initiative consists in a proposal for the ex ante regulation of very large online platforms acting as gatekeepers between businesses and citizens, with the goal being to complement competition law rules. This initiative forms part of the legislative package around the forthcoming Digital Services Act (so-called DSA Package), which will shape the rules of the digital services in the EU.[80] Notably, the DSA aims to address the posited current self-regulation model for online platforms. Depending on their structure, the activities offered and the data collected,[81] OI platforms could fall under the scope of application of this legislation. Energy companies or organisations

---

[77]   J. Harris, fn. 62, *supra*.

[78]   There are different types of platforms, and the literature distinguishes between intermediary platforms (two-sided, multi-sided, transaction platform), development platforms (industry, technology, innovation platform), and integrated platforms (function as intermediaries and also possess a large external developer network that plays a key role in creating the platform's value). 'Open Innovation Platforms – An Approach to City Development', 6Aika, 2016, 9.

[79]   Regulation (EU) 2019/1150 of the European Parliament and of the Council of 20 June 2019 on promoting fairness and transparency for business users of online intermediation services (P2B Regulation).

[80]   DSA homepage: https://ec.europa.eu/digital-single-market/en/digital-services-act-package.

[81]   The online intermediaries' services covered by the P2B Regulation involve direct transactions between business users and consumers (Art. 2(2)).

could be qualified as 'platform operators' when running the platform and be subject to a series of new obligations. Concerning the treatment of IPR, the P2B Regulation requires (using the wording 'shall') providers of online intermediation services to include information in their terms and conditions on the ownership and control of IPR of the business user.[82] In other words, this issue is left to the providers to decide in their contractual terms and conditions.

Certain aspects of the OI platforms may indeed be better addressed by contracts. The existence of different platform contractual terms and conditions could also increase competition between platforms, making some of them more attractive than others, including on the question of IPR treatment. For example, it is recommended to adopt internal safety measures on confidentiality to avoid risks of leakage of knowledge.[83] Those issues are normally part of the contractual negotiations between parties and would normally not be subject to legislative harmonisation.

To further harmonise practice, voluntary or mandatory certification or labelling schemes could apply to OI platforms, as they do for other platforms such as crowdfunding. Among the relevant tasks that OI platforms could offer and that can be subject to harmonisation is the IP audit.

4.3   The Role of Contracts in OI Models

The fundamental principle of freedom of contract enables parties to agree on a wide range of terms at two conditions: there is no harmonisation, or they want to derogate from the default regime.

As OI is still a practice in rapid evolution and in need of some flexibility, IP law may not yet address the needs of the partners. Contracts may fill this gap and provide a more tailored solution to the OI collaboration. For example, property law regimes directed at physical property do not have the appropriate tools to handle use of IPR that are not naturally exclusive. Even if the legislation defines some type of co-ownership regime and even defines co-ownership as a default regime, it will probably need to be supplemented with contracts on

---

[82]   P2B Regulation, fn. 79, *supra*, Art. 3.1(e).

[83]   As suggested by the European IPR Helpdesk, those measures could cover elements related to: setting up an internal filing system to track any creation of IP assets; documenting each IP element (laboratory notebooks, inventorship forms, etc.) – proof of ownership; creating an IP database and keeping it up to date; organising regular reviews of IP used; securing confidentiality internally and externally; third parties' IP rights (freedom to operate; infringement) (The European IPR Helpdesk, 'Intellectual Property Management in Open Innovation', fn. 19).

the further exploitation of jointly developed knowledge (e.g. via licensing).[84] Also, there could be many contributors in an OI process, and it might be challenging to allocate claims among them. Even if IP law usually provides for rules on co-inventorship and co-ownership, it does not provide for a system of prioritisation of the claims among co-creators/OI contributors.[85] This issue would need to be addressed by contracts. In practice, empirical research proves that firms active in OI prefer contract-based regimes for organising their IP relationships with other firms.[86]

The OI process is composed of many steps that will lead to the conclusion of not one contract, but a succession of contracts in which the different, previously identified IPR issues can be addressed.[87] Among the most traditional agreements encountered in the process are:[88]

- Confidentiality or non-disclosure agreements: This covers the risk of leakage, and the situation where some technology or knowledge is not yet protected.
- Confidentiality obligations may also be included in an MoU, instead of a stand-alone agreement. The confidentiality provisions could be staged.
- Consortium agreements can be signed by a large number of parties, and usually cover many aspects of the project collaboration, including background and foreground IP, IP protection and maintenance, IP monitoring, joint ownership and knowledge transfer, and conditions of exploitation.

Although this contract-based regime provides more flexibility to partners, it is not challenge-free.

First, there are important transaction costs in negotiating the contract, with a certain imbalance in terms of small actors in contrast to big energy companies.[89] As contract negotiations tend to be a complex and lengthy progress, it may be challenging for small companies to negotiate on an equal footing with

---

[84]   J. Hagedoom, 'Sharing Intellectual Property Rights – An Exploratory Study of Joint Patenting Amongst Companies', Indus Corp Change (2003) 12(5):1035–1050, at 1045.

[85]   N. Lee et al., fn. 28, *supra.*

[86]   J. Hagedoorn and A.-K. Zobel, 'The Role of Contracts and Intellectual Property Rights in Open Innovation', Technology Analysis & Strategic Management (2015) 27(9): 1050–1067.

[87]   See Section 4.1, *supra.*

[88]   The European IPR Helpdesk, 'Intellectual Property Management in Open Innovation', fn. 19, 6.

[89]   A. Gorbatyuk et al., fn. 25, *supra.*

large companies running OI platforms, and a standardised approach would be beneficial to them.[90]

Second, ensuring a transparent and attractive regime for IPR treatment will require consistency on the matter across the different agreements of this contractual value chain. This can be facilitated by the standardisation of the contracts. Different public or private organisations already provide relevant standardised agreements. For example, the European IPR Helpdesk provides models of a non-disclosure agreement and an MoU. The oil and gas sector also has a long tradition of standardising contracts, particularly in Norway.[91] The default regime described in the standard contracts is mostly protective of the company towards its contractor. It does not aim to promote innovation, but to envisage it, and it intends to attain a fair balance. In case the invention is developed based on the information provided by the contractor, the latter will be the owner, although they should compensate the company with a royalty-free, non-exclusive right to use inventions so created to the extent necessary for the object of the contract. The contractual solution described corresponds mostly to a bilateral contract, and innovation is not the primary objective of the collaboration. Nevertheless, it stresses the importance of reaching a fair and foreseeable solution for all parties. In the case of OI platforms, it can be presumed that they will offer standard contracts for their platform, and that, in the long run, some common standard contracts could be developed. There could also be competition between the OI platforms, where the contractual terms on IPR treatment can be part of their attractiveness.

The challenge of transparency and third-party exploitation of co-created knowledge raises the question of the role of IP institutions, such as WIPO or EPO. Gorbatyuk et al. recommend the level of transparency be increased by implementing an obligation to indicate patent ownership changes throughout the lifetime of a patent at national patent offices, and propose strict measures to ensure the effective enforcement of such a measure. Moreover, they argue that it would be beneficial if the EPO would register patent transfers during the lifetime of patents issued through the EPC system and not only during the opposition period. The obligation to register the contractually modified exploitation rules of co-owners at patent offices would also increase the level of transparency and legal certainty for third parties interested in obtaining access to co-owned patents and engaging in OI.[92]

---

[90]   On standardisation, see Section 4.3, *infra*.

[91]   The standard contracts for the petroleum activities on the Norwegian continental shelf (Norwegian Total Contract 2015 Modification (NTK 15 MOD)) contain provisions on the protection of property rights related to information, technology and inventions, in Art. 33.1.

[92]   Gorbatyuk et al., fn. 25, *supra*, 300.

Finally, contracts themselves should be flexible enough to accommodate all the innovation (tangible and intangible) created throughout an OI process.[93]

5. OI, IPR AND INTERNAL ENERGY MARKET: INTERACTION BETWEEN REGULATORY ECOSYSTEMS

The regulation of open innovation and IPR can hardly be envisaged in isolation, even less if it is applied to a highly regulated sector like energy. As put by Adnan Z. Amin, Director-General of IRENA, 'determining a suitable, tailored innovation mix for each country requires a systemic approach – combining innovations in technology with those in market design, business models and systems operation'.[94] Therefore, innovation law and policy in the energy sector should also take into account energy market design rules.

Indeed, there is a need to consider the interaction between regulatory ecosystems to better understand the impacts and constraints they have on each other. This should also prevent the risks of inconsistency across regulatory frameworks. The legal theory on the law of regulation, also called Regulation Law, has developed a methodology on 'interregulation' that can be applied in the present context.[95] The interregulation methodology refers to the process of connecting autonomous regulations while no process is in place to establish priorities between them, but a decision eventually needs to be made. Each regulation aims to reach an objective, has its distinctive logic, but different sets of regulations may apply to the same situation. In the context of the treatment of IPR in OI models in the energy sector, IP law will interact with energy law and internal market/competition law, at least. The reason is that OI involves collaboration along the energy supply chain, which may infringe unbundling

---

[93] N. Lee et al., fn. 28, *supra.*

[94] IRENA, 'Innovation Landscape for a Renewable-Powered Future: Solutions to Integrate Variable Renewables', 2019, 5.

[95] M.-A. Frison-Roche, 'L'hypothèse de l'interrégulation', in M.-A. Frison-Roche (ed.), *Les risques de régulation*, coll. 'Droit et Économie de la Régulation', vol.3, (Dalloz, Presses de Sciences-Po, 2005) 69–80.

rules,[96] and exchanging information or putting together patents (like in a patent pool), which may infringe competition rules.[97]

First, as concerns energy market regulation in Europe, the EU has developed an extensive legal framework on energy market design. As an example, system operators, and in particular distribution system operators (DSOs), will be on the front line to address the changes of a more decentralised, digitalised, decarbonised and democratised energy system (the 4 Ds). System operators are regulated actors and are obliged to act as neutral market actors and facilitators. In order to adapt to a changing energy system, they need to invest in innovation. Regulated actors like DSOs experience that the regulatory framework represents barriers to innovation, notably because they are regulated actors with constraints in terms of market activities and collaboration with other actors.[98] Therefore they have been asking for more flexibility in terms of participation of regulated actors in innovation actions, and the uptake of innovative solutions in their regulated activities.[99]

Second, from an internal market perspective, low-carbon energy innovation requires a well-functioning internal energy market and a robust competition policy, which gives newcomers an opportunity to bring their innovations to the market on an equal footing with incumbents. As stated by the EC in the context of the completion of the Capital Markets Union: 'A greater emphasis on OI and open science will lead to more opportunities, especially for smaller companies, to bring research results to the marketplace'.[100] If this is the goal, implementing OI may raise competition law constraints to the form of cooperation.

---

[96]   Unbundling refers to the separation of energy supply and generation from the operation of transmission and distribution networks. The unbundling requirement aims to avoid risks of discrimination in the operation of the network and of insufficient investment in networks that can arise when undertakings are vertically integrated. See Art. 35, 43–47, Directive (EU) 2019/944 of the European Parliament and of the Council of 5 June 2019 on common rules for the internal market for electricity.

[97]   As a way of addressing the possible conflicting objectives between IP law and antitrust law in the US, the US Department of Justice and the Federal Trade Commission issued the 'Antitrust Guidelines for the Licensing of Intellectual Property', explaining how the federal antitrust agencies evaluate licensing and related activities involving patents, copyrights, trade secrets, and know-how. The objective is to clarify conditions that can make IP pooling procompetitive (first in 1995, updated in 2017).

[98]   European Distribution System Operators for Smart Grids, EDSO Position Paper attached to the Response to the European Commission's public consultation of EU funds in the area of investment, research & innovation, SMEs and single market, March 2018. The Position Paper notes: 'Currently, throughout the EU, regulatory frameworks are rarely adapted to innovation frameworks and have the potential to prevent innovative behaviour from regulated actors.'

[99]   *Ibid.*

[100] Communication by the Commission, fn. 42, *supra*, 14.

Relying on small patent pools, clusters and platforms may entail risks of market foreclosure and inhibit change. On the one hand, OI collaboration between partners with a certain market power can raise risks of anticompetitive behaviour, such as fixing purchase or selling prices, or limiting/controlling production, markets, technical development or investment.[101] Similarly, a 'closed' SSO in which entry or exit by SSO members is restricted could raise antitrust concerns.[102] On the other hand, clusters are generators of new ideas and technology, but once established, they can also act to inhibit change because the concentration of similar firms gains market power and the ability to control or funnel resources to maintain the dominant technologies that they produce. This may decrease the likelihood of firms in the cluster developing or investing in radically new technologies.[103]

Companies and competent regulatory authorities will need to foresee this interaction between regulatory systems, and sometimes predict or adopt solutions to respond to this interregulation.[104] OI in those sectors may need regulatory flexibility and legal innovation too, such as the increasingly common use of regulatory sandboxes.[105]

6. CONCLUSIONS

With energy system integration, decentralisation, digitalisation and the economic backdrop following the COVID-19 pandemic, there will be, more than ever before, a need to revisit some aspects of innovation strategies in the energy sector. This will probably reinforce the need to support innovation through open models of collaboration, with a low threshold for sharing innovative ideas, but also for joining forces between actors having different economic capabilities.

Fruitful collaboration on innovation does not happen for free and in the absence of rules. Openness needs to be structured and legally organised. The move observed today in the energy sector consists in the development of more

---

[101] In the sense, for example, of Art. 101 TFEU.

[102] A. Chen, 'IP Strategy and Strategic Uses of IPRs: In Search of a Coherent Antitrust Balance', conference paper, Chung Yuan Christian University, Taiwan, 2014.

[103] Travis Gliedt and Kelli Larson, *Sustainability in Transition: Principles for Developing Solutions* (Routledge, 2018) Chap. 4.

[104] M.-A. Frison-Roche refers to this as ex ante intervention, while judges will also need to consider interaction between rules, but ex post.

[105] As put by IRENA: 'There is a need for the regulatory space that will allow levels of experimentation; one example is creating regulatory sandboxes that allow actors to experiment and test innovations without being restricted by the regulatory environment' (IRENA, 'Innovation Landscape for a Renewable-Powered Future: Solutions to Integrate Variable Renewables', 2019, 151).

structured and formalised OI models, where foreseeable and balanced IPR treatment is a key factor in attracting diverse inventors, accelerating innovation and securing benefits for all partners and society. This need for structure pertaining to collaborative innovation is revealed by the increasing use of OI platforms. Yet, the OI models and their legal environment is still under development. This generates complex challenges for OI regulation, particularly in already highly regulated sectors such as energy. This chapter argues that the regulation of IPR treatment in OI models within the energy sector is an integral part of the design of new business models for the energy transition, with benefits for companies and society in general.

Index